KEITH FERGUSON

TEXAS BLUES BASS *by Detlef Schmidt*

Forewords by Jimmie Vaughan and Billy F. Gibbons

ISBN 978-1-57424-306-2
SAN 683-8022
Copyright © 2014 CENTERSTREAM Publishing LLC
P.O. Box 17878 Anaheim Hills, CA 92817
www.centerstream-usa.com

**To Susanne,
the love of my life.**

KEITH FERGUSON
TEXAS BLUES BASS *by Detlef Schmidt*

Contents

Foreword by Jimmie Vaughan

I was asked to do an introduction to this book, but I don't know how to do one without just telling how I felt about Keith, how we met and all the things we shared and did together over the years.

The first time I ever met Keith Ferguson I was sitting on a parked car around the corner from The Vulcan Gas Company in Austin, which was on Congress Avenue, in 1969. I was waiting to get in the club to do my set-up. I believe we had arrived in Austin in Phil's car that afternoon and didn't have but a couple dollars between us. I had been playing around in different clubs with Phil Campbell, Jamie Basset and Paul Ray for quite a while in Dallas. We had played the Vulcan a couple times. But this time, when I met Keith, I was playing with Phil and Doyle Bramhall. This was way before moving to Austin. I didn't move to Austin until 1970. Jamie Basset had gone off to do something else, and we didn't have a bass player. So we went and got Stevie and I gave him my Barney Kessel to play. I tuned it down to C and told him he was the bass player. He was probably about 14 or 15 years old and had never played bass before. I think Phil and Doyle were out running around trying to score.

So I'm sitting there like a bump on a log, and up walks this stranger. He has a Schlitz tall boy in his hand with a bag around it, and he says, "Are you Jimmie?" He had the most unique walk I had ever seen. Very smooth, with big, big

Jimmie Vaughan in a post-Thunderbirds promo shot.

Courtesy of Jimmie Vaughan

steps -- almost like a glide. Like he was skating. He knew we were playing and told me he played bass with Benny Rowe in a band called Sunnyland Special. Well, I'd heard about Sunnyland Special from Benny as I knew Benny, and blues bands were far and few between in 1969. I hadn't heard the record yet, but they made a record at Robin Hood Brians, where I had recorded when I was 15 with The Chessmen, in Tyler. They had a harmonica player, Lewis Cowdrey, and a singer named Angela Strehli and a girl tenor sax player. Wow, I didn't know any girls who liked blues, much less could play them.

We small-talked a little bit and then he turned and walked off without saying anything. I'm still sitting on the car by myself. I think Stevie was around somewhere. So about 30 minutes later, here he comes again with a big, brown sack full of something. He says, "You looked hungry so I brought you a bag of cheeseburgers." Because you could get five cheeseburgers for $1.25 at the Galloway Cafe around the corner. So that's how I met Keith.

He was dressed crazy, like a rock star, with scarves all over him and boots. He was very flamboyant -- with the walk, the sunglasses and hair, the Rod Stewart hair and everything. He was wild; he didn't look like anybody else. He was walking with his big, long walk. If you ever knew Keith, he walked with this glide. So we talked a little bit, he brought me a bag of cheeseburgers then he walked off. What a guy!

I didn't see Keith for several years after that. Later, after I moved to Austin in 1970, I ended up playing with Lewis Cowdrey and Angela. I played with them for five or six years all over Austin. This is before the T-Birds. After I played with Lewis for a few years, I ran into Kim Wilson, who came down and showed up at some gig. I started thinking about putting together a band called The Fabulous Thunderbirds, and this is about the time I met Lou Ann in Dallas. The first night I saw her sing she was wearing her sister's dress, all stacked up and gorgeous. She sang a Little Richard medley and that was it: I knew some day we would do something together. I later called her up, sent her a bus ticket and she came to Austin and joined the band. She was in the original Thunderbirds.

We had several drummers for the Thunderbirds at this time. Keith wasn't in the band yet. I hadn't seen Keith since that first meeting. We had Otis Lewis and Andy Miller. We had several bass players. We had Pat Whitefield, who was the main one, but we also had Boo Boo Watson and a couple of other guys. I think Keith was out running around with Johnny Winter at the time. He showed back up on the scene in Austin. He found out where I was and showed up, and we sat around and talked. He really knew his stuff about the blues and had a lot of great records.

We became really good buddies pretty fast. He knew about hot rods and cars and we had a lot of the same interests. But, I wasn't really sure about his bass playing at first. It was very strange. It was totally different from anything I had ever heard. It was very rude sounding, percussive and very primitive. It took me a while to warm up to his playing because it was so different. He had his own thing completely. A lot of people would have describe it as being completely wrong, but he was a badass. It was left handed and big and crazy and percussive, but very mean sounding.

Around this time we met Mike Buck. Mike showed up at the One Knite and sat in. The first song I ever played with him was "Scratch My Back". I had met him once -- the night I met Lou Ann and Freddie Cisneros in Dallas at some gig. So that is when Keith got in the band, and then Mike Buck and the Thunderbirds started playing around town. We already had the Rome Inn, the One Knite and we played several places downtown. We also played Waco, Houston, and we played a couple gigs in Dallas.

Jimmie Vaughan on the German TV show Rockpalast, 1980.

Mike and Keith both had fantastic records. Between Kim and I, we had a lot of great records. But when we met Mike Buck and Keith, it was amazing because they had a bunch a crazy stuff that I didn't know about, hence a lot of The Fabulous Thunderbirds material. We started coming up with some stuff that most people had never heard. So that's where we found out about Frankie Lee Sims, Mercy Baby and all the Excello records.

So we started playing around town, and after a while Clifford opened up Antone's. It was really exciting. Clifford had a store where people would go jam after hours, and the word was out that Clifford liked blues and he was always asking everyone to come over and sit in. Finally, he opened up his club and all that started.

I was in my early 20s when the T-Birds formed. We had a really cool band. I'm the one who introduced Keith and Lou Ann. They seemed excited about each other right from the beginning and even got married later on. We had a great time and we started playing all around -- Austin, Dallas, Houston, San Francisco,

Courtesy of Michael Becker

and on and on and on. Muddy Waters actually got us on the East Coast. It was a real dream come true, musically speaking.

Keith knew people everywhere. He knew people in San Francisco. He knew people in New York and England and Europe. Keith was also very well read, and he could hold a conversation with anyone about anything -- and he did it all the time. I'd never met anyone like that before. Keith was the kind of guy that had a beer in one hand and a book in the other. He was always reading some book. Keith would sit around and read the dictionary from front to back. He would read technical books and crazy books. He was always reading. If he wasn't talking or walking, he was reading. He could converse with anyone.

When we played at the One Knite, you would pass the hat at the club. You didn't make any money, so whatever you could get out of the audience was what you made. So Keith knew some of the strippers at the Yellow Rose in Houston, which is the big strip club there. He got a bunch of the strippers to come to Austin and pass the hat one night. We made $300 to $400 each that night. This is when we really had the One Knite going and it was packed. Every Monday night it was jam packed -- people out the front door trying to get in, and it was really, really jumpin'.

and then we became the house band and Antone's, backing everyone you could think of from Chicago. The Fabulous Thunderbirds.

We really started tearing it up and actually met Muddy Waters, and he loved us. He started talking about us on the East Coast and we started getting gigs. That's how we met the Roomful of Blues. Muddy Waters talked to a club in Boston and told them they had to get The Fabulous Thunderbirds because they were the best young band he had ever seen and the harmonica player was like Little Walter,

When we started playing around and at Antone's, Ray Benson from Asleep At The Wheel moved to Austin and he introduced us to Denny Bruce. That's how we got hooked up with Tacoma Records. We made our first recording with Keith, Kim and Mike Buck in Dallas at Summit Burnett Recording Studio. That is where we recorded *Girls Go Wild*, which Mike Buck named. No one even argued with him when he said that that should be the name. We were like "OK," because except for Keith, the real name of the album should have been *We Don't Have Any Girls Here*. So we called it *Girls Go Wild*, thinking that might help. It was very cool at the time, and we were very excited about it.

So we went to Dallas and recorded pretty much live. Maybe there was some rhythm guitar overdubbing and maybe some background vocals and tambourine or something, but for the most part it was live. Bob Sullivan was the engineer. He was a real veteran who had earlier recorded Elvis at the Louisiana Hayride. He was the engineer on "Suzy Q" by Dale Hawkins and lots of great blues; he had recorded Eddie Taylor. So it was a real godsend that we found the right guy to record us. I had always had trouble in the studio because I couldn't get the guitar to sound the way I wanted it. It didn't sound as cool as the old records that I was listening to. So Bob allowed us to try things like room microphones for more of a live sound. Bob Sullivan had made great records, and we were all very excited to be working with someone like that. He knew what we were talking about, sound wise. We made "Los Fabulosos Thunderbirds", the song which was like a giant Mexican blues poster from cross the border. Everyone should go listen to that song. That's Keith doing the narrative in that.

After the first record or two, we really started traveling around. We went to Canada and Europe, and Rockpile hired us to come open their tour in England. All this time, I had developed a really nasty drinking problem. I started drinking at 14, and by the time I was 18, I was out of control. For the most part, I was able to play the gigs pretty good and didn't really screw up too many gigs. But after the gig -- watch out. I had a truly fabulous time with The Fabulous Thunderbirds and am very proud of the 10 albums we made and all the music and touring we made together. It was amazing. The reason I threw that in there was that Keith drank beer all the time. From the time he got up until he went to sleep. I don't remember ever seeing him legless or drunk. He would get a little buzz going, but he never got drunk.

I think he started in with the heroin and all that stuff before he came to Austin. Chipping, a little here, a little there, but not doing it very much. I think he was afraid of it at first. I know the only time that I ever did it, it totally freaked me out because I didn't want to do anything. I didn't want to play music, so that really scared me. By God's grace, I didn't get into heroin. But I think Keith started fooling around with it periodically in California before he came. After years and years, he got to where he didn't want to go on the road anymore. He openly told me that he didn't want to go out of town because he didn't want to leave his connection. It was too scary for him, and he was becoming more and more dependent on that stuff. I tried to talk to him about it, but like I said, I was an alcoholic and I couldn't really say anything to him about what he did. We went on tour in Europe, and he would nod out in between songs on stage but still standing there. He'd wake up for the song and then sleep between songs; stuff like that. It was a pretty bad scene. It got really bad, and there was no way around it.

Keith didn't want to travel and he didn't want to quit. And we were a band. I had to look for somebody else. Keith was very hard to replace, as you can imagine, but I was so concerned about the music. Keith had the look and his personality was big and he was great, but other things became more important. So I picked Preston Hubbard, who was a fabulous bass player and also played upright, which is something I always wanted. I hired Preston over the phone to play bass and talked him out of his gig with Roomful to come with us. I didn't realize it at first, I had heard rumors, but Preston was into the same thing. He was a great musician, but I was in denial about his habits. My one-track mind was thinking about his bass playing. Preston, for years and years, was able to maintain and it didn't really affect the band too much, but eventually it did -- as it does everyone.

That is when Keith and I parted ways. It was a combination of he didn't want to leave town, but he also didn't want to leave the band. You can't have your cake and eat it too. Everyone was up in arms. All of Keith's friends and fans were like, "Jimmie, you're a horrible guy. You fired Keith." Even my best friend Tonky said, "You can't fire Keith. You have to keep the band together."

So I tried to talk to Keith about going to treatment. So I talked him into going to a hospital in Austin with the help of my doctor, to do a fast clean out, like a pre-treatment clean-up in the hospital. But it was tough on Keith and everybody. All the doctors would come around and look at Keith, tattoos, etc. -- they treated him like some kind of circus freak. Anyway, that didn't work out. It was scary and really hard. And I really

loved him as a friend but didn't have a better idea. So there you have it.

Keith sued us one time. We got a gig doing some songs in a Disney movie starring Matt Dillion called *Tex*. Keith hired these attorneys, who were allegedly into the same thing he was, and they sued us because they said we had stolen all the money from Keith, which wasn't true. So some sour grapes going on about Keith getting fired is what it boiled down to. The judge dismissed the case, because Keith called his attorneys and said he was done with this and that he had "better things to get dressed up for". So that was one of the low points of the Thunderbirds.

I few years later, I got a message about Keith and that an infection had ruined his kidneys and he was in the hospital dying. So I got back from the road and went to see him. It was really great to see him. It was bizarre because here we were in the hospital -- his mother was there, a lot of his friends, all the people I had known all these years. Keith knew he was dying and there was nothing that could be done. The first thing that he said to me was, "I really missed you." And I said, "I really missed you, too," and, "Sorry about all this." And we hung out for a while. He then passed away, I think the next day.

He was a great friend and musician and he was a great part of the Thunderbirds. But the drugs and the drinking and the traveling and the loneliness of the road, as we all know, can reach out and snatch you at any moment. One minute you're on stage sounding great -- they love you. And the next minute you're in your motel room by yourself, alone, wondering what happened. So that's why so many musicians end up at the bar and maybe end up with people that they may not want to run around with. But they're just lonely. But anyway, that's what happened.

His mother, Margaret, was beautiful and smart, and she loved Keith very much. Keith had that house over in South Austin. His mother and grandmother lived next door. His mother bought the house. The first thing Keith did was paint it turquoise.

Keith was a very, very charming guy when he wanted to be. He could charm the president if he wanted to. One time, we ran into Mel Torme, the famous jazz musician, in the airport. Keith could hold a conversation with Mel Torme and keep the conversation going. He learned a lot about music from his dad, who was also a musician and a serious record collector. He worked at Starday and the big record distributors in Houston and taught Keith all about the record business when he was a kid. Keith's dad was an encyclopedia of jazz and blues. Every time we played Houston, his dad would come and sit out front and be the proud father of Keith. Even though his parents were divorced, they both supported his music, loved him -- and he loved them very deeply.

It was a real experience to meet his parents and all his friends in Houston when we'd play there. It was like he knew everyone. He introduced me to Joey Long, the great guitarist, and a lot of other Houston greats. He knew about the whole Gulf Coast blues scene, beginning to end. Like I said, he was very charming.

One common thread that I noticed in all these stories is that everyone liked Keith and had great times with him. All the people in this book really loved Keith and thought he was cool and wanted to hang out with him because he was so much damn fun. You never knew what he was going to say or do, and he was always just a giant personality on his own. I'll never forget him as long as I live.

As you will notice in these short stories, whether he was giving you something to eat or he was just walking away, everybody in this book thought a lot of Keith. All the stories I read, nobody said that they didn't like him. I think you will really enjoy this read from all of his friends. I really miss him and think about him all the time.

-- Jimmie Vaughan

Foreword by Billy F. Gibbons

Keith Ferguson:
Master of style and attitude

As those who know Keith through his work behind his now infamous early '52 Fender Precision bass guitar, it's fair to say that his sense of entertainment, dark as it may have been perceived, stands as the valuable sliver in the persona that propelled his playing into realms of realism, always one step ahead of the masses.

As a left-handed player, it allowed Keith that unusual advantage of appearing "backwards" which, of course, immediately set him apart from the norm, a setting which, no doubt, was much to his liking.

And perhaps the best part of that unexpected advantage is simply that Keith possessed immediate passion and a wealth of rare examples of splendid recordings from his vast collection and was intimately knowledgable of the best in blues, the best in western swing, and at the far end of the extreme, his intimate connection with Tex-Mex music -- Keith's way of what was considered the best part of spinning and spending a day.

Keith's disturbingly droll demeanor still remains one of his most memorable traits. And those that know tend to agree -- Keith Ferguson was thunder and lightning in a tall Aztec frame.

ZZ Top guitarist Billy F. Gibbons.
Courtesy of Billy F. Gibbons

And here is the opportunity to dig in and dig out the eccentricities which remain in the ethos, eccentric energies that constantly visit any number of unexpecting individuals who suddenly "feel" something excitingly foreboding. As it was once said, "Yeah, man, Keith's out there." And the response? "Yeah, and he's out there 'cuz he's known out there!"

Rock on, Keith.

-- Billy F. Gibbons

Author's Introduction

Detlef Schmidt, of Germany, has been a guitar and bass collector since 1984. He wrote a book about early Fender Precision basses and writes articles for a German bass magazine. As a bass player, he tours with bands in Europe. He recorded and toured with U.S. blues artist Louisiana Red and one of Germany's leading blues acts, the Matchbox Blues Band.

The author playing a 1970 Fender Telecaster Bass with a Seymour Duncan Quarter Pounder pickup.
Courtesy of Charly Phillip

Writing a book about Keith Ferguson without ever having met him? Writing it living in Germany? OK, how come?

It's a long story. Being a bass collector, I wrote a book about old Fender Precision basses in 2010, "The Fender Precision Bass 1951-1954". During the research, I contacted Preston Hubbard, the bassist in The Fabulous Thunderbirds after Keith Ferguson. He told me that Erin Jaimes, an Austin bass player and singer, has Keith's old Precision bass now. I contacted Erin, and she gave me a little information on the bass, which I featured in my bass book.

Then, at the 2010 Arlington Guitar Show in Texas, which I attended to promote the book, I met Mark Hickman, a former bassist for Anson Funderburgh. He told me that he had owned an old Fender Precision that later was played by Keith Ferguson, and he told me the serial number, #0069.

A Canadian friend told me of a Facebook group about Keith, and that someone had mentioned #0069. I finally contacted Scott Ferris from Dallas, who owns the bass now. Through a misunderstanding, Scott thought that I was writing a book about Keith. I told him I wasn't and that I was just researching the bass. He replied that I should write a book about Keith. **The idea was born.**

This was in summer 2011. Scott then gave me contact to Gerard Daily in Fort Worth, who had sold the bass to him. Gerard helped getting me in contact with Liz Henry, who had lived with Keith. Liz put me in touch with Margaret Ferguson, Keith's mom, who was 91 years old at that time. Margaret was very kind and gave me her support. She gave me some initial contacts, most importantly Conni Hancock, a former girlfriend of Keith. I made a lot of phone calls, and I exchanged some handwritten letters with Margaret. **The plan was born.**

In October 2011, I flew over to Austin, did the first interviews and was given access to a Lubbock archive, to which Margaret donated all of Keith's papers and old letters that she had kept. I met a lot of his old friends. Scott Ferris supported the project by driving me around and helping with interviews.

Craig Higgins, who had started a book about Keith in 2008 but had to stop the project because of his studies to become a doctor, supported me with all the interviews he had done at that time while he was living in Austin -- and he had done some great interviews. I returned with a lot of material and lots of personal impressions.

The material collection continued in 2012 and 2013. Again, I flew over to do interviews; again, Scott was driving me around. I was not sure if I should tear the interviews apart to fit them into the timeframes the parts would fit, because a lot of people knew Keith over long periods. I talked to Margaret about that problem, and she said to leave the interviews together.

This leads to the structure of the book. It's a chronological history of Keith's musical career and life so that the reader gets an overview, followed by interviews separated in the chapters Houston, California, early Austin, Thunderbirds, Tail Gators and late Austin years. Then a chapter on his basses and some notations to shed light on Keith's role to blues bass players all over the world.

My personal highlights during the research for this book have been so many that it is hard to select a few. Reading Keith's letters to Margaret from the years 1968 to 1976. A visit by Armando Compean and his wife to Germany. (Armando showed Keith how to play bass in his Houston days, and he has turned into a real good friend of mine since.) Meeting Jimmie Vaughan, Lou Ann Barton and Johnny Winter when they did concerts in Germany. Meeting Omar Dykes in a bookstore in Austin, and he knew who I was and he knew about the book. The blues sessions with Erin Jaimes in Austin; meeting Anson Funderburgh in Fort Worth; talking to Danny Turansky, who sadly died last April; and, most of all, finding and being able to play the basses Keith used: #0171, #0172, #0069 and the cowhide bass, a '56 Fender Precision.

Receiving an email from Billy Gibbons from ZZ Top, with greetings from Texas and him expressing his will to support the book with an interview, was another highlight. Bill Ham, former manager of ZZ Top, was so friendly to answer some of my questions via email.

Doing all the interviews, meeting lots of old friends of Keith, who were all very supportive and contributed hundreds of pictures out of their private archives, was just fun. Some of the evenings I will never forget. I was impressed by the number of loyal friends Keith had, all really nice people -- and with some, I really became friends with over the years.

And I remember the great times Scott and I had down in Port Arthur with Carlos, Billy, Phil and Glenn -- just an unforgettable evening with good food, blues music and drinks.

I received a deep inside view of Texas blues music and read a lot of books. Mike Buck from Antone's Record Shop in Austin was very educational (got a lot of vinyl records for my collection).

Writing this book was a big experience for me. I hope while reading it you have the same fun as I had compiling it.

-- *Detlef Schmidt*

With A Little Help ...

The book would not have happened without the following people: Gerard Daily, Scott Ferris, Conni Hancock, Craig Higins, Neil Meldrum, Kathy Murray and Cal Stone.

Gerard Daily at his house in Fort Worth, 2014.
Courtesy of Gerard Daily

GERARD DAILY was a good friend of Keith in his late days and is also an established Texas musician. He not only contributed an interview, he also offered to overlook the whole project by reading all the interviews, helping me with historical correctness, and making sure the book is respectful to the memory of Keith. He and his wife, Lois, accommodated us while we were in Fort Worth -- a big thanks for this, also.

SCOTT FERRIS is a member of the Dallas Blues Society. Scott gave the initial idea of the book. His help during the trips to Texas was invaluable. He volunteered to drive me around, helped me with the interviews and the scanning of the pictures, and did some interviews of people that I could not reach during the times of my visit. Scott was my contact in Texas and did a lot of phone calls to talk to people to get interviewed. He is just a great help, a great person to talk to, and a good friend. I would not have been able to write the book without his help. Nothing is nicer than to have somebody who picks you up from an airport in a foreign country (you don't have to do the driving while suffering jetlag) and to have someone to share your thoughts after the interviews. I also want to thank his wife, Valeria, because they accommodated me so many times in their house. Scott has

Scott Ferris with his Fender Precision #0069 that once was used by Keith.

Courtesy of Scott Ferris

a great YouTube channel where he puts all the videos of all the concerts he has recorded. Look out for "TeeBeeFerris".

Mike Steele, Conni Hancock, Margaret Ferguson and Scott Ferris, 2011.

CONNI HANCOCK a former girlfriend of Keith, was my contact to Margaret Ferguson. Being out of a music family herself, she had come to the idea of storing all of Keith's things in an archive in Lubbock. Through her, I got access to the archive, and the permission to use everything came through Margaret. The archive was so nice to scan all the documents, and I received 14 DVDs full of material. Also, Conni Hancock is responsible for some interviews about Keith that she organized in 2009 in her house and that were recorded by Lubbock University.

Craig Higgins playing a Thunderbird Bass
Courtesy of Craig Higgins

CRAIG HIGGINS is a bass player from New Orleans who lived in Austin for a while and had started to write a book about Keith. Being in town, he got some great interview partners. He had to stop his book project because of his studies to become a doctor of physics. And he was so nice to contribute all of his material -- his typed interviews, all the addresses and telephone numbers that he had collected. We stayed in close contact during my research, and Craig always was a great help. I hope we meet in person some day.

Neil Meldrum in his house in Scotland.
Courtesy of Neil Meldrum

NEIL MELDRUM was the one who nominated Keith to the Walk of Fame. That plaque pictured in the book very well might not be there outside of Palmer Auditorium if it wasn't for Neil's thoughtfulness. Neil gave me the initial start to the book by sending me a huge album of newspaper articles he had collected over the years.

Kathy Murray on her veranda in Austin, 2011.

KATHY MURRAY offered to do a final proofreading. As an Austin musician who was around at the times, she knows the names and spellings (which was sometimes difficult when names were mentioned to me in interviews and I wrote them down phonetically).

Cal Stone playing upright bass.
Courtesy of Bill Bresler

CAL STONE and I met through my bass book, "The Fender Precision Bass 1951-1954". He sold me an old gig bag, and while emailing, I told him that I started a book about Keith. An editor for a Detroit-area newspaper and bassist, he offered to do the proofreading and editing of this book and help with the layout. I had bought the layout program Indesign, and with the help of my Spanish friend Alicia, created a basic layout; the fine tuning was done by Cal.

Chapters
Introduction

Keith was born July 23, 1946, in Houston. His parents, Margaret and John, divorced when he was a baby. He grew up living in apartments with his mother. His father worked for a record store, so Keith got into contact with music early and already had a large record collection when he was in his teens. He spent his summers in New Braunfels, Texas, at the house of his grandmother Effie. He sang in a choir in his high school, which he graduated in 1964.

He had friends out of the music scene, and it was Armando Compean who taught him to play bass. A lot of his friends were Mexican-American, and Keith started to learn to speak Spanish and begin his interest in Mexican music (which maybe became his main love later on). He was hanging around musicians; Johnny Winter became his friend in about 1966. Both were blues lovers. He was married in 1966 for a very short time (the marriage was annuled); got his driving licence (but later on decided not to drive); was not drafted into service; and worked a very short time in a record shop.

Keith had a deep interest in blues music and good connections to the English blues scene. That would lead to a flight to England in late 1968 with Johnny Winter with the intention of getting Johnny a record contract with an English blues label. This journey had a huge influence on Keith, coming back with English clothes, boots and a shag haircut. During this time, he also made friends with Billy Gibbons and Dusty Hill, who later formed ZZ Top. Around 1968, he started to play in bands, bought his first bass, a 1952 Fender Precision that he kept playing most of his career.

Like lot of other Texas musicians, he went to California in the late 1960s. His mother bought him a car, a Rambler Station wagon, in which he travelled to Californa to join Sunnyland Special, a band with Angela Stehli and Lewis Cowdrey. They made their first 45 records while they were touring Texas. He later played in various bands in California, making friends with other musicians and the roadie from Jefferson Airplane.

A young Keith with Santa Claus.

Courtesy of Margaret Ferguson

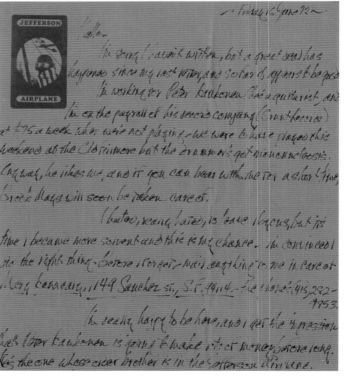

Keith's letter from California in which he reports on his work with Peter Kaukonen from Black Kangaroo, June 26, 1972.

Courtesy of Keith Ferguson Collection

I recall seeing Lipscomb, having looked at his pictures again. It was during summer school last year and he and Hopkins were standing outside this rec studio about a block from school. I remember because he was nearly toothless and wore a hat. He ...carried a guitar that could've been electric. Mc Cormick was with them. They all went in and I forgot about it.

There is a ......preacher shoe shine boy named Walter at the airport. He knows some blues (He won't sing blues "devils music") and many spirituals. I know because Sunday before last I was out there with .... And I started whistling "Motherless Children". He started ... singing and said that they sing it in the little church where he preaches. I ended up with a free shine. He is a cool guy.

Above: Keith's letter to his mother, undated, in which he talks about Lightnin' Hopkins, Mance Lipscomb, manager McCormick and blues. Top right: Keith's letter from England, writing of his trip to England with Johnny Winter, October 24, 1968.

Courtesy of Keith Ferguson Collection

Below: Keith with Muddy Waters.

Courtesy of Watt Casey (www.wattcasey.com)

The Jefferson Airplane connection let to a deal as a touring bass player in 1972 for Black Kangaroo, the band of Peter Kaukonen, younger brother of Jefferson Airplane guitarist Jorma Kaukonen. He also kept his friendship with Johnny Winter and visited Johnny in New York. He joined him as a sidekick on tours, including one in 1970 to England where Keith stayed a few months longer to find work as a musician.

Around this time he got to know Jimmie Vaughan and visited Austin, which was just beginning to attact musicians from all over. Around 1973, Keith moved to Texas' capital city, starting to play in bands there. Life as a musician was hard; not much money made. Keith played in numerous bands -- Storm with Jimmie Vaughan, The Nighcrawlers with Stevie Ray Vaughan, and a band named The Texas Sheiks. When Clifford Antone opened up his club, Antone's, in 1975, Keith was around and played with numerous black blues musicians like Muddy Waters, John Lee Hooker, Eddie 'Playboy' Taylor and Hubert Sumlin, especially when he joined The Fabulous Thunderbirds. During that time, he was also playing with Rocky Hill, the brother of Dusty Hill and one of the most underrated guitarists in Texas.

In 1976, Keith joined The Fabulous Thunderbirds which originally included Lou Ann Barton (later Keith's wife) and bassist Pat Whitefield (who left and Keith joined). The Thunderbirds -- now with Jimmie Vaughan, Kim Wilson, Mike Buck and Keith -- started their touring, first going to the East Coast, using Antone's club and Austin as a home basis.

They got their first recording contract in 1978, started touring England together with Dave Edmunds, and had TV appearances in Germany. Fran Christina came in as the new drummer. The band made three more records and played on an album of Carlos Santana's, *Havanna Moon*. Lots of musicians liked the way the Thunderbirds approached the blues, amoung them Eric Clapton, The Rolling Stones and Robert Plant. The Thunderbirds later toured with Clapton and opened up two concerts for the Stones in Texas. Keith influenced the Thunderbirds by his dress style and his huge knowledge of the blues. He also was an influence on Stevie Ray Vaughan.

During that time, the Thunderbirds were constantly touring. Being on the road for more than 15 years, Keith didn't like the touring anymore. He wanted to be home more; his drug habits interfered with trav-

Advertisement poster for the single "The Crawl".
Courtesy of Keith Ferguson Collection

The Thunderbirds with Nick Lowe, the producer of the album *T-Bird Rhythm*.
Courtesy of Keith Ferguson Collection

***Real Blues*, June/July 1997**[36]

"In the mid 1960s, when British blues researcher Mike Ledbetter traveled to Houston, Texas, to investigate the local blues recording scene there, his guide was Keith Ferguson. Ledbetter ended up buying a large protion of Ferguson's rare Houston 78s and Keith took the money and bought a Fender bass and the rest is history."

Grammy nomination from 1985.
Courtesy of Keith Ferguson Collection

elling. His mother had bought a house for him. He married singer Lou Ann Barton in 1980, but they soon divorced. Then Conni Hancock, also a musician in The Supernatural Family Band, became Keith's girlfriend, and they were together until about the time he was out of the Thunderbirds.

Keith left the band in 1984, being replaced by Preston Hubbard, then bassist for Roomful of Blues. Keith played bass on The Leroi Brothers album *Check This Action*, then joined The Tail Gators with guitar player Don Leady. With that band, he recorded five albums and also toured. During that time, Keith received a Grammy nomination for his playing on the album *Big Guitars of Texas* together with Mike Buck, Don Leady and Denny Freeman.

Around 1990, Keith left The Tail Gators, again not wanting to travel anymore. From then on, he mostly stayed around Austin, playing in local bands like The Excellos and The Solid Senders with Hector Watt and Spencer Thomas. He was also booked for pickup gigs and for recordings, mostly together with Mike Buck. He spent his days out on the porch of his house, a meeting point for local musicians and friends. Keith died April 29, 1997. The official cause: liver failiure. Lots of his friends were at his death bed when he passed away, among them Conni Hancock, Daniel Schaefer and Jimmie Vaughan.

Painting of Keith (most likely done by Rolling Stones guitarist Ron Wood), which his mom, Margaret, had kept in her collection.
Courtesy of Keith Ferguson Collection

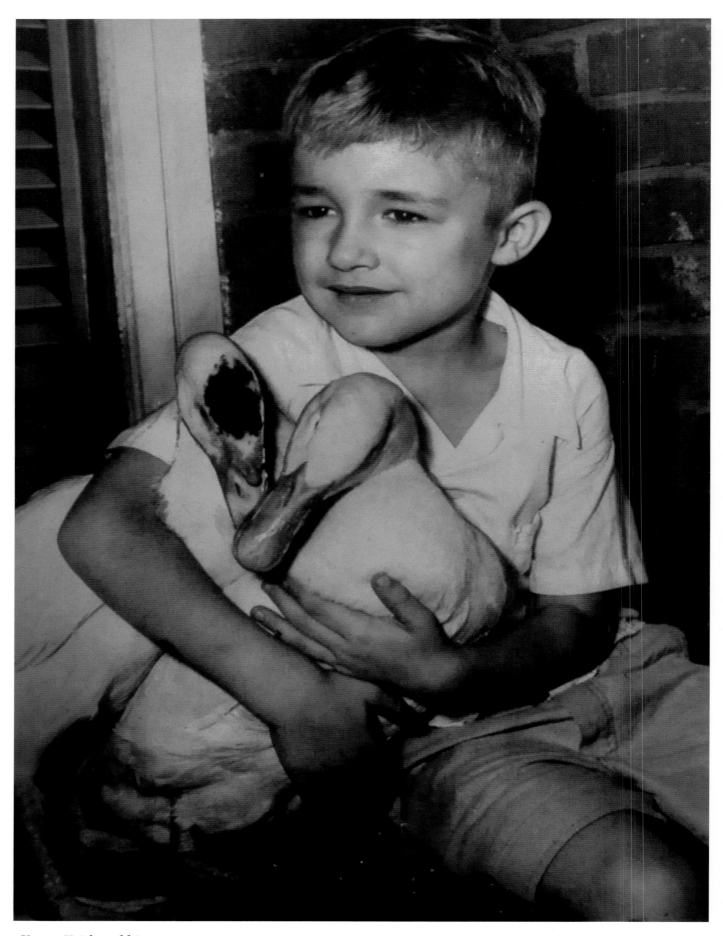

Young Keith and his geese.

Courtesy of Margaret Ferguson

Chapter 1

Houston Days

1946-1968

Chapter 1

Houston Days 1946-1968

Growing up in Houston

Margaret Ferguson
Interviewed by Detlef Schmit, October 2011

Keith's mother, Margaret Ferguson, was 91 at the time of the interview.

I was born in Osage County, Oklahoma on August 9, 1920 (the town is now named Barnsdall), then we moved to the southwest Oklahoma. My maiden name was Talbutt.

I graduated from high school in Oklahoma City and then we moved to Houston in 1937 during the Depression. I liked living there. Houston was different, and I loved going to Galveston. I worked as a secretary for Exxon.

Keith was born on July 23, 1946. His pop wasn't interested in a baby boy. Keith was a baby when we divorced. His father's name was John. He died in the beginning of the '90s.

We did not know John's family very well. There were two brothers; both ran away from home. Their mother was very mean. His father did not want much to do with Keith, but his father spoiled him later on. Keith did not know his grandparents on his father's side. Keith's grandfather was a postman.

Keith and I had a garage apartment. He would go out in the alley and pick up really big worms to keep. He went to a private school next door, and he had been out collecting them. The bell rang, and as he went upstairs, he just stuck the worms in the teacher's pencil container.

He would ride his bike across town and sit outside the black churches to listen to them singing. He liked to watch TV and to make model planes, and they hung all from the ceiling. He had friends from different racial groups, which was uncommon during the '60s. One of them was black; this made me proud.

Keith was really close to his grandmother Effie. His

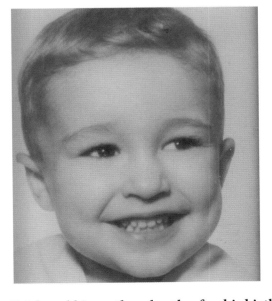

Top: Keith and his mother shortly after his birth; (middle) as a toddler; and (bottom) growing.

Courtesy of Margaret Ferguson

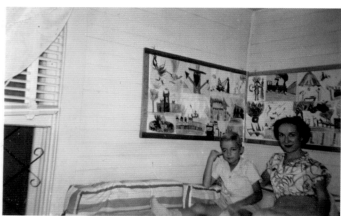

Some family photos of young Keith. Margaret: "On the last photo below, Keith was told not to look into the camera."

Courtesy of Margaret Ferguson

grandmother spoiled him. Grandmother lost a son, so when Keith was born she took over. She lived near San Antonio. Keith went to her in New Braunfels in the summer and loved it.

We both loved the zoo in San Antonio. We hit the snakes first thing. There was a black cobra -- really tall and it spit venom at the window. I took Keith to Amarillo to my brother Dillard when Keith was 13. My brother helped straighten Keith out. Keith wrote me a letter saying, "I will study if you let me come home." Keith stayed long enough for Dillard to be a good example.

He went to San Jacinto High School. He had an Hispanic friend named Mando Compean. They were well-known Houston musicians. This friend of his needed a bass player. Keith played the bass guitar upside down.

I took Keith to New York after he graduated. We were on our own and never took a taxi. We went to the Museum of Natural History. We went out late at night to see an oud player in a club. I have fond memories with Keith of listening to the player. We had a friend in Greenwich Village back in 1965. The club where the oud player played was featured in a magazine.

Keith enjoyed my traveling. I would bring him scarves. He loved the berets I brought him from central Asia. At mother's house there was no attic, just a little space, and there was this huge gecko. The sounds they made was "fuck you". Keith was so delighted. He would put a folding chair out in the yard, and it happened around twilight, and he would invite guests out there. He would invite guests over to hear the gecko.

I was not going to interfere with his career choice. I wish that he would have pursued his art more. He did what he wanted to do, and he did it quite well. He had many talents. I am just sorry that he didn't do more with his artistic abilities. He liked customizing everything -- clothing and instruments. He would have been a good teacher.

Central Church continues to grow in the grace of singing. Two choral groups meet regularly at Central. They are called on to serve in radio and television work, weddings, funerals, and in special teaching situations. The purpose of this work is to give opportunity to those who are talented in singing to use that talent more fully in the service of God. The separate work of these two groups has the natural result of improved congregational singing when the whole church comes together for worship.

This chorus meets weekly under the direction of Nancy Taylor and Peggy Miner. They are taught to love and appreciate the best hymns and to sing in two- and three-part harmony. This group also appeared on television in 1955. Plans for 1956 include television work for both this and the adult chorus.

First Row: John Collins, Keith Ferguson, Allison Gainey, Susan Bivins, Gaylene Cayce,
Second Row: Paul Gainey, Charles Cayce, Cecile Cogswell, Carol Welsh, Carol Cayce,
Third Row: Mike Carter, Sherri Roberson, Morgie Callender, Lee Catherine Garner,
Sally Easley.

JUNIOR CHORUS

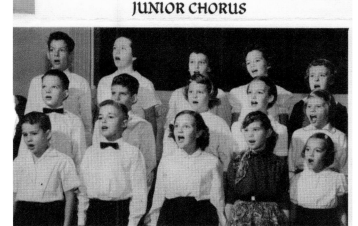

Keith (second from the left, front row) was a member of a junior chorus at the age of 11.
Courtesy of Keith Ferguson Collection

SAN JACINTO SENIOR HIGH SCHOOL

CLASS MOTTO: *"Happiness is the full use of your powers along lines of excellence in a life affording scope."*—An Old Greek Proverb

PARK PLACE BAPTIST CHURCH

4101 Broadway

THURSDAY, MAY 28, 1964

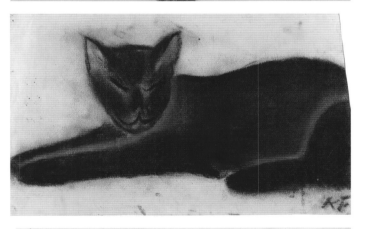

Above: Keith graduated from San Jacinto Senior High School. Right column: Pictures drawn by Keith; his love of cats started at an early age.
Courtesy of Keith Ferguson Collection

Searching the archive

Keith's mom, Margaret, gave full access to the archive in Lubbock, Texas, where most of Keith's papers are stored.

All the items used in the book will be cited in the short form Keith Ferguson Collection. The long form is Keith Ferguson Collection, Southwest Collection/Special Collections Library, Crossroads Music Archive, Texas Tech University, Lubbock, Texas.[1]

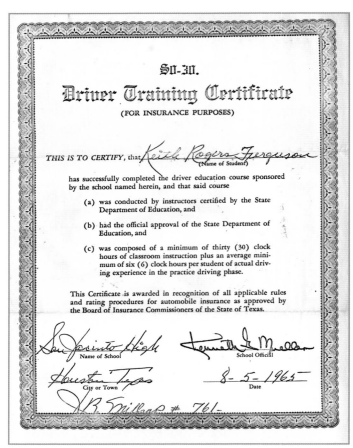

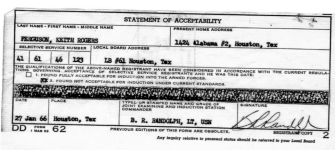

Top: Keith's high school diploma, 1964.
Above: Keith was not drafted into the military, which was a good thing at the time of the Vietnam War.

Top right: Keith's Driver Training Certificate, 1965.

Right: A certificate of his first marriage in 1966. It did not last long and was annulled in May 1967. The last name was erased by the author.

All courtesy of Keith Ferguson Collection

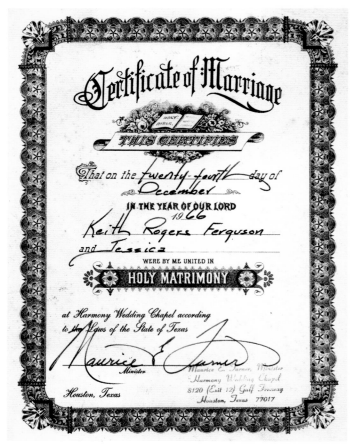

The 1969 registration (above) for Keith's Rambler station wagon like the one shown below, which he drove to California.

Courtesy of Keith Ferguson Collection

Tuesday (undated)
Pulliam and Walter ... gave me a call Monday night a week ago. Talked for '5 minutes. They played some Blues records over the phone. They sounded as crazy as ever.

Keith's love of blues music can already be found in his early letters. Playing records over the telephone -- definitely different times.

Courtesy of Scott Ferris

May

The car gave me not one bit of trouble the whole trip — tires, everything shipshape. Unbelieveable.
In between here and Houston is some really pretty country — nearly all excellent roads. It's very pretty here — air's real nice, too.

Most likely the first letter that Keith sent to his mother from California, May 1969.

TEXAS DEPARTMENT OF HEALTH
BUREAU OF VITAL STATISTICS

FILE NO. 74182-46

NAME Keith Rogers Ferguson

DATE OF BIRTH 7-23-46   SEX Male

PLACE OF BIRTH Houston, Texas

FATHER John William Ferguson   MOTHER Margaret Faye Talbutt

DATE FILED 8-9-46   DATE ISSUED 3-24-88

This is a true certification of name and birth facts as recorded in this office. Issued under authority of Rule 54a, Article 4477, Revised Civil Statutes of Texas.

A copy of Keith's birth certificate, issued in 1988.
Courtesy of Margaret Ferguson

Left: A young Keith at Christmas.
Courtesy of Margaret Ferguson

27

Learning to play bass

Armando Compean

A friend of Keith Ferguson since their teenage days in Houston. Armando Compean -- bassist, vocalist, composer and band leader -- boasts a

career with a countless number of collaborations and musical partnerships. He has worked with Oscar- and Grammy-winning producer T-Bone Burnett, playing the bass on such films as *Walk The Line*. Armando can also be heard playing the bass on numerous recordings with artists Taj Mahal, Jennifer Warnes and Coco Montoya, as well as singing vocals on jazz guitarist Joe Pass' *White Stone* record.

Armando Compean playing a Strat in the 1960s.
Courtesy of Armando Compean

I first met Keith in high school, in the ninth grade when we were 13 or 14. Because we were both loners and had our own unique style, we were considered weirdoes in school. As a result, we naturally gravitated towards each other and became good friends and were almost inseparable between the years of 1961 and up to1968, right before I moved to Los Angeles, California.

Keith was a troubled child and that could have been due to the fact that he had a very strained relationship with his parents who had already been divorced when I met him. Since I had never known anyone with divorced parents, it was a foreign situation for me. Keith did not speak well of his father during our teenage years. He thought of him as weak and as not having a very strong character. Even though I always experienced his father as being polite and proper, their relationship was tense and uncomfortable. I recall an exchange between them one time that accelerated and became volatile and ultimately physical. This appeared to be a much needed blowout for both of them because that confrontation seemed to ease the strain between them and, years later, I

was told his father attended many of the concerts of The Fabulous Thunderbirds. The bond between Keith and his father became much stronger as they grew older. Keith was in his 20s when he found out that his father had been a classical pianist.

During our high school years, I was a guitar player in a blues and R&B band, and that drew us together even more. He started coming to my gigs, hanging out and soaking it all in. He told me how well I was playing the blues. Although it was nice to hear that, I didn't know what I was doing. I was just playing. As our friendship deepened, he became part of our family. He would come to my home every day after school, including some weekends, and he enjoyed the fact that we were always surrounded by good food and music because my entire family was musicians. After school, Keith would watch me practice an hour of classical piano, while quietly picking at my dad's nylon string guitar, holding it upside down, since he was left-handed. He loved talking to my sad who taught and played classical violin and upright bass, and who enjoyed Mexican boleros and classical music. My father had been born in 1893 in San Luis Potosi, Mexico, and as a kid played snare drum in a marching band that supported Pancho Villa. Keith was fascinated and curious and couldn't get enough information from my dad about the old style guitar playing of the days of the Mexican Revolution. He spent hours at our home, watching, listening and asking questions. Houston, like New Orleans, is divided into wards, and my family lived in the Sixth Ward, which the Latin community calls El Sexto. Although Keith was born and raised in another part of Houston called the Montrose area, he loved the vibe of the Sixth Ward. So you could say that during those years he was practically raised there.

Our family took regular trips to Laredo, Texas, where we had relatives. Keith accompanied us. While there, we snuck across the border to Laredo, Mexico, and found our way to the red light district called Boys' Town. We were fascinated because this particular part of town was swarming with clubs, bars and women for sale. It was the first time we had ever experienced anything like that and, if I remember correctly, probably the first time we ever got laid. In fact, we had such a good time that we repeated the jaunt another time by lying to my father that I had to go on a trip with a high school band. So, Keith and I got on the road with our friend John in his car and couldn't wait to get down to Boys' Town again for some more drinking, clubbing and women. Those were good times.

After we finished high school, I got called to play bass with one of my favorite bands named The Perry Mates. Although I was technically not yet a bass player, I could play well enough to get through a gig. So, I fudged the truth a bit and accepted the gig. In order to play, I convinced my dad to buy me a bass and amp. He did, and my first bass was a used blond 1962 Fender Jazz bass with a brand new black Fender Bassman amp. I was styling. The gig was a six-nighter and Keith was there every night and, as usual, watching, listening and learning. After a week of playing bass, I was hooked and never came back to the guitar.

David Tristan, bass; Armando Compean, guitar; and Ralph Saldiva, sax.

Courtesy of Armando Compean

The Sultans: David Tristan, bass; Ralph Saldiva, tenor sax; Johnny Pena, trumpet; John Gonzales, tenor sax; and Armando Compean, guitar. Armado: "To this day, I do not remember the drummer. He was subbing for Eddie Rodriguez, who could not make this concert because he was being punished for receiving a failing slip in school."

Courtesy of Armando Compean

Many nights after The Perry Mates gig, we used to go to an after-hours place called The Upstairs. It was a gay club where all the go-go dancers, musicians and people working at the local bars would go to party. It was a great place. We used to love to go there. Some nights I would sit in with Johnny Winter with whom Keith became very close friends. Even though by now Keith had begun to play bass, he was not yet playing professionally, but he continued to check out as many bands as he could.

Going back a bit, when I was still a guitar player, I was playing with my band, The Sultans, at a college frat party. In a future interview, Keith stated that it was at a high school dance but I beg to differ. He probably had a memory lapse. It was definitely a college frat party. In any case, this is what happened. My bass player had been overserved. In other words, he got blasted and could not continue playing the gig. We tucked him in the car after trying to revive him with a few slaps. It did not work. So, I had to think fast. Since I knew Keith had enough natural musical instincts and a good feel, I felt I could teach him something quickly. We went over four licks -- a

basic shuffle, a pattern for playing ballads, a simple walking bass line, and a basic boogaloo funk. Because he had heard the band's material enough times, he was able to grasp everything quickly. In order to accommodate his left-handedness, he had to flip over the bass and play upside down. But forward we went. Although at first it was a little rough and he was in a bit of a shock, he finished the night and did a great job. It was his first gig on bass and he was elated.

Shortly after that life-changing night, his mom bought him a brand-new, left-handed Fender Precision bass. It was beautiful, brand-new, shiny and with a sunburst finish, probably made between '63 and '65. I don't remember exactly. It was Keith's first bass. Years later, he got his second Fender bass, which was an older Fender Precision bass (most likely a '52) which he liked a lot. I personally was not fond of it because the neck for me was a bit too thick and I was used to playing the Jazz bass, which had a smaller neck.

When I met Keith at the age of 14, he was a meticulous collector of blues albums and he would correspond with blues enthusiasts all over the world. He was already familiar with blues artists not yet discovered by the mainstream, broader audience -- artists like Lightning Hopkins, John Lee Hooker, Sunnyland Slim, Muddy Waters, B.B. King, Freddie King, Albert King, to name a few. Even though blues was Keith's first love, he later came to appreciate the local Tex-Mex conjunto music and became as passionate and equally knowledgeable about that genre. As the English music invasion evolved, he became interested in The Beatles and The Rolling Stones. He was particularly enthusiastic about Jimi Hendrix because even though Jimi was considered a rock guitar icon, he was basically an amazing blues man.

By 1966-1967, Keith was renting an apartment in the Montrose area. He began to let his hair grow and it was on the long side. Keith's father worked for what was considered at the time a high level record store, and Keith always had a lot of information about the various albums. He had an amazing ear and was good at remembering melodies. Quite often we would sit around his place and listen to the current Top 40 records: James Brown, Otis Redding, Wilson Pickett, Albert Collins and Little Johnny Taylor.

Among the many things Keith and I enjoyed, were

seeing Lightnin' Hopkins at a place called Bird Coffee House, as well as seeing The Beatles live at the Houston Coliseum. What an experience. It marked our lives.

I was fortunate in that the majority of my gigs were in the black part of town. Not only did I play at these places, but we would also go there socially to listen to music and to dance. One of our favorites was the El Dorado Ballroom. It was a huge room with a big stage and a 10-piece R&B band that featured a musician named Spooky Dance who played the B3 organ, saxophone and sang like a soulful angel. We always felt privileged to be part of this great musical circle and environment. You could find the real authenticity and depth of blues and R&B in these places. Another wonderful musical adventure was at the Palladium Ballroom where we saw Little Richard, Bobbie Blue Bland, Little Junior Parker and many others who had a distinct influence on us. There would be a group of about six of us. We would get all dressed up in expensive suits, try to look cool and older than our teenage years. It never seemed to bother anyone that we were teenagers and the only non-blacks there, and we never experienced any problems in these clubs, only fun times. These were some of the most enjoyable times of our youth.

Young Keith with an unknown friend. This photo came out of an album that Keith had given to his friend Becky Stapleton Crissman

Courtesy of Becky Stapleton Crissman

Johnny (Winter) took such a liking to Keith and enjoyed his company so much that in the late '60s, he invited him as a sidekick to England on his first big tour there. If I remember correctly, either Ike Sweat or Tommy Shannon was the bass player at the time. When Keith came back from that trip, he seemed to be a changed man and had morphed into a British rock star. He was wearing rings, scarves and snake skin or leopard boots. This was the complete opposite from the pachuco persona he ultimately ended up with for the rest of his life.

The last time I saw Johnny Winter was in the early '80s in Houston where he was hanging out at a Thunderbirds gig. The reason I remember it so distinctly is that when Johnny saw me there, he was so happy to see me that he ran up to me and gave me a big hug which broke my glasses. Even though I was unable to see clearly the rest of the night, it was great to unite with him again.

Speaking of Johnny Winter, I also had the pleasure of playing with his brother Edgar for a short time when I was still with The Perry Mates in 1967. The last time I saw Edgar was in the early '90s, when I played in the house band at the China Club in Hollywood, where he sat in singing and playing the alto sax. He brought down the house with an absolutely stellar performance.

Another person Keith was very fond of was Eddie Rodriguez, who played drums in my teenage band, The Sultans. Eddie was a big guy whose sense of humor kept us constantly laughing. Even though Eddie wasn't the best drummer, when he played a shuffle, he played his ass off. Eddie also played with Jimmy Reed, among many others. Eddie and Keith also played together with Johnny Winter and Sammy Highburger, and they also worked together in the Dallas band The Werewolves with Brian and Seab.

Keith had many girlfriends and love affairs. One day, in 1966, at an after-hours club, he confessed to me that he had been having an affair with a girl I had been seeing for a while, Jessica. Since I had entrusted him to look after her during my gigs, needless to say, this news did not sit well with me and I felt betrayed. We had a heated exchange of intense words but, ultimately, managed to straighten it all out and remain friends. Shortly after, he called me and said, "I may have fucked up. I married Jessica." They continued to have an on-and-off relationship for a few years but it was never a model marriage. During that time, Keith

***Record Mirror*, March 1980**[18]

Keith remembers seeing Jimmy Reed: "The first time I saw him, was in a night club in Mexico -- a giant Mexican nightclub that held 2000 people -- and he was there on Halloween Night and the place was packed."

A shot of a young adult Keith.
Courtesy of Margaret Ferguson

also fell in love with my niece, Laura, who was the oldest daughter of my brother, Robert. That relationship fizzled away as well, and Laura, unfortunately, died shortly afterwards. Substance abuse was suspected.

There seemed to be always something going on in Houston at that time, somewhere to play and hang out. My friend Rudy Flores played guitar in his own band called The InCrowd. His grandmother owned the Cadillac Bar and his father a bar called the Red Rooster. Every Sunday there were jams going on and sometimes fights would erupt. These were funky and rough places but the rougher they were, the more Keith seemed to gravitate towards them.

As I recollect my friendship with Keith, many memories have surfaced -- both happy and, especially sad that Keith is no longer with us. But when it comes right down to it, these were some of the best times in my youth and I would not change a thing.

Teen Canteens

Frank Sarro
Interviewed 2011/2012

Frank was Keith's friend during their teen years. Frank played drums, congas and sang for The Vanderas, a band Keith used to listen and go to their concerts. Frank currently lives in Houston and collects vintage drum sets.

Another friend of Keith, Eddie Rodriguez, also played drums in The Vanderas. With Eddie, Keith would later play in other bands. Eddie passed away in 1986.

The Vanderas in 1962.

Courtesy of Frank Sarro

I first met Keith through Armando Compean when I was about 15 or 16. I think Armando may have been teaching him to play bass at that time, but he wasn't yet accomplished enough to play in a band. I was in a band at the time called The Vandaras, and we played the same teen clubs that Armando's band, The Nite Owls, played. It was at one of those teen canteens where I met Keith. In the early '60s in Houston, there were several teen canteens where all the local young bands played -- Taylor Hall, Teen Hall, Mason Park, Love Park, and Wood Park.

We remained friends up until his untimely death. I would visit him at his home in Austin -- which, by the way, was painted '57 Chevy Aqua Blue -- spending the night and going with him to his gigs. At the time, he was playing with The Tail Gators and later The Solid Senders, groups he played in after the Thunderbirds.

I believe Keith was married for two weeks to a lady named Jessica, who was originally Armando's girlfriend. Keith worked as a rack jobber for the same Cactus Records here in Houston that his father retired from after 30 years. That was the only non-playing job Keith ever worked. I am not really sure what his responsibilities were, but that job lasted only slightly longer than his first marriage.

He had a very small apartment in the Heights here in Houston, Texas. Keith was a clothes horse. He was a fashion trendsetter. He loved his tattoos even before they were popular like today.

Keith's first real bass was a '52 Fender P bass. He bought it from Texas Tom Slaughter (Mickey Gilley's bass player) who worked at Brook Mays Music store here in Houston. Brook Mays was the happening music store here all through the '60s and '70s. My friend Jim Fulton was the manager at the one on my side of town. He actually sent a lot of jobs my way, and I played in several bands with him.

I believe Keith's first working band was with Sammy Highburger (piano), Jim Fulton (guitar) and Eddie Rodriguez (drums) -- Sammy Highburger & Company -- a typical Texas roadhouse band, Jerry Lee Lewis style; solid rock and roll. Eddie Rodriguez was like an older brother to me.

Houston's Cactus Music

The Daily brothers' father, H.W. 'Pappy' Daily, opened a downtown store, selling coin-operated jukeboxes. He moved into the record business in 1946, opening Daily's Record Ranch, a store that sold records for under $1. Daily sold the store to his sons Bud and Don in 1959. The Dailys opened Cactus Records in 1975. The store had several retail outlets.

I knew him from when we were 13 years old. He basically taught me to play drums. The Vandaras was the first band for both of us, and we took turns on drums/bongos/singing. Most of the concerts I went with Keith to were the back-to-school concerts that had multiple acts. I did see The Beatles with Eddie.

Around '72, he played with the former guitar player from The American Blues, and Dusty Hill's brother, Rocky Hill. The Rocky Hill Blues Band was a three-piece band with a drummer named Turtle from up north, I think Boston. Rocky was a monster guitar player, every bit as talented as Billy Gibbons, but he had a problem with depression and drugs. I think that's part of the reason Dusty and Frank (Beard) left him and their group, The American Blues, to team up with Billy G to form ZZ Top. Keith played with him for a few years around '72-'73.

The Werewolves were a fellow named Seab played guitar; Brian was the singer; Keith on bass; and a friend of mine, Eddie Rodriquez on drums. They were not together for very long and played mostly at a club here in Houston, Texas, called The Cellar. The Cellar was a famous rock dungeon in which The American Blues also played. Keith was friends with Dusty and introduced him to me as a perfectionist.

Keith's father was an avid music fan who possessed a huge record collection. He worked at a local music store here for over 30 years and was constantly buying every blues record he could get his hands on. He was very egocentric about his collection in that he would open a record, play both sides and never allow it to be played again. He was a buyer of classical records. I don't know anything about him being a musician.

Mr. Ferguson was a very meticulous man. He dressed impeccably and was always very neat and well groomed. His influence on Keith's musical taste was indeed profound. I visited his home many times, and he would play some of his col-

The Vanderas: Eddie Rodriguez (left) and Frank Sarro (right).

Courtesy of Frank Sarro

lection for us. His stereo system was first class; you could feel the bass in your chest. All tube type stuff. As far as I knew, he and Keith got along just fine. Keith's parents divorced when he was very young, and Keith was not above playing them off against each other to get whatever he needed at the time.

I believe it was in the late '80s when Mr. Ferguson passed. As far as I knew, Keith always had a real good relationship with him. He left a massive stereo unit and his record collection to Keith. I'm not totally positive, but I believe Keith donated the collection to Rice University here in Houston, Texas. I know he sold all the stereo equipment, but the record collection, to the best of my knowledge, was donated to Rice University.

The main thing that upset Keith's dad was Keith's inability to let go of some bad habits that interfered with his responsibilities to the T-Birds. I'm fairly certain that his dad was trying to practice what was known at the time as 'tough love'. He definitely wasn't breaking ties with Keith because of his departure from the 'Birds; however, that might have been how Keith rationalized it.

Keith and The Werewolves

Frank Sarro: "I actually only saw him play one gig with The Werewolves at the Cellar Club here in Houston... I remember that very well because Keith introduced me to Dusty Hill that night... I do not know whether or not he played with The Werewolves on a regular basis or was just sitting in for that night."

Bobby Baronowski (Werewolves drummer): "Keith did not play the New York Dolls gig with the Wolves. Keith just played one gig that I believe may have been Mother Blues, when Bucky Ballard was on guitar because Seab Meador had left temporarily to move to NYC."

The Vanderas performing a Back to School Dance for KILT, a Top 40 radio station in Houston.

Courtesy of Frank Sarro

The Vanderas: Tom Prado, guitar; Jim Reeves, guitar; Frank Sarro, drums; Bill Ross, bass; and Alfred Arespie, singer; backstage at the Sam Houston Coliseum.

Courtesy of Frank Sarro

"Keith was a clothes horse. He was a fashion trendsetter. He loved his tattoos even before they were popular like today."
-- Frank Sarro

Hispanic Friends

Lucy Cullivan
Interviewed by Craig Higgins, 2008
Lucy was a friend of Keith in the 1960s. She gives some interesting insights into his early years.

I met Keith in November '64. I went to a club with a girl who graduated with him. He came over to talk to her and she introduced me to him. He asked for my phone number and I gave it to him. About a week later, he called me. I never met his mother in the early days, only later when the Thunderbirds came to town and she attended the concert.

He always had his friends over -- his friends from school -- and they were all Mexicans.

I used to come and watch him practicing, and he would play records for me that he had bought and they were all in Spanish -- musica nortena, from the north of Mexico. That's all he ever played. The only friends that I knew that were friends of his were all Hispanic.

The guys that he hung around with were mostly musicians, Armando Compean and others. Armando's father was a music teacher and all of Armando's brothers played an instrument. Mando played the guitar and he also played the piano. Keith wasn't playing the bass yet when I met him.

He left Houston and was going to California because he wanted to play with someone.

Keith and Lucy Cullivan.
Courtesy of Rudy Flores

He mentioned Johnny Winter. He would send me postcards all the time. He never wrote letters; postcards all the time. Wherever he went, he would send me a postcard.

My kids just loved him. When they grew up, they would say, "Where is my dad?" to Keith.

He played with Johnny Winter and Rocky Hill. It was before he would play with the Thunderbirds, when he was in Houston. He would call me and I would pick him up and drive him to Rocky's place.

When they (meaning the Thunderbirds) came in, we were always on the guest list -- my kids and their friends. I guess he just loved to have us around.

I met Lou Ann one night when he played at Fitzgerald's. He said, "You can call me any time when you want" and I said, "But you are married." And he said, "It doesn't matter. They know who you are." And when I met Lou Ann, she said, "Oh, my god, you're Lucy."

My children were at the memorial service for Keith. Rosanna was there and Mark was there.

Keith grew up in Magnolia; that's near the Port of Houston. They were living in an apartment. I knew John real well, the father of Keith. He worked over there at the record store.

One time at the Richmond Barroom, Johnny Winter came in to see the Thunderbirds. My son Mark was in the Air Force and we were backstage when Johnny Winter came in. I think he came out twice to see the Thunderbirds. Keith toured in Europe with him. I remember he sent me postcards from all over.

When he came back from California, he came by my house, knocked on the door, and I said, "Who the

A signed photo of Keith, Lucy Cullivan and Rudy Flores backstage.

Photo by Tracy Hart/ The Heights Gallery; Courtesy of Mark Cullivan

hell is that?" I didn't recognize him. He was totally a different person. When I heard his voice, that's how I recognized him. I said, "Oh, my god. Why are you dressed that way?" I had just seen him in his suit with the tie when we were going out. He was wearing these boots, and I think they were kind of patched, different colors; some crazy jeans and a striped T-shirt that looked like it had had been torn. And he had a thing around his head, like a headband. And he had long hair, which I had never seen him wear.

My mother came in and looked at him and he said something to her in Spanish. He spoke Spanish to my mom. I said, "Where did you learn this?" He said, "I told you, one day I would know how to speak Spanish." When I met him in the '60s, I don't think he did know a lot of Spanish. He was always sitting in the kitchen and my mom was talking Spanish to him. I knew he'd say, "Si." And she talked Spanish to him all the time. I asked him if he understood her. He said, "Sometimes I do and sometimes I don't." So I said,

"Be careful what you say 'si' to."

He never would drive a car. He said, "I know how to drive, but I don't want to. I don't like to drive." And he would never drive. I thought that was real funny. No matter where we went or what, I would be the one to drive. Mark did live upstairs for a while. Effie moved to Austin in the early '80s. His friend Rocky Hill told me that Keith really loved me. I took him over one day, and we went in and drank two beers.

The first time I saw Keith playing with the Thunderbirds in Houston was at the Juneteenth Festival. They would play at the Miller outdoor theater. He called me and told me, "Go!" We went and the curtains were closed and you heard … there comes this music from behind the curtains, and I went, "Wow, who is that playing?" I thought this was some black band, you know. And all of the sudden it starts to open little by little, and there were these white boys. Everybody in the black audience started screaming.

I don't remember when I met Keith because I was only 7 years old, but I do remember him as always being very nice to me and giving me a lot of attention. He would always talk 'to' me as opposed to most others who talked 'at' me. When Keith would come and visit he would always spend time with me drawing pictures of guitars, guys playing guitars and cats. I loved cats and that was one thing we had in common right from the start, because he loved cats, too.

When I was a senior in high school (I went to the same school Keith did) -- after not seeing Keith for quite some time -- he came back from California to see mom. What a way cool thing that was to see him. I went up to the door and there he was, wearing these killer boots, jeans with a hole near the crotch and long shaggy hair. I also had long hair that year, as did my friends who were over hanging out. We welcomed him in like he was a hero. He told us all about his travels and about how Carlos Santana cut off all his hair and became a Jesus freak. When I retold the story the next day at school, all my friends thought I was telling this big old lie until it came out later in the magazines and the radio -- no Internet then, of course. I was one of the coolest dudes at school after that because I always knew a lot of what was happening in the music biz because of Keith.

After I graduated high school, Keith was not over that much. He was off doing his music thing trying to get a band together and eventually moved to Austin. Much later he told a story about one of those nights when he came to visit after he came back from California. He and Dusty Hill were walking over to our house one night when they were stopped by the cops. The cops had a field day with them making fun of their hair and the bag Keith had. When they got out of the car and threw Keith against the hood, Dusty went nuts and started screaming, "Oh, hell no, I didn't serve in Vietnam to come home to this!" Keith thought, "Oh shit, we're gonna get our asses kicked now." But instead, the cops told Dusty, "Hey man, calm down, it's OK. You can leave." Dusty never served in Vietnam, but it worked anyway. After that, the cops took Keith's bag and dumped it all over the street, shoved him into the back window of the car, rolled it up on him and started beating him. They let him go after they had their fun. Keith told me he'd had enough of the Houston cops after that, and that's

Mark Cullivan in the Air Force, 2013.
Courtesy of Mark Cullivan

when he decided to move to Austin. That was the tipping point.

Another weekend, I was visiting Keith. He gets this phone call, and afterwards he closes all the curtains and told me not to answer the door. He said Johnny Winter was coming over and he didn't want anybody there when he showed up. Johnny arrives in this giant tour bus, gets off and the bus leaves. We hung out all afternoon and then climb into my car and go over to Rollo's place to get Johnny a tattoo. He gets this huge Phoenix on his right thigh. The feathers were all the colors of the rainbow, including yellow. Keith said he was jealous because Johnny's skin was so white that even yellow shows up real good. Johnny's girlfriend gets a tattoo of his autograph on her hip.

I lived upstairs from Keith when he died and spent many nights alone with him talking on the porch. I didn't realized he was so sick at the time. He never said anything other than he was sick. He told me about how he really regretted not joining Billy Gibbon's band. That always ate away at him. Billy, Dusty Hill and Dusty's brother Rocky would call Keith all the time. One night, Rocky called Keith and asked him to join his band he was putting together or do a little tour or something. Keith gets off the phone and says, "Can you believe it? He wants to use electronic drums and play with a prerecorded backup guitar. I ain't doing that shit." Keith said Rocky told him some of the stuff he wants to do is impossible to play without a backup recording. Keith says he told him to get another guitar player, but Rocky told him he wanted to keep it a three-piece. Keith said he liked the idea of keeping it a three-piece because you don't have to split the check as much, but didn't like the electronic drums and prerecorded music even more. I didn't think it was a big deal, but not Keith. No way!

There were two important things Keith told me that I remember like it was yesterday. He said there was only one person in Austin that always came through for him no matter what. That was Ralph Ritchie. Ralph genuinely loved Keith, and the feeling was surely mutual. I remember Ralph told me one day, "I can't figure out if Keith thinks of us as his little brothers or his kids." We had a good laugh over that one. We were always getting in trouble with Keith. I think we were more like his kids.

On another night, we were talking about the T-Birds and what everybody was doing. No animosity or anything remotely resembling that; just reminiscing. Keith begins to talk about Jimmie Vaughan, nothing profound, just little things. He finally tells me how much he missed hanging out with him. Other than when we lost Stevie, this was as emotional as I had ever seen Keith. Then he says, after a short pause, "I really miss him. I love Jimmie like a brother." He said "love" as in the present tense. It was very difficult for me because I could feel his pain. I knew how much he was hurting, and there was nothing I could do to help ease that pain.

I can never fully explain how much of an influence Keith had on me and how much I loved him. He was like a father and big brother rolled into one. He never lied or said anything to hurt me. He was gentle, kind, caring and always generous. Anyone who really knew Keith knew this. He had his demons, not just his addiction, but very deep emotional burdens as well. Fate dealt him a rotten hand, and I, for one, felt it was way more than anyone of his caliber deserved. We lost a wonderful human being, and some of us will never overcome that grief. I miss him every day and always will. I love you, Keith.

Mark, Vicky and Keith in 1985.
Courtesy of Lucy Cullivan

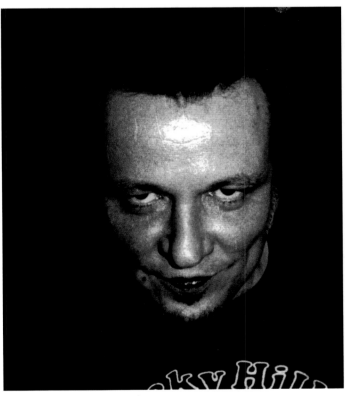

Keith wearing a Rocky Hill T-shirt, 1985.
Courtesy of Mark Cullivan

Cadillac Bar and Red Rooster

Rudy Flores
Interviewed by Detlef Schmidt, 2012

Rudy Flores, a friend of Keith since the '60s, is an artist, guitar player and photographer who took some great shots of Keith.

I knew Keith from about 1966 on. With my band, The InCrowd, we played the Cadillac Bar in Houston from about 1963 to 1968, then we all moved to California. Armando (Compean) already had left to California a few months before me. In 1969, me and the band packed up everything and we moved up there; 1970 we even played in Las Vegas.

Keith was sitting in with us; he came over to the Cadillac Bar. The Cadillac Bar was my grandparents' bar. They lived upstairs, had a bar downstairs. Then my dad opened up a lounge called the Rooster Lounge. They had jazz on Sunday for lunch, and he let me play on Fridays and Saturday from time to time. Keith would come over and jam; Armando would come over; everybody in town would come over. I don't remember what bass Keith did play at that time. I think it was a Jazz bass he got from Armando.

I knew Armando helped him a lot. Armando taught him some things, lent him some instruments. Once Keith was on, he had his own instrument. He played with Sammy Highberger, and there was another guy who had a little band where they played some rock 'n roll. Keith was jamming with them. When he moved out from Houston, I was already in California. I didn't see Keith for a long, long time. I think he moved from Houston to Austin and then to California.

My friend Charles, who was playing keyboards in the band, him and Keith were always fussing around. We all liked Keith very much. We had this inauguration thing going on in the band. Somewhere in the middle of Main Street, we all grabbed him and put his trousers down -- some of that teenage shit. But Keith was really cool. All the others tried to pull their trousers up really fast, but Keith was cool. He said,

"You fuckers," and then pulled up his trousers real slow with no hurry.

At that time, Keith did play with Edgar and Johnny Winter, and that is how I met Jimmie Vaughan, through Keith. Later on, when I was in California and I came back to Houston to visit, I saw him with the Thunderbirds and with The Tail Gators. We would hang out and drink some beers.

His Spanish was pretty good but he was still learning. He could understand, but later on, he got better. He already got his first tattoos when he was in Houston. It was that gang type of thing at that time. Armando and I were not into those things. We were born American; always speak English unless you went over to grandma's house.

Lucy Cullivan, her mother lived next to my house. Lucy's family knew my family. Lucy's son Mark was visiting Keith when I was visiting him in Austin. Mark used to visit Keith a lot.

The Catacombs and the Cellar

Tommy Dardar
Interviewed by Detlef Schmidt, 2012

Tommy Dardar, a vocalist and fiery harmonica player from Houston, has been doing this a long time and gigged with Lightnin' Hopkins, Mississippi Fred McDowell and Juke Boy Bonner.

Keith and I first met when I was playing a gig with my band on the steps of the Houston Art Museum in '68 and became friends for the most part after. Billy Gibbons did sit in that day, and so did Keith. I don't remember who Keith was actually playing with at that time, and Gibbons had not started ZZ Top.

The Catacombs was a popular teen club here at that time in which I had first seen The Moving Sidewalks, which was Gibbons' first band that I knew of at the time. It was also the first club that I met Jimmie Vaughan, who played with the Chessmen at that time. Doyle Bramhall was their lead singer. These guys really rocked the house.

The Cellar was a late-night strip club that I and many others in the area played in the old Market Square in Houston where the girls danced on stands on each side of the stage. That's when I met Rocky and Dusty Hill. They had a band called The American Blues, and all had dyed their hair blue. Thus came my association with Rocky, Keith and (Unc) Uncle John Turner, drummer of Johnny Winter's band. I guess we kind of ran in the same circles, so to speak. Me and Rocky and Keith played a few gigs together at Irene's in Houston, but I always had my own band for the most part and played harp for Lightin' Hopkins. We did a lot of shows together at the old Liberty Hall here in H-Town.

I went to Georgia, were I met The Allman Brothers Band, then Austin and New Orleans, then back to Houston sometime later. Keith got with the T-Birds and did real well for a while. I got in trouble with the law and disapeared for awhile, but like birds of a feather, we all seem to come back together towards the end then.

The Tommy Dardar album *Blues Fool.*

© LocoBop

I heard about him and Unc going to Amsterdam with Alan Haynes, and they dissapeared when they got there. Hell, if I would have been on that gig. I'd have been right beside them.

My favorite story is when I would come to Austin and go sit in with him at some joint on Sixth Street. The last time I had seen him before he died, I called him and he said he had to see me. So I went down to south Austin, sat on the front porch of the old house with the checkerboard tile inside, and we talked for a while. His leg was pretty messed up, but he wouldn't say a thing about it. I said, "You ever see Jimmie or any of them lately?" He said Jimmie did come by and talk with him for awhile, as if to say their peace with each.

Then he gave me this double CD, *Different Tacos* -- a bunch old live performances of old T-Bird stuff he played on -- and said, "I want you to have this." So I said, "Well, I hope you signed this so when you die, it will be worth something," to which Keith said, "Yeah, I wrote something for you inside." So I hugged him goodbye and left. Later, when I got to the house, I opened it up and it said, "Best wishes, Orson Wells". I laughed my ass off.

The first band

Jim Fulton
Interviewed by Detlef Schmidt, October 2012

Jim Fulton is a music store owner and a repairman for the famous music store Rockin' Robin. He was the guitar player of the first band Keith played in. He worked for the Houston music shop named Brook Mays, where Keith bought his first amplifiers.

Jim Fulton in his music shop, October 2012.

I met Keith somewhere in the '60s. I left the Air Force in 1966, got a job at the music store in 1967. So it must have been probably 1968 or 1969. He bought his bass directely from the guy I was working for, Texas Tom. He was so proud of this bass. I was running another store at this side of town and he brought it by and showed it to me. He had some Rotosound strings and wanted me to put them on. They barely fit on there backwards. They were round-wounds and everybody was using flatwounds right there.

I don't think the bands we played together had any names. We just got together and somebody got the gig and we would go and play. We were not making much money back then. You made $90 a week on a six-nights gig. That's a week pay -- and you were glad to get this, too.

We played some pretty rough places over at Harrisburg, which was kind of a rougher area back then. I remember a place where the owner pulled out a chrome plated pistol and started chasing some guy in the bar and shot it while he was chasing around. It was all concrete walls in the inside. Nobody got shot. Ray Hall was the saxophone player, Eddie Rodriguez played drums, Keith played bass and I played guitar. Keith and Eddie were always jivin'. They were really funny to be around. It was a lot of fun.

Keith wanted to be a Mexican, so he spoke Spanish with this real kind of a Spanish accent. Eddie has passed away. Eddie was a really good drummer back then, and he sang. I knew Eddie a little bit more than I did Keith. Keith did have long hair; he always dressed very special. He was really cool, wearing the Beatle boots and all that stuff. He was always pacing;

he would pace back and forth when he would talk to you. And when he was smoking a cigarette, he had it between his little fingers. He was just a different kind of person.

We would go to his apartment. It was furnished with records -- the whole wall had nothing but racks of records. He would pick one out, put it on and start pacing back and forth. "Listen to this." Before it was finished, he would pull another out. He was definitely into music, 100 percent.

And he was kind of guru everywhere he went. People would always respect Keith. His father worked for a record shop. I never met his father, but I met his mom. She signed for him, I believe it was an amplifier. She was in there in the music shop and filled out a credit application. She was a real nice lady.

I saw him when he came back from England with Johnny Winter. I still worked at the first store. We went to lunch and were sitting together and talked about England and Johnny, about where they were hanging out and things. That was still at that Brook Mays store. I don't know if Keith ever played with Johnny Winter, but they were buddies.

We did mostly do the blues. When we played with Sammy Highberger, we also did some Jerry Lee Lewis rock 'n roll, some slow songs. We played some clubs, the 55 Club in Baytown. Somebody got the gig, and we would put a band together and play.

Keith was a good bass player; he always had a good feel for the bass. Later on he was into Kay and Har-

mony hollowbodies, but I think he got the best sound out of his Fender bass. The first Thunderbirds album was great. When Keith went to Austin, I kind of lost track.

I met Keith later on at a Rolling Stones concert in Houston. It was the Thunderbirds, ZZ Top and the Stones playing. I had sold an old Fender amp to Ron Wood and the road manager brought me backstage. Then I met Keith and I had somebody to talk to. The Stones had a different backstage area.

In my first store, Billy Gibbons taught guitar there. I think it was before ZZ Top. It was when he played in the Moving Sidewalks. He didn't have a little studio to teach. They were sitting on the stairs to the room where they kept the cases. He always had these vintage guitars. He'd bring his old Strat down while he was teaching to change strings.

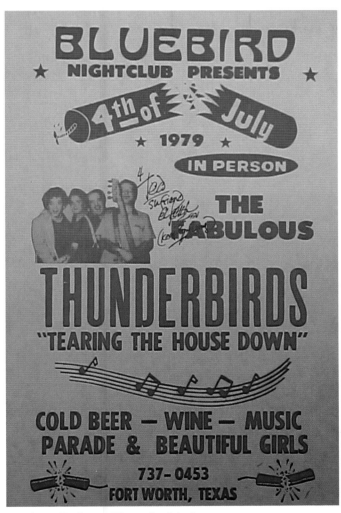

Early Fabulous Thunderbirds posters.

Courtesy of Ted Tucker

43

Old pictures from a rehearsal room. Top: Rob Franklin (with guitar in striped shirt next to Keith) and other unidentified musicians. Below: Keith's 1952 Fender Precision bass had no stickers on it yet.

Courtesy of Becky Stapleton Crissman

The Port Arthur connection

Philip Samuels
Interviewed by Detlef Schmidt, 2012

Phil is an old friend of Keith who knew him
since the mid 1960s in Port Arthur.

My parents' house was here in Port Arthur. My
neighbor that lived in the garage apartment behind
our house was Chick Powell. They called him Highway Blues Powell, or Chick the Texas Highway Man,
a famous blues musician. That's where they were
hanging out, all these musicians from Texas. Johnny
and Edgar Winter would come out. My mama would
call me and say, "Hey, the blond boys are here. They
want to use the phone. Do you want to say hi to
them?" We had a phone in the garage. All used the
phone. My father worked for the government. He
said, "If you need to make some long distance calls,
just tell me." Johnny and Edgar, every time they came
over, they were on the phone.

Or Lightnin' Hopkins, all of them would come to the
house. My mama would cook for all of them. And
that's how I met Keith. Keith would walk to the store
and get cigarettes. This was about 1966 or 1967. I
was about 11 or 12 years old when I met him. They
always jammed at the house; daddy would let them
crank it up.

Every time they were playing on the chitlin' circuit,
that's where they were staying. It was an earlier band
before Storm. I try to remember. It was a pickup
band that used to get guitar players from around
here. That's how we developed our friendship back
then. My brother was a big fan of The Storm. I
remember they played at the One Knite, must have
been early '70s.

I considered Keith more like an older brother. He
never drove; he quit driving, and I remember him
telling me. When he later played in Beaumont with
The Tail Gators, he would stay at my house. We always had a huge library of books, and the first thing
he would do when he came over was to go to the
library. Keith was a big reader. When he came after a
gig, and he wasn't that wasted, he would start reading.

**Little Ray, Philip and Joe Mendoza in Port Arthur at
a gig of Joe Mendoza's blues band, Joe Mendoza and
The Shuffle Kings, 2012.**

When he was driving from and to California, they
were always carrying some pills back to Austin. One
time when he drove back, his car flipped on the highway and all the pills scattered all over the highway.
That's when he stopped driving. You always had to
give Keith a ride. He had a bench from a church on
the front porch of his house. And he was walking in a
funny way. Had a lot of good memories with Keith.

I met his father a few times in Houston. His father
was a real educated man, an accomplished musician.
I met him backstage at the Rockefellers in Houston,
when they played there with the Thunderbirds in the
late '70s or early '80s.

His mother was really nice. We all went to his funeral, the whole crew from Port Arthur. That's where I
spoke the last time to her.

Before I would move to Austin in the late '70s, I
did visit Keith occasionally. This was when he was
together with Lou Ann. We would all start drinking.
Keith would never sit down.

Brothers in blues

Quote from Jim Franklin, Austin artist who is Johnny's friend, talking about the Vulcan Gas Company in Austin. (There is more about the club and the cistern in "Raisin' Cain"): "I had some conga drums, a sitar, and then there was some flutes. It was a marvelous chamber, because you could be sitting right next to someone. And if you hit the note, it would resound off the wall. You don't hear it coming from the person; you just hear it coming from the wall. After his first national tour, Johnny came back and did a gig at the Vulcan. He came down from Houston, and Billy Gibbons came along with him. He wanted to see the cistern. He'd heard about it; word had really gotten around. So they go down the ladder -- it was Johnny, Keith Ferguson, Uncle John (Turner) and Tommy (Shannon). Billy and I were waiting for them to get down the ladder; 12-foot or 14-foot. So we went down there, and it was just enough people to line the wall and soak up all the echo. No magic effects -- there were too many of us down there. There'd never been that many people in the cistern."

Quotes from Uncle John Turner, Johnny's first drummer: "Keith Ferguson was one of the most unique people that any of us knew. He was wicked unique. He had a little twist to him. He was different than normal -- a beatnik, a trendsetter. He came back from England with the first shag haircut we'd ever seen, the first pair of bellbottoms we'd ever seen. Keith had a cross and a rose tattooed on his chest. Me, Johnny and Stevie (Ray Vaughan) got tattoos, too -- all mimicking Keith.

"When I got with Johnny, there weren't a lot of blues collectors. I didn't know Johnny was a blues collector until I started hanging out with him. Keith and one other guy were blues collectors -- the only ones I ever

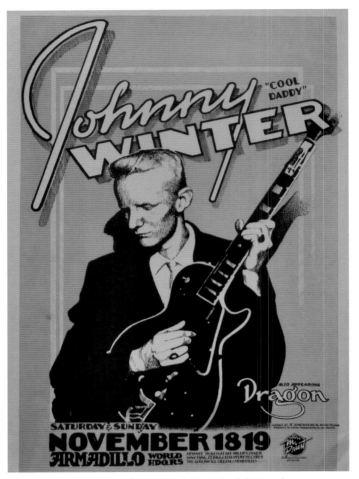

Gig poster at Austin's Armadillo World Headquarters.
Courtesy of Kathy Murray

met. Keith and Johnny had blues in common when no one did. They were islands in the stream with their blues collections. They could talk about Mississippi John Hurt or Fred McDowell, people like that. There wasn't anybody else to talk to, to share information with. I never heard of any of those people until I met Johnny and Keith."

"Me and Keith Ferguson went to Johnny's house in Beaumont (Texas) one Christmas. I didn't have any family there, so we all stayed at Johnny's house, upstairs. Me and Keith Ferguson spent the whole three days there tape recording off of Johnny's 45 collection. Brought that back to Austin and that was the backbone of The Fabulous Thunderbirds' repertoire – Johnny Winter's record collection."

From "Raisin' Cain: The Wild and Raucous Story of Johnny Winter": Johnny also met Keith Ferguson, a musician who shared his love of the blues and later played bass in The Fabulous Thunderbirds. Johnny was playing in the Phil Seymour Band at an after-hours gig at a gay club when drummer Eddie Rodriguez introduced the two like-minded musicians.

"Eddie played that gig and he knew I loved blues and he knew Keith loved blues and he got us together," says Johnny. "We were about the same age and we both liked the same music. He had a big record collection, a lot of 78s that his daddy gave to him and he was sellin'. He was the only white person I knew in Houston that was into blues."

Through Ferguson, Johnny was introduced to Cactus Records on Alabama Street, where Keith's father, John William Ferguson, worked as a classical music buyer. The elder Ferguson was also a musician; he had been a concert pianist with the Chicago Symphony.

"I bought a lot of records in Keith's father's store," says Johnny. "It had a better selection -- a lot of the old reissues on albums, 45s made into albums. I had a Philco set with six or eight inch speakers. I listened to records all the time, straight blues and a few of the hippie records like I listened to records all the time,

straight blues and a few of the hippie records like Firesign Theatre and *Psychedelic Lollipop* by the Blues Magoos. I usually bought records I couldn't hear on the radio. I bought Hendrix -- the first records -- *Are You Experienced*. I bought Bob Dylan albums -- electric and folk -- I liked Dylan a lot."

Ferguson, like many of Johnny's close friends and fellow musicians, died young. He died of liver complications at age 50 on April 29, 1997, but talked about his initial meeting with Johnny in an interview the previous year (Josh Alan Friedman).

"Since blues was all Johnny liked, these local musicians thought it would be hysterical if we got together: 'Let's put these two freaks, these two mutants, together,'" said Ferguson. "Johnny flipped out; he never saw that many 78s in his life. He had records too, but I had more." Ferguson recalled being dazzled by his new friend's virtuosity and said he had to remind himself not to stare when Johnny cranked out a scorching solo in the middle of a song."

"Keith wanted to go to England to see what it was like, so we went together. He had enough money saved and I had enough money saved with Carol

Johnny and Keith comparing tattoos backstage.

Courtesy of Rudy Flores

Johnny, Keith and Lucy Cullivan backstage.

Courtesy of Rudy Flores

working. So we flew out of Houston and went just to see what it was like."

"We had already gone all around the states and it seemed like there was a better deal in England for white blues artists. We went to a lot of different record companies here, though we never did try Chess or those kinds of labels because they were black labels. They didn't care about white blues artists in the states and they did in England. There was no other white blues artist in the states that I knew about at that time."

Johnny and Ferguson stayed in England for two weeks, sleeping on people's floors, chairs, wherever they could find a place to stay. Although they didn't know anybody in England, they had the name of a man who owned a blues record shop. The shop owner let them hang out at the store during the day, use it as their home base, and sleep there if they didn't have anywhere else to go. They spent a couple of nights in London at the home of a clerk who worked at the shop.

"I remember it was November and starting to get cold. The guy had a coal furnace. I didn't know how to work a coal furnace, but I was damned sure gonna try to keep it from being cold in there. We slept in chairs in front of the coal furnace, so I learned to shovel coal in it and light it.

"We saw Jethro Tull at a small club – they were just starting out. I had no idea that I'd be playing festivals with them in another year, but I liked them a lot. We also saw a girl named Jo Anne Kelly who was real good. She never did end up making it. She died of cancer, I think, but she was real good."

Johnny Winter interview (He met Keith Ferguson in 1966 when Johnny was 22): "I bought a lot of records from Keith Ferguson's father -- his father worked at a record store in Houston. He knew a lot about black records -- he turned me on to a lot of records. He was a musician."

"I met Keith in Houston – I had this drummer – we worked a gay club after hours and this drummer played that gig and he knew that. I loved blues and he knew Keith loved blues and he got us together. We were about the same age and we both liked the same music. He had a big record collection. He had a lot of 78s he was getting rid of -- he was sellin' -- that his daddy gave to him, 78s. I can't remember what they were, but he did turn me on to some records I had never heard."

"Both divorced at the same time. He had his own place. His wife was supposed to have been pretty bad. She just ran the show pretty much. She ran around on him too. He was the only white person I knew in Houston that was into blues. So we could play records together."

"Keith Ferguson's father's record shop -- I don't remember the name. He didn't own it -- he just worked there. That was a great record shop though. He got me a lot of great records out of that store. I met Keith from a drummer friend of mine -- Eddy Rodriguez. He knew we were both into the blues, so he introduced us."

"I have three of the Alan Lomax Library of Congress records -- music goes back to the '30s and '40s. Saw them in Keith's father's record store when I was living in Houston. Mance Lipscomb -- he's a Texas musician -- played guitar. Heard about him in Keith's daddy's record store."

Johnny Winter about when he was in River Oaks Hospital in New Orleans for heroin addiction: "Some of my friends came to see me. Uncle John (Turner) came to see me. Keith Ferguson -- the guy who was in the Thunderbirds -- they all came to see me. Nobody from New York came to see me -- Not Steve Paul, Teddy or Rick Derringer -- just my friends from Texas."

Quote from Mike Vernon of Blue Horizon Records: "I met Johnny in November 1968 when he and Keith Ferguson came over (to England) to discuss the realities and possibilities of Johnny recording for Blue Horizon. We may have met over lunch or dinner or at our new but shabby office/record shop in Camden Town in London."

Dick Shurman, Johnny Winter's producer: In 1984, when Johnny was in Chicago and Keith was in town with the Thunderbirds, they got together and showed each other their new tattoos and knives.

Quote from Bobby Caldwell, drummer in Johnny Winter And: "I don't think anybody outside of his own family and maybe Keith Ferguson -- would know how brilliantly smart Johnny is. Yeah, he's got his opinions you may not agree with and that's fine -- but I'm talking about intellect."

First Johnny Winter album.

© Columbia Records

Chris Wellards Records, London

When Keith and Johnny were in England 1968 to get a record contract for Johnny, they stayed at the record shop of Chris Wellard. In the late 1960s and early 1970s, the record shop in New Cross was one of the local hubs for the cultural underground.
Chris Trimming of the London Blues Society. used the shop as a mailing address. This is maybe how Keith got in contact with the record shop. Keith later gave the address to his mother.

Johnny and Keith and an unknown girl backstage.
Courtesy of Rudy Flores

Rocky Hill connection

Joy Hill (Rocky's wife): "Keith, Rocky Hill and Turtle (he played drums; his name is Randy De Hart). Rocky once asked Keith how he got girls. His response -- 'I always ask them for their first and last name when I meet them.'"

Courtesy of Joy Hill

Chapter 2

California Years

1969-1972

The early California days of Keith.

Jamie Howell: "This was a serendipitous shot photographed by John Verbeck from Elyria, Ohio in probably 1968-1969. John was a film editor and a graduate of the Royal Academy of Film in London.

The front row is Danny Thompson; Mary Kennealy, one of the most beautiful girls in Hippiedom; Carolyn Lindner. Her second husband was Jimmy Gillan, the drummer who played with Keith and Peter Kaukonen in Black Kangaroo and had played with Johnny Winter. At the time, she was married to Bob Lindner, the guy in the far right front who was a great recording engineer at Coast Recorders in San Francisco. In between Carolyn and Bob is Rosie from D.C. (no last name).

The second row is Michael Casady (the brother of Jack and the main roadie for the Airplane); Cliff Lundberg; Norman Lombardo (a great musician who was the bass player and singer in my band, Dry Creek Road); my wife, Heidi Howell, who was the head of public relations for the Ariplane's record company, Grunt Records; and a girl named Betsy.

The top row is Debbie Dole, Heidi Howell's little sister; me (leaning back); and Keith."

Photo by John Verbeck; Courtesy of Becky Stapleton Crissman

Chapter 2

California Years 1969-1972

The first recording

Interview with Benny Rowe

Benny played with Keith in his California days and also was a member of Angela & Lewis with Sunnyland Special, with whom Keith did his first recording. Benny had also played with The Wig with Rusty Wier and Boz Scaggs. Later he played with John Lee Hooker.

I met Keith about 1969 in San Francisco. I think we came together through a guy named Tom Schiffour, but I'm not absolutely sure. Tom and I got together through Bob Simmons and Henry Carr. Bob was fairly influential in the music scene in San Francisco then and wanted to help his Texas homeboys however he could. Even though Tom was from Chicago, he seemed like a Texan (laughs). Shortly after Tom and I met, we started playing together in a band named Cross Country. And around that time I met Keith -- definitely a Texas boy…though I must confess, I can't remember exactly how our meeting went down.

Keith and I were first in a band together called Angela & Lewis with Sunnyland Special. Angela (Strehli) was a fantastic singer, and Lewis (Cowdrey) was

a pretty kick-ass harp player. They got together in Austin and then moved to California. Keith was in the band at that time. Angela & Lewis had a guitar player -- I think his name was Robert Franklin. Robert left the band and somebody had recommended me, maybe Bob or Henry. Anyway, I joined Angela & Lewis with Sunnyland Special and Keith was the bass player. There were actually two entities: Angela & Lewis and their backing band, Sunnyland Special -- us. They were based in L.A. mostly. So I went down there and played some gigs with them. I kind of hit it off with Keith pretty well. He was not married, but I was. But we did have similar minds. He was definitely a unique person, especially since he was left handed. It was like having Paul McCartney in the band, but with a blues feel. On the surface, he was a no-bullshit guy. Inside, he was very intellectual.

I remember him telling me a story about when he was playing in New Orleans one night. Some drunk in the crowd invaded his personal space, and Keith put the back of his bass in the guy's face. So, Keith was not the guy to put up with any crap. He was an amazing bass player. The reason was his sense of bottom and keeping the rhythm. His relationship with the drummer was very important to him. He

The first 45 Keith appeared on: "My Back Scratcher" by Sunnyland Special with Lewis Cowdrey, Angela Strehli and Benny Rowe.

Courtesy of Ted Tucker

Early promotion photo of Benny, Cecil and The Snakes with Keith Ferguson sitting in front of a barber's chair.
Courtesy of Benny Rowe

really held the low end, the beat, and the meter of the song -- almost better than anyone I'd worked with. His bass lines were also very tasty. He was no Jaco Pastorius, but he was always so solid, and always hit the right notes -- very complementary. One of the best bass players I have ever played with.

We did a mini-tour of Texas -- Angela & Lewis with Sunnyland Special. We played in Austin, Houston … and we might have played in Dallas, too. I remember one of the gigs we played in Houston. We had this woman sax player in the band, Robin. Jensen was her last name, I think. We were all in the same dressing room, and Robin had no problems in taking her top off and changing clothes with the rest of the guys. Back then it was pretty unusual, but she was an excellent player, and cool to hang with. And, of course, there was a lot of drinking and a lot of drugs and a lot of good times, but never much money.

When we were in Texas, Angela and Lewis booked some time in a studio in Tyler, Texas, which was kind of regionally famous. I think it was Robin Hood Brian's place. And so we went over there and recorded "My Back Scratcher". I think the B side was called "Do Something for Yourself". "My Back Scratcher" was recorded in 1969, to the best of my memory.

We were all pretty happy with the way that turned out. I don't think the record ever did anything sales wise, but there are probably still some copies floating around. I thought it was a pretty good recording. I'm pretty sure not very much ever got recorded with Angela at that time, and I don't remember us doing any other sessions. Those little micro devices with which you can make good sounding recordings like they have today didn't exist back then.

So we did that and went back out to California. Actually, before we left, when we were still in Texas, Angela and Lewis told us that they were busting up the band. They fired us all. Basically, they left, and the rest of us kept going. The drummer was George… I can't remember his last name. Keith was the bass player and I was guitar player. So the three of us stayed together and went back to California. Sometime after we got back to the bay area, George left the band. I don't remember why. Probably because we weren't gigging. But before George left, we had put together some kind of a musical thing -- I don't recall the exact configuration -- and that was the beginning of the next band in which Keith and I played together: Benny, Cecil and The Snakes. We played locally (San Francisco area) for a few months, making no money. I eventually left to join John Lee Hooker's

Benny, Cecil and The Snakes, with Keith Ferguson on the left side.

Courtesy of Benny Rowe

band, with whom I played for six months or so and did two recordings. I think Cross Country was after BC&S but had some of the same members, including Keith and Tom. He'd played drums with The Shadows of Knight in Chicago. I didn't play in Cross Country but jammed with them, and we were good friends. For me, there was a lot of overlap between BC&S, Hooker and other musical projects in which I was involved, and the times/dates are a bit fuzzy ... to understate it. You know ... musicians sometimes play in two (or more) bands at the same time.

Benny and Cecil came from, of course Benny -- that would be me -- and Cecil Cotton, our singer. There was a cartoon show, a kid's program, maybe back in the '50s; it was called *Beany & Cecil*. We thought this was a clever play on words, so we started this band. The drummer was Steve Karnavas for a time, and then Tom became the drummer. At some point later on, Keith left the band but Tom and I stayed together. Cecil also quit before Keith did. So, for a while the band consisted of me, Keith, and Tom playing drums.

I think Keith left not too long after Cecil, but we had a while together with Tom on drums. After Keith left, Tom started to play bass, and we went through a succession of drummers and played several rather informal gigs.

Bob Simmons was a promoter of sorts. Well, I guess he was a promoter; he did a lot of stuff. He worked with Mother Earth some, if I remember correctly. Bob really tried to help all of the bands I was with -- Cross Country, who I never really played with but would have if we'd had some gigs. And Keith played some with CC as well. And Benny, Cecil and The Snakes. He and possibly Houston White (of The Vulcan Gas Company fame) got us some gigs with a printing company called Rip of Press. They published a lot of comic books, I think. These guys would have outrageous parties from time to time, and Bob helped us to get a job as the house band. We'd play for a while, and then all manner of other folks would come up and sit in -- some famous, some not. It was always crazy, though. Simmons was also a radio announcer, and a very good one, with, as I remember, KSAN in San Francisco.

We had a friend that Keith met through me, a drummer named Sammy Piazza, who was the drummer for Hot Tuna. And I think that there was this other lady from Houston; her name was Sally. I believe she might have been the girlfriend of the drummer for Jefferson Airplane.

Henry Carr was always around the music scene. He was involved in the management end of the business. We talked to Henry about managing one of our bands, but it never happened. Henry had reasonably good success in the music business. I think he was a partner of Travis Rivers at one time. Travis and Henry co-managed the Mother Earth band for a while, I think… maybe. Travis was their main manager. Powell St. John was one of the people that started the band (Mother Earth), and I think he and Henry had a close connection.

Keith and I came back to Texas -- I forgot whatever reason it was, maybe it was while we were playing with Sunnyland Special, -- and we went out to a bar named The Jade Room in Austin. Maybe it was Keith that inspired me, but I had bought myself a pair of purple velvet bell bottom britches, and I had this bright red shirt on, and my hair was long. Texas was still a pretty redneck place at that time.

I had gone down to see an old friend of mine (Rusty Wier) play in the bar, and we were just sitting there having a beer and watching the band. Something hit me on the head. It felt like someone had thumped me, you know like with their middle finger, like your teacher used to do. Well, I looked around and no one was there. So I felt it again, and this time located the source. It was a Big Luke -- this 6'6", 250-pound guy that was throwing ice at me out of his glass. He probably had a hundred pounds on me.

Well, next time he reached in his glass, I was ready for him and stared straight at him. Big Luke pulls his hand out of the glass, slams it down on the table as he's striding across the room, and says "Ain't no hippie gonna look at me…" and proceeded with one punch to knock me clean out of my seat. I got up a bit dazed, and after a bit more tussle, Keith, who was standing nearby took what looked like a can of Gillette Right Guard spray deodorant out of his bag, and handed it to me. He said, "It's mace" The next time the guy tried to whack me, I sprayed it right in his grille. And it worked. Then some people came and intervened and wonder of wonders, the cops came and hauled those yokels off to jail. I think Keith might have saved my life that night. I know he saved my ass (laughs).

This was around 1969. Back in those days, hippies did not mess around with rednecks. There were actually two of those bastards, and I remember at one point they dragged me around the dance floor by my hair. That was a disadvantage of having long hair. Except for getting chicks, it could be a real liability.

There is an old story of an Indian rule: never let your hair grow so long that you could be strangled with it.

Another sorta weird thing about Keith is that he didn't like to drive. He had a car, but he was one of those kinds of guys where there was always something mechanically wrong with his ride -- even if there wasn't. He could drive if he had to, he just really, really didn't want to. Mostly, he got women to chauffer him around. What a trip.

Keith played this old Telecaster-style bass (an old Fender Precision). I never saw him with another axe. He always changed the stickers on the bass, and he hung scarves on it as well as on himself. Keith would always dress like the gypsy rider. Stevie (Ray Vaughan) might have gotten some ideas about cool threads from looking at Keith; he was a trendsetter. He had this really long hair, and the chicks dug him immensely. Yeah, he was quite the lady's man. I can't really explain how awesome he was. We were always sitting there with mouths open and watching how easily he could pick up women. It was partly the way he dressed. I never saw him wearing a hat. Head scarves, yeah. But he was too proud of his hair to cover it up. Dude loved scarves. Some would mistakenly call that feminine clothing. Outrageous, maybe. But not really feminine. And the more radical the clothing, the more chicks he got.

The blues scene in Texas, I mean the white boys playin' blues, was just getting popular in 1967. People like myself started getting into it. I started learning guitar with a Freddie King record called *Let's Hide Away and Dance Away*. I played Ventures' stuff too, but Freddie King was the man, as far as I was concerned. That kind of stuff was starting to get pretty widely noticed in about 1965 and 1966. And Keith was at about the right age to be influenced by it, and I know for a fact that he was. There weren't a lot of white bands playing blues and R&B; most wanted to play pop music. What was often called black music (blues/R&B) was happening to some extent in Austin, but I know it was going stronger in Houston and in Dallas. Phil Campbell, Jimmie Vaughan and Paul Ray were the guys that I knew from Dallas. And it was just starting amongst the pasty boys up there -- not so much in my crib, but I loved it. I didn't know much about the Houston scene, but I know it was happening big in Houston. Houston was a bigger blues scene than Dallas or Austin. I'm sure Keith was exposed to it in a massive way because it dominated his style. And I'm convinced that he knew and played with a lot of excellent practitioners well steeped in that tradition, because he was so good at it. In Austin, we used to go to the east side just to get us a reality check. But Keith had all those legends like Lightnin' Hopkins, Bobby Bland, Albert Collins, Arnette Cobb ... way too many to list. No wonder he played like that!

I do seem to recall that Keith maybe played for a bit in a blues band called The Storm in Dallas and possibly Austin, or perhaps not. In any case, it's a good story. Jimmie Vaughan was the guitar player and Paul Ray was the singer. Originally they called themselves Texas Storm, and later maybe just Storm -- memory is obviously failing me right now. The drummer was this guy Phil Campbell that I mentioned earlier. Phil was crazy, but an awesome drummer -- he had a shuffle like no white boy I'd ever heard. I remember these guys were really good. It was a four-piece band -- three instruments and Paul Ray, the singer. Paul is a tremendous singer -- way soulful, but also technically as good as anyone. There was a deejay/radio personality who really saw Storm's potential -- he was very popular, and whose name, I think, was Jimmy Rabbit. So this guy helps out the band, and they were supposed to get a major record contract ... I think it was Columbia, but I'm not sure. They had one of these showcase gigs at the Whiskey in L.A. It was supposed to close the deal. The band was going to come in and blow the audience away. And they were that good. Well, Phil got so screwed up on drugs that they blew the whole gig -- never showed up, the way I heard it. So they didn't get the record contract and then they broke up. Or so that's the story that was told to me, as well as I remember it ... some 40 years later. And if Keith didn't play with them ... he should have. They'd a been that much more awesome.

We also did a lot of jam band stuff in San Francisco back in those days. We often played with Ibicus. It was not a band. It was the name of a guitarist who put together a jam band with Keith, Tom and myself. A really flashy dude. We used to open at various San Francisco jazz rooms, though we played more fusion-rock than jazz. Personnel moves between bands were pretty common at that time. Then, at some point, I left the music scene. I was married and had a baby at that time and realized that I was not supporting my family like I needed to. Music was just not doing it financially. Baby girl had to eat. That was also around the time I was playing with John Lee Hooker, and I made more money playing with John than I did with all the other bands. But John was not

that generous either. In fact, he was downright cheap. My jam bands played a lot for free; the competition was strong at that time, and we weren't really writing that many songs or trying to form a "group". And, like I said, I didn't make enough money playing with John to take care of my family either. So sometime in 1971, I decided that the music business was not going to be what I was going to do anymore. I quit playing, and moved from San Francisco back to Texas, to Dallas, and got into construction. It paid the bills ... well, better than music anyway. After that, I kind of lost touch with Keith for a few years.

I moved to Houston after about a year in Big-D. Keith was from Houston, and through another good friend, Becky Crissman, I met Keith's father, John. He was a really cool and interesting man with an incredible record collection. And through Becky, Keith and I began to re-establish our connection. He was living in Austin at that time, I believe. I saw him in Houston a few times back then. This was probably between 1975 and 1980. Since that time, I had also remained friends with some of my old musical comrades from Austin and Dallas. I was good friends with Jimmie Vaughan and Paul Ray before I ever met Keith. Jimmie always had a good reputation as a guitarist. He was kind of a young prodigy and quite famous throughout the state. People from all over knew who Jimmie Vaughan was when he was 16 years old. He was really quite good.

Jimmie and Kim Wilson started The Fabulous Thunderbirds in the early to mid '70s and got Keith to play bass for them. And since they were playing in Houston from time to time, my friendship with Keith endured. Then eventually I moved back to Austin in about 1981. We would still hang out, but I was pretty established in the construction business, so I wasn't too much into the music scene. But I'd see Keith from time to time. I'm not quite sure what happened with the Thunderbirds, but Keith ended up leaving the band. And, of course, he and I kept in touch. But for his last few years, he began to isolate. Keith always drank a lot, but he could drink a lot and still play well. He was not a junkie when we started playing music together, but later he got more and more into that lifestyle. No matter what he was doing, though, he was always Keith -- a true original. There's never been, nor will there ever be, another like him. He obviously had a self-destructive streak that finally took him. But I'll always remember him with fondness. He was one-of-a-kind -- a tremendous bass player, a very generous person, and a good friend.

Keith's letters

All letters courtesy of Keith Ferguson Collection[1]

Wednesday, May 21, 1969

I live in an ample trailer with our guitarist, he's graduating from Long Beach State (sculpture) and we enjoy privacy and every other comfort and necessity.
We are booked solidly, enough to be more than comfortable — we've got a budget and all is fixed so no welfare is necessary.
We played San Fransisco this weekend — that's the only place to live, really — soo times better that New York.

I've needed an extra bass and they're priced excellently out here — the need increases with all our travelling around and we get more jobs all the time. If anything happened to mine I'd be up the creek, being left-handed. (The reason they're cheap is because working musicians automatically get 10% off on new Fender instruments).

I'm working and no one bothers me so I'm not stagnating and that's precisely why I left Texas again. Out here I pay for what I get.

Friday, June 27, 969

I am, in all truth and honesty, doing well — I have plenty to wear (costumes and everyday are combined, you see) and have more to eat than I need. Our singer is a superb cook and health freak, see and is a zealous disciple of the balanced meal.

Wednesday, July 30, 1969

We've got confirmed booking throughout August and there should be no letup — workworkwork etc. We are back in L.A. for a gig starting August 13.

I found another bass and the band-leader got it for me - $75 and as long as I like to pay it off. It's really necessary as I've been breaking strings right and left for two weeks now. The whole performance must come to an end whenever this occurs, resuming when I've replaced the broken string. This type of occurrence naturally destroys both my nerves and the continuity of the evening and I couldn't allow it to continue — with the purchase of an extra instrument this problem is rendered to nonexistent. I will have the bass paid for within the month with no strain.

Thursday, August 9, 1969 (written on Jefferson Airplane letterhead)

Eddie Rodriguez came out here yesterday to see me — he was on vacation in L.A. and I was really freaked when he came over.

Tuesday, August 19, 1969

Here's an address for San Fransisco that's a lot more permanent.
My relationships with the fairer sex have become too numerous to have my mail sent through one of them, so James (Howell) will gladly and reliably take care of it all.

Sunday, December 14, 1969

San Fransisco was very nice, but there is much more work here, so here I am in Long Beach.

Friday, April 3, 1970

I may have told you this before — do you remember my making a record in Texas with the band Sunnyland Special?
I heard it on a jukebox out here and it's not bad at all. One side was a song that I and most of the band didn't like or want to record, but the other one is quite nice. People have said (and they don't know me) that I make the record good — this is very nice to hear. It's a 45 on Armadillo records (really) called "My Back Scratcher". You'd like it — very danceable and all that.

Johnny has been working almost constantly for the past few weeks — he's leaving for England on or about the 13th. He will do the Royal Albert Hall and recently learned that the tour has been extended to include Paris, Switzerland and points there around.

Monday, May 18, 1970

I hung out with Chris Strachwitz the other day (the Arhoolie record man) and I've turned him into a Mexican-music addict. He's just gotten back from the border and says it's all he wants to record now.
Inspite of this, however, I'm to play a recording session Saturday (for this label) with a black Cajun band from Louisiana. They're nice older guys with thick French accents.

Tuesday, June 30, 1970

The group I'm in is getting more work (starting next week) a fact with which I'm well pleased. We learned five new songs in one day (the day I had the flu) stopping long enough for me to go and throw up every now and then.

Wednesday, May 27, 1970

I went Sunday to a Chris Strachwitz recording session with a black Cajun band — they wanted me to play it, but it would've been too loud, so it was done without bass.
I really miss Mexico badly — until I'm through looking the way I look, I'm unable to go, of course.
I really envy Chris his trips down there. Early next week, I'm to go to his house and transcribe a bunch of "corridos" for him — no one he knows can speak the dialect but me (and write and spell it). My historical background is also rather vast concerning the Pancho Villa era (thanks to José Compean Sr.).

Saturday, September 19, 1970

It's awful about Jimi Hendrix — I really feel lousy about that. People who shoot heroin are in constant danger of killing themselves and often do exactly that. It's so sad that it happened to such a genius (guitar-wise). I just hope that it wasn't suicide — accidental overdoses are pathetic enough. In his case suicide is so uncalled for — I really feel a sence of loss when something like that occurs.
Johnny is doing incredibly well — he took me to San Diego with him for a weekend. It's like an overgrown Corpus Christi and has excellent hotels. He's been doing weekend concerts in places like Paris and Hamburg — really a rough life.
…reports about race riots…
England is so civilized and safe — I'll keep you posted on my progress in that direction.

60

Friday, October 23, 1970

I'm working with a group called Cross Country now, and occasional jobs with my last group, Benny, Cecil and the Snakes. The Snakes were (are) made up of Benny, myself and two other guys ... to whom music is but a hobby. Benny and I are serious, however which is why we're both with Cross Country now. Cross Country's made up of a fellow from Texas and his wife... I'm the band freak, a Martian whose intelligence alarms them all.

I'm looking forward to making enough with this group to go to England.

As far as my plans go, I still intend to go to England once I secure a work permit. Any Christmas presents should be selected with this in mind. I intend to go around Christmas, or the first of the New Year or whenever I have the necessary cash. Our band manager lives at the address on the envelope. His name is Henry Carr.

Saturday, February 27, 1971

Letter on paper of The White House Regents Park, London N.W.1

I am giving this letter to Johnny's girl and you should have it by Wednesday. I had to borrow $200 from Johnny – I've gotten very sick since a week ago or I wouldn't have asked for so much. (Keith mentions a Johnny Winter tour and Johnny leaving to the airport.)

March 16, 1971

I've talked to a few more people here, rather prominent musicians, and the general idea of most of them is to pretend to get a group together without ever really doing so or wanting to. They can afford it, but I can't and I'm growing a little tired of their constant screwing around when all I want to do is work.

I'm to do some work for Johnny Winter in the next couple of month either in his band proper or studio work on his LP which he's to record before summer and that's much better than trying to force work out of a bunch of overpaid English cream puffs.

Wednesday, March 3 (?), March 1971

I stay with Mr. and Mrs. Bill Crawmer and their 15-year-old daughter of Vancouver, B.C. and Kingsport Tenn.

.... the daughter is a Johnny Winterfreak who sometimes talks Johnny and myself into having dinner at their home one night.

.... Europe is so strange, and England too. The thing I came here to escape – chiefly oppression, is indeed missing, but so is something else, that I can't quite put my finger on. The people my own age I find largely dull, but the older people are usually really good.

.....When the day comes that I'm able to take something in my hand besides a guitar in an attempt to take of myself, I'll probably die of relief, until then I'll try to remember what it's like to pay rents and phone bills and such all by myself. Being a gypsy is quite often very miserable, you know. in spite of what everybody thinks.

At the beginning of 1971, Keith stayed a short time in England in order to find work as a musician over there. He came as a sidekick with Johnny Winter and was hosted by a family named Crawmer, also Americans. He spoke with some English musicians but then returned to the U.S.A.

March 24, 1971

I'd like to come home now if it's at all within your power.
Everything's fine, but there are things I must do and I can only do them in the States unfortunately.

Monday, May 31, 1971

Chris Strachwitz (of Arhoolie records) just got back from there and I'm to go visit him on thursday. He always brings back great records and this time's no exception. Lots of great Mexican stuff. I have turned him into an irreparable polka-freak.

923 CHURCH STREET
San Francisco, California 94114
Thursday, June 10, 1971

Henry Carr, since you asked, is chiefly a music publisher, he has publishing rights to several songs; the royalties therefrom enable him to live comfortably in a very nice house. A few years ago he managed some rock n roll bands but he doesn't like doing that so he doesn't do it anymore. He's from San Antonio, where I used to listen to his program on KMAC radio in ,61-'62.

923 CHURCH STREET
Thursday 15 July 71

As for a driver's license - I've let mine lapse, due to the fact that, in California, traffic is so heavy and laws so stringent that driving's economically out of the question as far as I'm concerned. I'm considering getting one in Texas but I'm not at all sold on the idea, since it's more difficult to run over someone (or wreck) while you're walking. I'm still thinking about it, however, and I've by no means discarded the idea.

Thursday, May 11, 1972

The white train help hated my amplifiers but were unwilling to refund money, so I'm here with all my equipment. The colored trainmen are without a doubt the best people connected with the company, they were a great help.
Los Angeles, you can call Jimmi Gillen. He lives nearby and will come over in his car with any message of extreme import.
L.A. hasn't changed much, except that there are more people around looking like I did when I first came here, with jewelry and scarves and all that crap. It's nice not to be worried by police and weird people whenever you leave the house.

Information from Jamie Howell

Henry Carr was a deejay in San Antonio in the pre-hippie '60s and I think may have managed the Conqueroo in Austin during '65 and '66. He moved to San Francisco and managed to stay in the music scene through his connections with Powell St. John and, through him, Mother Earth. He was a charming scoundrel and a good friend of Keith's. I don't know how they became friends but did, and Keith often stayed with Henry while he was in San Fransico.
Keith never had a connection to the Airplane members but was friends with the staff. Henry had nothing to do with getting Keith the job with Peter Kaukonen. I co-produced Peter's album, *Black Kangaroo*, and put together his road band.

Jillian Bailey: "Henry and Ellen Carr, 15th and Guerrero Street in the Mission, San Francisco. Keith lived with them and their cat, Squink. That's where I met him. They were really his family in SF."

Courtesy of Jillian Bailey

Sunnyland Special

Lewis Cowdrey

Promotion photo of Lewis Cowdrey.

Lewis Cowdrey
Interviewed by Detlef Schmidt, 2011

Lewis was based in L.A. in 1968, leading a blues band featuring Pee Wee Crayton. He also worked with Johnny Otis on a belated recording project before returning to Lubbock where he met Angela Strehli, who admired his record collection. Lewis also was co-founder of The Storm, a legendary Austin blues band that boasted Denny Freeman, Jimmie Vaughan, Keith Ferguson and W.C. Clark. His 1994 CD on Antone's, *It's Lewis*, was called the best Texas blues release of the last 25 years by the *Real Blues Magazine*. Lewis now lives in Wichita, Kansas.

Keith played with me in the band Angela & Lewis and The Fabulous Rockets. The record companies didn't like the name, so we changed it to Jets and later to Sunnyland Special. Sunnyland came from the general slang term for southern California as "sunnyland" as well as a subliminal nudge to listeners to think of the American south. Nothing really to do with Sunnyland Slim. This was all advertising and marketing for a general audience, as in those days there was really no blues audience as now. To sell records it was necessary to appeal to everyone, which was our plan. When we played folky-type venues in southern California, we sounded more like what The Cowboy Junkies did later. When we played surfer joints or hippie places, we sounded more like James Cotton and Muddy Waters *Live At Newport* era. When we played black clubs or events, more like Johnny Taylor and BB King. At that time, Keith played more funky than with the Thunderbirds.

When we started The Storm, we had Danny Galindo as a bass player. At that time, our band was kind of badly organized, so I got Keith in. Keith was the funkiest and loudest bass player available -- and a great friend. He was more an artist than a musician. At 6 a.m., he was ready to go to a gig, never looked like a square. This was around '72, '73. Everybody

The original The Storm 45 "The Doo-It".
Courtesy of Ted Tucker

Poster for Lewis and the Legends.

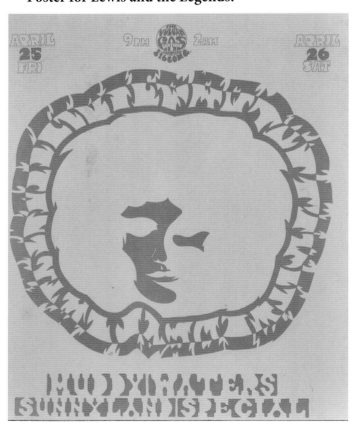

Poster of Sunnyland Special playing with Muddy Waters at the Vulcan Gas Company club in Austin.

learned from The Storm. At that time, a good audience was about 75 to 100 people; an average audience about 35 people.

Keith was a big heavy metal fan. He played with Black Kangaroo on the West Coast. He liked Randy Rhoads. He liked a band named NRBQ. He also played with a Dallas band named The Werewolves. They opened up for the New York Dolls, but Keith didn't play this gig. Bobby was their drummer; the name of the singer was Brian. It was a Clash/Rolling Stones type of music. He also played with Benny & Cecil in San Francisco and in a band named Queen in Los Angeles. He often was taken for his looks. He also played in a band named Aleph Baze and the Jungle Brothers in Orange County. They pre-dated War and may possibly have been an influence. They were extremely rhythmic. Their style was like War, kind of funky and lots of congas.

Keith worked for a record distributor, wholesale. His father worked in retail. Keith took Johnny Winter to England to get a record contract for him. Keith had the connections. This was around '67 or '68. He came back better dressed than ever. Keith and John-

LEWIS COWDREY
"IT'S LEWIS"

Born and raised on the secluded plains of Lubbock, Texas, Lewis Cowdrey never quite fit his middle-class cowtown upbringing. His parents supported his individual spirit and his long-haired style of relaxed indifference to his surroundings. In the 1960s Cowdrey broke out of the confines of Lubbock and headed West with blues companion Angela Strehli. Once on the coast, the two worked with several bands including The Fabulous Rockets and The Jets. Together, Angela and Lewis recorded at Kent Studio and later for Johnny Otis.

After returning to Austin in 1969, Cowdrey recorded a 45 under the name Sunnyland Special and played local clubs (The IL Club, Vulcan Gas Co., The One Knight, and the Jade Room), immersing himself in the booming music culture of the city. He later constructed what would become a legendary Austin club band, The Storm. The Storm's members fluctuated, but consistently proved themselves some of Texas' all-time great musicians. Guitarist Jimmie Vaughan, drummer Doyle Bramhall, guitarist W.C Clark, and bassist Keith Furguson each have claimed membership in The Storm at one time or another. With The Storm, Cowdrey recorded a 45 on Connie Records, and became established in the vanguard of the Austin blues boom.

Lewis & The Legends was Cowdrey's next collaboration and was a joint venture with Don Bennett in the late '70s. Bill Campbell originally played guitar for the group, with David Murray eventually taking over as guitarist. Together, they released an EP on Amazing Records with Ponty Bone.

For some years, many fans of Cowdrey's have felt that his unique brand of Texas blues has been overlooked and under-recorded. His self-titled debut solo album on New Rose Records satisfied an old craving for true fans. Now with an upcoming release on Antone's Records, Cowdrey once again gives the audience what they crave--honest blues, shot straight from the soul.

Known for his raw soul and searing harp chords, Cowdrey is also a guitar wizard and has played with some of the blues greats of his time. He has shared a stage with Pee Wee Crayton, Earl Hooker and George Harmonica Smith and has recorded with Jimmy Rogers and Pinetop Perkins. Drawing on his colorful career, which includes touring Europe with "The Texas Harmonica Rumble," Cowdrey creates music reflecting the varied background of his experience. His second solo album, "It's Lewis," is set for release in 1994. Cowdrey is a self-described "down-home blues guy" and his music is as sinful, sweet and satisfying as a Texas praline.

ANTONE'S RECORDS
500 SAN MARCOS
AUSTIN, TEXAS 78702
512/322-0617
FAX: 512/477-2930

Press kit for Lewis Cowdrey's *It's Lewis* release.

ny played a lot together. Keith was a member of his band, Johnny Winter but ... This was after The Storm, as I recall. Keith also played for a short time with Doug Sahm.

Keith was very much into reptiles; had a huge knowledge. He also was very much into cats. The Fabulous Thunderbirds got their swamp sound mostly from Keith's ideas and his record collection.

Later on, I co-produced an album for The Solid Senders. Keith also played on my record *It's Lewis* on Antone's Records, together with Mike Kindred. He played his blond Telecaster bass (early Fender Precision). I remember that Keith met Jimi Hendrix in a session, and Keith's bass was the only instrument that was tuned for left-hand, so Hendrix took the bass and played it. I have also seen him with a Harmony bass. He played an Allen cabinet and a black Fender Bandmaster. He also played Gibson amps, one meter tall. Later on, I bought him a Danelectro Longhorn bass. The basses he used in his last years were kind of junk.

His dress influence on other people was big. He was kind of an American idea of Brian Jones. In the beginning, he sounded way different than with the Thunderbirds. He developed his own style. Keith was extremely intelligent. He was much fun to have around. He was not talking anybody into drugs, like others did.

The Storm: Lewis Cowdrey, Sally, Diana Ray, Paul Ray, Ed Vizard, Doyle Bramhall, Jimmie Vaughan and Jeff, early 1970s.

Courtesy of Burton Wilson

The original The Storm single "Lost On The Ocean Part 2".

Courtesy of Ted Tucker

Lewis Cowdrey and Keith Ferguson.

Courtesy of Liz Henry

"The Fabulous Thunderbirds got their swamp sound mostly from Keith's ideas and his record collection."
-- Lewis Cowdrey

Angela Strehli
Interviewed by Detlef Schmidt, 2014

Angela is a great Texan blues singer who later worked for Antone's and has several albums of her own. She lives in California.

I met Keith when he joined Lewis and myself in L.A. when we started the band Sunnyland Special. We had some good gigs there, but in the meantime Austin had become more hip, and we missed Texas. Later, he played in Lewis Cowdrey's band, The Storm.

I do remember that I played "second guitar", which was when you played bass lines on a guitar. That was when country blues had not become urbanized with bass and drums. I remember Muddy Waters complimenting me about that when our band, The Fabulous Rockets, opened for him at the Vulcan Gas Company on Congress Avenue (Austin). That large venue preceded Armadillo World Headquarters. I had met Muddy in Chicago in 1966.

Anyway, I guess I was still doing that when Keith joined Sunnyland Special and we were working in California. He finally insisted that I give it up, which was reasonable, because two different bass lines could be conflicting. I was crushed, however, because it was so much more fun to be playing with the band than to be out front with nothing but a dinky microphone. I still feel that way.

Years later, Keith gave me a cool Japanese bass, a Conqueroo, which was a hollow body, which meant that I could hear it without an amp. I used it to compose riffs for songs on it. I remember that Sunnyland made a 45 rpm at Robinhood Studios in Tyler, Texas, and they had all Danelectro amps and instruments to use -- really cool and perfectly funky. That was the first-ever Armadillo record. Nice of Spencer Perkins to want to do that. Just imagine that Austin didn't have a decent studio at the time!

The most important and soulful connection I had with Keith was his extensive knowledge of the "Mexican blues" (my term). I was fairly fluent in Spanish.

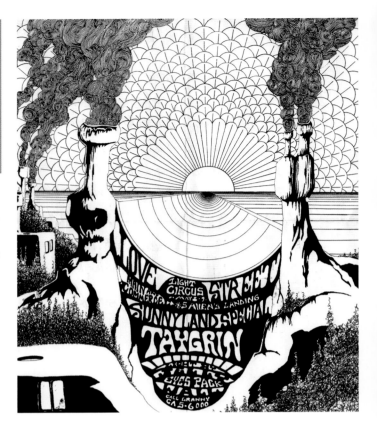

Early Sunnyland Special poster.
Courtesy of Keith Ferguson Collection

3rd Coast Music, April 2002

From Jesse Taylor: In 1967 or '68, the bass player had decided to leave Sunnyland Special and at his last show in Houston, Jesse Taylor went outside for a smoke and when he came back, he told Angela Strehli and Lewis Cowdrey that he'd found a replacement -- and that's how Keith Ferguson came to move to Austin. "He was just so hip, I figured he had to be a good bass player."[20]

He had a huge collection of the norteno-, conjunto-style bands. Some of the best artists, notably Los Alegres de Teran, would tour in southern Texas. And I was thrilled to go to those dances out in the country in halls with huge dance floors. I also remember a nice party in Austin for Lydia Mendoza, the most recorded female singer of that genre. It was heavy to get to meet her. Maybe Chris Strachwitz of Arhoolie Records hosted that party. Keith was an invaluable asset to Chris' research and recordings.

"He was just so hip, I figured he had to be a good bass player."

-- Jesse Taylor

Sidekick and New York

Tommy Shannon
Interviewed by Detlef Schmidt, 2013

Tommy Shannon was the bassist for Johnny Winter and recorded the first three Johnny Winter albums with him and played Woodstock in 1969. Tommy joined a band named Krackerjack. Later, he became Stevie Ray Vaughan's bassist in Double Trouble and recorded all the albums with Stevie. Tommy still lives in Austin and plays locally just for fun.

Tommy Shannon with his white 1963 Fender Jazz bass playing with Stevie Ray Vaughan.
Courtesy of Scotty Ferris

I was playing with Johnny Winter in 1968, I believe. Johnny and Keith were already good friends. I met him then and we became friends. Keith was the coolest person I have ever known. I have never known anybody as cool as him. He just had this groove going all the time. He was real smart. I met Keith before he was going over to England with Johnny. Johnny, a little later, got his recording contract; the first album came out. After we got that recording contract, we moved up to New York. Beautiful home we had, real big. Almost like a mansion. We all lived together there. There were several bedrooms and a rehearsal room. It was nice. I was this guy from Texas. I knew about nothing. I moved up there, and in about a year I grew up about 10 years.

Keith and I went through all this period together. We became good friends, real good friends. We would go out shopping together, clothes. Back then we were wearing velvet bell bottoms, shag haircuts. Just everything was cool.

Keith came down and stayed a while in New York. He would stay with us in New York some time and then go back to Houston. Keith did play bass at that time. He was learning. He played his early Fender Precision bass. I didn't see another bass with him at that time.

There was this club called The Scene. Our manager, Steve Paul, it was his club. You couldn't walk in just off the street because it was full of famous musicians and beautiful girls. When we went up to New York, there were two girls waiting on us at the airport; one of them was Janette Jacobs. She was Jimi Hendrix's girlfriend. Keith came in the club one night, wearing Jimi Hendrix's scarf. Jimi Hendrix got a little frustrated, I guess. Janette had all these clothes from Jimi Hendrix, and she gave Keith this scarf. Keith never played with Jimi nor did they know each other personally. They just knew each other from seeing Janette. Keith had a closer relationship with the girlfriend of Hendrix. He hung out with her all the time. In 1970, when we went to England with Johnny, we took Keith as a sidekick, as a friend, on this tour. Keith travelled with us on that tour.

Keith was so cool, but underneath he had the biggest heart. He was a good human being. We always had deep talks. We had a band called Krackerjack. We got together in 1970. It was Bruce Boland, Jesse Taylor, Uncle John Turner, Mike Kendrick and me. We were a good band and pretty popular in Texas. Keith never played in Krackerjack.

Keith played with Rocky Hill, but I never heard them together. Keith and I kind of lost touch with each other at that time. Keith also jammed with Johnny Winter, but he never played in a band with him. I remember Keith and Stevie playing with The Nightcrawlers. That was a good band. It was a blues-oriented band. They did some soul music and blues. I also remember a band named Texas Sheiks which

Tommy's white 1963 Fender Jazz bass he was playing with Stevie Ray Vaughan and Johnny Winter. There even exists a photo where Jimi Hendrix is playing this bass.

Courtesy of Scotty Ferris

"Soul to Soul" -- Tommy's 1956 Fender Precision bass that was presented to him by Stevie Ray Vaughan.

Courtesy of Scotty Ferris

Keith played in. It was with Bruce Boland and Randy Banks, but it didn't last very long.

The Nightcrawlers were under the management of Bill Ham, ZZ Top's manager. Later on, I was playing in a band called Fools. We also signed with Bill Ham. We almost starved our asses off. He did the same to The Nightcrawlers. He'd send them around, but they didn't get any money.

In the Thunderbirds, Keith used his old Fender Precision bass and he also had an old Telecaster bass. Both of them were good basses. The Telecaster bass was a blond color bass. Later on, I gave him a bunch of basses. I brought them over to his house because people gave them to me. Some Tokais, Robins, stuff like that. He would go and hock them. I kept giving him basses even after that.

I talked a lot with Keith when he was out of the Thunderbirds. He was very resentful. Later on, he sued the Thunderbirds, but he lost in court. He didn't like touring. I hate touring now, too. I quit doing it. I just play locally and for fun only, not trying to be sucessful.

Keith loved cats and so do I. I also saw Keith playing with The Tail Gators. It was a good band.

Something that really bothers me: I was playing with Storyville and we were on the road. I got a message from Keith to give him a call. Back then, I waited two or three days to get back to somebody. Well, I thought, I'll just call him when I get home. I found out that he was in the hospital and had died. I feel really bad that I didn't call him before that. I was shocked, and it still bothers me till this day that I didn't call him. I am still in connection with Johnny Winter. We don't talk as much as we used to, but we are still friends.

Stevie gave me that bass. He did the engravings himself with a woodburner: "Soul to Soul". It's a '56. It's a real cool bass. It sounds really good and is real loud; just with that one pickup. I do also play guitar.

Back of the the album *Texas Flood:* (left to right) Tommy Shannon, Stevie Ray Vaughan, Chris 'Whipper' Layton, and John Hammond Sr.

© CBS

68

Black Kangaroo

Keith's letters to his mother give a very good impression of his thoughts and the dating concerning this time.

All letters are courtesy of the Keith Ferguson Collection, and used by friendly permission of Margaret Ferguson.

Monday, June 6, 1972

A rather interesting development occured last weekend that I will endeavor to describe in some detail, for openers, I was flown up to San Francisco by a record company to listen to tapes of one of their bigger artists who needs a bass player. The record company is owned by Jefferson Airplane and its product is distributed by RCA Victor.

The artist is the younger brother of a member of the Jefferson Airplane, and he has a great deal of money behind him. He plays guitar very well and sings, and needs a bass player for two Fillmore West jobs in mid-June and a tour thereafter. This week he's com-

 **RECORDS**
P.O. BOX 99387
SAN FRANCISCO, CA 94109
(415) 221-7412

Peter Kaukonen & BLACK KANGAROO

(l-r) Keith Ferguson, Peter Kaukonen, Jimmy Gillen

Promotion shot for the Grunt Records label.

Courtesy of Becky Stapleton Crissman

ing to L.A. to make final preparations for release of his record and to hear me play. The latter reason is considered almost superfluous by his advisers, who consider my membership in his group to be an already established fact.

I must admit that their proposition is very attractive and a great temptation to me, I detest living in L.A., and, regardless of the fact that I'm now playing what is certainly the best music I've ever done, I find it impossible to ignore an invitation from an artist as well established as this fellow in San Francisco.

Johnny Winter all but ordered me to go on and do it in San Francisco, as did everyone I know up there. I'm still torn between a desire to either play what I am most attracted to or to go with an organisation that's already equipped to take very good care of me. I wish I could combine the two, but that never seems to be case.

Friday, June 16, 1972
(written on Jefferson Airplane letterhead)

I'm working for Peter Kaukonen (he's a guitarist) and I'm on the pay roll of his record company (Grunt Records) at $75 a week when we're not playing, we were to have played this weekend at the Old Fillmore but the drummer's got mononucleosis.
I hated, really hated, to leave Ibycus, but it's time I became more solvent and this is my chance. I'm convinced I did the right thing.

I'm really happy to be here, and I get the impression that Peter Kaukonen is going to make lots of money before long. He's the one whose older brother is in the Jefferson Airplane. Everyone in the company treats me really well and I get the impression that I' important for once, which is new, strange and I like it.

Peter Kaukonen's album *Black Kangaroo*.
© *Wounded Bird Records*

Oh yes, Peter's a lizard freak and owns several really strange ones, an African Sungazer, a foot long and covered head-to-toe with sharp horns, like a Moloch. It's really a beautiful animal and very affectionate for a reptile. Having gone to Stanford (among others) Peter is not one's average rock n roll guitarist. He has a gold earring (a lizard) that doesn't hang but perches on the ear like the one on your green vase. It looks alive. Peter's wife is the Airplane's secretary and comes from Liverpool.
Coming up here appears to be what I needed.

Maybe this is my home, I don't know. L.A. was just too rank.

Tuesday, July 25, 1972

Things are still pretty much the same. Peter's record will be out in August and we'll do a tour with the Jefferson Airplane. Until then things will continue at the normal snails pace. I suppose I'm to relax until the tour and I probably will since there's little else to do but rehearse.
Johnny Winter is still in L.A., but says he'll visit me and Henry Carr in a day or two. He's doing fine.

Labor Day 1972

It is very expensive living on the West Coast and I'm learning how to cope with this. I appreciate your being of assistance to me with this, however, and I'm doing the best I can right now (by no means as good as I intend to do, though.)

I wish we'd hurry the hell up and go on the road. I'm getting very impatient for travel and the financial increase involved.

Wednesday, October 4, 1972

We start work this weekend, but I won't be getting good money until I go to New York around the 20th of October, that will be about three weeks' work in the New York area. We may be sent south after that, but I'm not certain.

After the tour I'm not certain what I'll do, but my plan at this point is to get out of debt and trade in my Brook Mays amp on something cheaper that won't need fixing all the time, and is easier to carry around. My equipment for the tour will be furnished, including an extra bass. That's big of them.

This gig has become a real chore, but I intend to last it out, until I can get some better money anyway. Three years ago this high-level rock n roll business was great fun, but being in it now isn't much fun. Perhaps the money will make it worth the trouble, but it's not the kind of playing I enjoy. My present job feels too much like a bad day at Records of Houston.
Peter's wife got herself a large young indigo snake from Texas.

Monday

New York is a busy, interesting place. I like it there but it becomes hard to handle after a while.

November 8, 1972
The Gorham Hotel

We are, I think, touring the Midwest two weeks after we return to San Francisco.
Thus far I'm having a grand time (on $ 10 a day). I really enjoy being in New York, but Johnny and I are both at a loss as to what it is.

Johnny's manager (Steve) has an incredible mansion in upstate New York. It's for sale, only $ 180,000. He's looking for another one with an indoor pool. Nice ...

Saturday, December 30, 1972

I'm not yet certain about our next tour, dates therein and such. I'll let you know in plenty of time, however, whatever pertinent information I can get. All I know at this time is that it's slated for mid or late January.

Third of all, I'm thinking of quitting as soon as I'm able to ascertain (roughly or otherwise) what my tay return will be and when I'll get it. I'm told, however, that it should be substantial. I'm also told that this job has me eligible for unemployment compensation should I care to pursue it.

At any rate, I don't intend to make any sort of major move until I'm better covered financially than usual, and I can bide my time (salaried) until I decide.

I don't really relish coming to Texas, but I don't really like living with other people, no matter how safe it is for me here. I also don't like playing super loud rock n roll exclusively either, playing with Rocky made more sense.
I may have already told you, but the record company spent a good deal of money recently repairing my guitar (it's 20 years old, you know).

Peter Kaukonen
Interview by Detlef Schmidt, 2012

A San Francisco Bay area guitarist, Peter Kaukonen has played, toured and recorded with Black
Kangaroo, Jefferson Airplane, Jefferson Starship,
and Johnny Winter. Peter also was a founding
member of Hot Tuna.

He continues composing his deeply personal,
engaging, challenging and eclectic music, which
he records in his own facilities. He currently
lives with his wife and twin sons in Mill Valley, California, where he bicycles preposterous
distances on and off the road and takes great
pleasure in growing roses.

When Keith was with me in Black Kangaroo, he
played his Precision bass through an Acoustic 360
amp, possibly one of the worst sounding amplifiers
ever made. But that's what we had. Robby Krieger
of the Doors played through them for a while. They
were considered on the cutting edge of technology
because they had an oscillator built in that would
generate a tone you could, theoretically, tune to.

If Keith talked about the bands he played with prior
to joining me in Black Kangaroo, I don't recall. I
had no contact with Keith after his departure, and
it wasn't due to ill feelings, because there certainly
were none. It was just that I didn't write or call and
neither did he. I'm trying to recall if he came back to
San Francisco and if I might have seen him then, but
nothing's coming to mind.

Keith did not record for me, but he was able to play
the parts. He was not, however, a rock 'n roll bass
player, whatever that might be. He had the look -- his
sense of style was, I think, extravagant and prescient,
but he did not have the aggressive edge, that manic
energy that seems to help a power trio. He was a
good groove player, but a lot of what I envisioned for
Black Kangaroo called for opening the gates and let-
ting the horses go tearing down the track at full tilt.

Jimmy Gillen provided the introduction to Johnny

Winter. Jimmy was an excellent blues/shuffle player;
again, not the best suited for power trio.

I replaced Keith with Michael Lindner, with whom I
still collaborate, 39 years later. Black Kangaroo went
out on some other ill-fated tours. Grunt Records, the
Airplane record label, was quite inept at distribution
and promotion and publicity, and did not service
areas that were playing the record. It was very frus-
trating and, for better or worse, I didn't renew my
contract with them.

Keith was personable, likeable, imperturbable and un-
flappable, and I wish there were more like him. Funny
thing is, I've never heard The Fabulous Thunderbirds.

I don't remember him as being problematic: he never
showed up drunk or blasted; he was punctual for
rehearsals; he learned his parts, he played them and
he moved on.

I do remember him as a fashion plate: He had Rod-
the-Mod Stewart haircut; flowery patterned jackets
and low-cut shirts; scarves hither and yon; tattoos at
a time when tattoos were unusual; and a very long
pinky nail on his right hand. He was on the cutting
edge, and had no shortage of opinions. "Ya gotta git
yerself a Flyin' V," he said. So I did -- a '59.

About his bass: one that almost substantiates the
mystique of "vintage" instruments, although if you
think about it, give a guitar 20 or so years and voila!

Keith played with me briefly in 1972. I had just
completed an eponymous album and was out on
the road, trying to push it into public awareness. We
spent a lot of time on the east coast; in New York City
we were booked into Max's Kansas City, a cultural
mecca to be sure, a watering hole of the effete and
elite. As I say, events are blurred and I can't recall if
we were opening for Steely Dan or if they were opening for us. But I do remember an after-the-show dinner that featured its own floor show: a man
standing on a table, posing and preening and
getting a blow job. The sounds of the city: slobbering
and sucking and gagging; an interesting obligato to
lobster and steak.

"Keith was personable, likeable, imperturbable and unflappable, and I wish there were more like him."
-- Peter Kaukonen

The house Keith lived in during his early Austin days, a duplex at 914A W. Annie.

Keith standing in Kathie May's living room door coming from the kitchen, early 1970s.

Courtesy of Kathie May

I don't know if heroin was a mainstay in Keith's pharmaceutical regimen while he was with Black Kangaroo, but there was clearly no shortage of other central nervous system depressants on the scene. Quaaludes were just making their presence known, impacting awareness and consciousness. Cocaine was just starting to become visible and available on the scene. It was also a time where we answered the question "What does this pill do?" by saying, "Shit, gimme 20 minutes and I'll tell you."

There we were, after another show, dining in the Max's first floor dining area. Keith was seated opposite me with a bowl of lobster bisque in front of him when his eyes closed and he, with all the gravitas of a felled redwood, pitched slowly forward towards his soup. I caught him with one hand before he splashed down -- like a NASA reentry vehicle -- and laid his head gently on the table. Why wake him? And why interrupt a good dinner? But I don't remember how we got him out of there or if, in fact, we did.

Kathie May about the house and Keith:

Keith Ferguson was my neighbor in the early to mid '70s. We lived in this duplex at 914A W. Annie, Austin, Texas.

I lived in front. He lived on the side. I was in my early 20s and I think he was early 30s. He really intimidated me at first with his long nails, tattoos, earrings, attitude and kimonos.

Later, I learned he was my protective, big brother. I took care of him, too. I always seemed to crack him up -- young, dumb blonde syndrome, I guess. I imagine he was quite grateful when I moved in. Lots of times I did his laundry and he was always in my fridge getting snacks. No one locked their doors back then or had A/C. He would come out his back door and around to mine, which was in the kitchen. I would see him get into the fridge and get out a hunk of cheese, which he loved! He loved *Kung Fu* and would always come over to watch that show.

When he left town for gigs, he always wrote me very descriptive letters. His handwriting was as artistic as he was! He was also very popular. A lot of female visitors and friends, too, like the Winter brothers and Billy Gibbons. Keith was a non-conformist, for sure. A true bohemian.

He walked everywhere, unless someone gave him a ride. Did not own a vehicle. He was tall and lanky and took big steps and talked with his hands a lot. Very dry humor and funny. We had a lot of fun in those days.

It was so hot we would all stand out in our front yard in the sprinkler eating watermelon. We drank alot of beer, too. Jax beer! We would stay up all night after gigs and sleep until noon. Then back to the store for more Jax.

Sometimes I would cook Thanksgiving dinner for Keith, and a lot of the other guys would show up -- Stevie Ray Vaughan, Denny Freeman.

The night I found out he died, it broke my heart. Loved him!! RIP, sweet friend.

A very rare live photo of Black Kangaroo (note Keith's Precision bass and Acoustic amplifier).

Courtesy of Becky Stapleton Crissman

Chapter 3

Early Austin Years

1973-1975

Early Austin scene: Doyle Bramhall in the middle; Fredde Walden in the back; Keith on left; and Lou Ann Barton (with a raised can) on the right.

Photographer unknown

Chapter 3

Early Austin Years 1973-1975

Moving to Austin

Herman Bennett
Notes in his own words, 2011

Herman Bennett was a singer who moved to Austin and was a roommate of Keith from 1974.

I met Keith in the very early 1970s, when he still lived in Houston and I still lived in Port Arthur. There was a club in Beaumont named Our Place where he would show up in his 'English' garb to play the occasional gig. He was different, but then again, so was the bar. The local hippies rubbed elbows with the frat boys -- both of those groups were looking for fun. And the local Bandido Motorcycle Club members and the occasional visit from the state troopers -- both of those groups were looking for trouble.

But it was amazingly peaceful. My jug band, Mama's Home Cookin', was the house band at the bar.

Keith had a palpable charisma. He was a beautiful guy with a perfect smirk, a sharp wit and style that never screamed 'poser'. He was comfortable in his own skin and people -- guys and girls alike -- would flock to him to buy him drinks. He was the epitome of cool.

We'd chat occasionally. He was, in short, likeable. And he was smart. And he was a hell of a bass player. I moved to Austin in 1974 to be a rock and roll singer, supported in my day job as self-employed plumber. I ran into Keith at a little bar on Sixth Street, which was beginning to rise from its reputation as the worst street in town as the Ritz Theater was renovated into a music venue. Then one boarded up

Herman Bennett and Keith Ferguson standing on the porch of Herman's house in Austin, early '70s.
Courtesy of Herman Bennett

building after another supported me as the plumber of choice and provided a stage for live music. I worked days and played nights. I helped with the Ritz and then Antone's as an actual 'scene' began to take shape.

Keith recognized me. We reminisced about Our Place, and he mentioned that he was making the couch circuit and was looking for a place to crash. I offered him my little screened-in back porch for as long as he wanted for $20 per month to help with my electric bill. He moved in the next day to sleep on an Army cot type metal-frame bed. Lynn 'Floyd' Moore occupied the other bedroom.

He was thoughtful … a good roommate. His 'uniform' was simple -- a pair of bell bottom jeans graced with a belt that was meant only for decoration, which had two silver hands that hooked together as a buckle. He always wore boots -- sort of Beatle boots but flashier -- and a T-shirt with a logo, often topped with a see-through shirt. You could see his pack of Kools in the pocket.

We would usually stay up drinking at a club or at the house. Keith was always the last to go to bed and would generally be up at 5:30 the next morning listening to his Mexican music, with the volume turned down (like I said, thoughtful) and starting on his daily diet of beer and Kools.

As my plumbing work increased, Keith offered to answer the phone for me during the day. He was good -- got all the necessary information. But his habit of pacing while he was on the phone would tangle up the wire and we developed an evening ritual of straightening it out.

I was well aware of Keith's view of me. On one hand, I was a square -- a guy who worked for a living. On the other hand, I was also a struggling musician who partied into the night and got up the next day to earn some money. We had a mutual respect for each other. Keith was generous with what he had, but he had very little. He said, "All I ever think about is having fun." Sex, drugs, rock and roll. Women flocked to him. People bought him drinks and food and cigarettes. He played pick-up gigs for a few bucks each week and put that aside for a new pair of boots. He called his mother every month to ask her to send him his $20 rent. She loved her son and he loved her. Indeed, when she moved to Austin, she bought three houses in a row -- one for her, one for Keith, and one

to rent. He lived there until his death. Now that he had his own digs, he put up our friend 'Floyd' when he was between houses and another friend who died of liver complications while living there.

He had a pet lizard, something Amazonian or tropical, if I remember correctly. Its main diet was roaches. Keith said, "I had a real roach problem until I got that lizard. Little by little, the roach problem dwindled. In the middle of the night, I would hear the lizard jump from the kitchen counter to chase down another morsel and, after awhile, the only roaches I saw looked very, very scared. Billy (Gibbons) came by to visit one time right before ZZ Top was headed out on tour. The lizard was in the windowsill basking in the sun. Billy reached out to touch it and I reminded him that the biting power of that little fellow had crushed many a roach and could do the same to a finger. Billy pulled back as the lizard opened his mouth. The tour was saved."

Over time, I heard some of the back story -- when and where he got his tattoos; the fact that he had been asked by his old friend Billy Gibbons to play bass with ZZ Top; the fact that he could have played with his old friend Johnny Winter. He said, "I didn't want to play music with those guys. I just like hanging out with them. I wanna play with Jimmie Vaughan."

So this reminds me of a story from back at the Our Place bar. New Year's Eve. The owners decided they would invite all the regulars and lock the doors. A private party of sorts with Mama's Home Cookin' playing -- remember, we were the house band -- and whoever else wanted to play to fill in. Keith showed up with Billy Gibbons, Johnny and Edgar Winter, Uncle John Turner (Johnny's drummer). Billy Gibbons played harmonica that night, by the way. It was an unforgettable night.

He told me how he learned to play bass. A fellow who was playing in a band showed him the basics one day. Keith played his first gig that night. The fellow loaned his bass to Keith. Because Keith was left-handed, he restrung the instrument making it, as he said, "upside down and backwards." And he restrung it before he returned it the next day.

He said he hung out with Hispanics when he was growing up -- even wanted to be a pachuco -- and he learned to speak Spanish (at least Tex-Mex) fluently. And he was comfortable enough to walk into the most Mexican of bars along Sixth Street, a place named The Green Spot where dances were sold for a quarter; old men paying for the pleasure of a dance with a young chica. Keith was probably the only person in there who could speak English, but his charisma and fluency won him many friends before he left.

Onstage, he was definitely not a showman; more the John Entwistle model -- just standing there and playing, never singing backup, never doing any rock and roll faces, hardly moving, except to take a drink or light a cigarette. But eyes were drawn to him, this ultra cool pretty boy with perfect hair and perfect slouch and charisma. Of course, it helped that he was a consummate bass player of the blues, providing that perfect bass bottom. Someone described it as an elephant trunk swinging from side to side, clearing out the underbrush so his bandmates would have a foundation for their efforts.

I will say that Keith was what they call a 1-3-5 guy. He offered to play bass with my Austin band one night at a little club. Our band, Uncle Uh Uh and the Uh Huhs, played more eclectic stuff written by our guitar player … nothing straight C-F-G about it, indeed, with 7th and minor chords and wacky structure. Keith was out of his element -- the only time I ever experienced that sort of thing. Since we hadn't practiced any of the tunes with Keith, he politely bowed out after a couple of songs.

Keith used to wear a head scarf at times. He said, "When I learned to tie one of these, my troubles were over." It was simple. Not a doo rag, not a bandana.It came to be called a 'Keith Hat'. He showed me how to tie it and, indeed, my troubles were over … in that regard anyway. As a plumber, I often have to crawl under houses and into attics. My long and unruly hair was a problem, but -- and to this day -- I keep a Keith Hat in my back pocket to be available when necessary. And a couple of knots later, my troubles are over.

He had an idea for a production bass -- the neck an erect penis and the body the scrotum, complete with crabs serving as the tuning knobs. He said, "I even sent a letter and a drawing of it to Fender and Gibson, but their polite reply letters basically said, 'Thanks, but no thanks.'"

I imagine he was surprised to live as long as he did, but he did it on his own terms … and I respect that.

Jillian Bailey: "I took that photo of Keith and Floyd backstage at an Edgar Winter concert in Houston, 1976. Keith and Floyd had two bands -- Gars From Mars and Crawfish Et Yo Face."
Courtesy of Jillian Bailey

Floyd Moore, Otis Lewis, Keith and Kim Wimberly.
Courtesy of Jillian Bailey

Keith and Floyd Moore in the 1980s.
Courtesy of Billy Cross

The Austin music scene

Denny Freeman
Interview by Andy Wilkinson, May 24, 2009
Courtesy of Keith Ferguson Collection

Denny Freeman is an Austin guitar player who saw the early days of the Austin blues scene. He played with Jimmie Vaughan in The Storm, with Stevie Ray Vaughan in Paul Ray and The Cobras, and with Angela Strehli and W.C. Clark in Southern Feeling. Later on, he toured with Taj Mahal and Bob Dylan. Denny now lives back in Austin.

Denny and Johnny Nicholas at the Saxon Pub, 2013.
Courtesy of Scott Ferris

Keith moved to Austin in about 1971, maybe 1972. He was really handsome. He wasn't a rock star in the sense that he was in a famous band. He was a musician and had played in bands, but none of them were famous. But he looked like a rock star and hung with them and looked like one and was one without being one. Long hair, the snakeskin boots, that rock and roll bag at all the rock 'n rollers used to have. I don't know what they had in it -- scarves and jungle gardenia fragrance, fingernail polish.

Keith had his own sense of style. He had a lot of different looks. The first one I saw was that glamour boy look. Later on, he was a white American who turned into a Mexican.

People went over to his house a lot; it was just something to do. He was funny and he was nice and he was interesting. Guys liked him. And girls. Everybody just liked him.

I moved to Austin in 1970. A bunch of Dallas people moved here, too. Dallas was not a good place to be if you had long hair and all that. Austin was ... it was like an oasis. It was some kind of a paradise. There were a lot of long-haired people for such a small place. I didn't come here for the music scene. It was that sub-cultural vibe that was drawing musicians. Jimmie Vaughan and Doyle Bramhall moved down here a month after me, and another month later, we were playing in a band together. This was the first Storm band, and I played with them for six months. We almost couldn't get a gig. And Jimmie already

had a name regionally. I thought, we were living in Austin and I am playing with Jimmie Vaughan -- we were going to rule. But it just did not happen. The Armadillo Headquarters had just opened up, and they would hire us. So we were either playing in the Armadillo Headquarters, the best venue in town, or in a joint over at the east side of town with about four black folks and five hippies. We were going home with about three dollars a night, unless our bar tab was higher than that. But nobody really cared. And about a year later, that was when Keith came down.

I left The Storm and Lewis Cowdrey joined. Paul Ray and I were trying to form a band, but we could hardly find any musicians that wanted to play the blues.

When Keith came here, he knew people that I knew. He knew Angela Strehli, who is from Lubbock, and Lewis Cowdrey, who is from around Lubbock. Keith had played with Angela in Los Angeles, and they had just arrived here. And when Keith got here, he also knew a lot of Austin people, too. I guess Keith had spent some time in Austin before he lived here. And so I met him pretty quick after he got here, because he wanted to play. And so he was immediately in our little cult -- our little music, blues cult. He knew about blues and wanted to play with us -- that was Jimmie, Stevie, Doyle Bramhall, W.C. Clark. We were just like-minded people who had found each other.

John Lee Hooker and Walter Horton at Antone's with Denny Freeman on piano and Keith on bass.
Courtesy of Burton Wilson

Keith knew more about blues than any of us did. Keith was a Brian Jones type character. And we were all about the same age.

Keith was so exotic. He made me seem square and conservative. Keith had played with Black Kangaroo, so when Keith moved here, he had that nice 8x10 photo of that band. I was kind of surprised that Keith would want to hang out with me. But we found out that we had a lot of things in common, like we both were into Excello Records. That's all you needed to know at that time.

Keith grew up around Mexicans in Houston. Mexicans liked the blues and Mexican music. Keith was very exposed to Mexican culture. He knew all the roots music, liked country music. He knew about a lot of things. You just enjoyed hanging with him. He was nice and he was funny. A lot of times he just enjoyed turning me on to some things he thought that were cool. I was a willing audience for him. He was always watching the latest *National Geographic*. For my birthday, he gave him a rainforest pygmy album. I only listened to it once.

He never had a job, didn't go to college. He played with Angela in San Francisco. He wasn't affected by

Keith, Lou Ann Barton and Denny, about 1975.
Courtesy of Denny Freeman

the draft. He got out of high school in 1963, maybe '64. He was hanging around with Johnny Winter.

It is just a guess, but when he lost the gig with the Thunderbirds before they appeared on *MTV*, I think he was really bitter about it. He lost the gig, and then all of a sudden they were on *MTV*. I think Keith was causing the Thunderbirds problems. He just wanted to stay home and didn't want to do the thing that needed to be done, the roadwork and all that stuff. They loved him, and they knew that there was going to be a firestorm when that happened because Keith had a lot of devotees. I saw both sides really, and I didn't take sides. I understood that sometimes you had to do stuff like that, as sad as it is. Brian Jones was fired from the Rolling Stones, too.

From then on, life wasn't the same for Keith anymore. He was in some cool bands after that, but he was out of the spotlight. And then he saw them getting some success and ending up with some money. And you would turn on the TV and see them. And it wasn't him, it was Preston.

Keith had turned into an icon by the time I left town in 1989 or, really, a long time before that. Keith influenced a lot of people by the way he dressed. He was one in a million; not a versatile player but a bass player who exactly knew what a band and the song needed.

Denny and Keith around 1974.

Courtesy of Denny Freeman

Kim Wilson, Muddy Waters, Jimmie Vaughan and Keith in Austin, April 1977. The photo was used on the cover of the photo book "Picture the Blues" by Susan Antone about the first 10 years of the Antone's club.

Courtesy of Watt Casey; www.WattCasey.com

Southern Gentleman

Lois Loeffler
Interview by Scott Ferris, 2013

Lois is the wife of Gerard Daily and knew Keith from the early 1970s on. She was a waitress at some of the clubs he played.

I first met him in 1971. Keith was playing with Storm, I think. I was a cocktail waitress, working my way through school at UT. I was 20 or 21, Keith was 25. It was really interesting because I was a young, slim, pretty little girl back then. All the boys were hitting on me. Keith kind of just watched me and did never really hit on me. Then, that first night that he played, he actually came up and talked to me. I was in that little hallway, was kind of resting, and Keith came up to me and kind of leaned against me and said, "You have got bad breath." I said, "You are rude", and pushed him and walked away.

Later, I thought that was very calculating. He just worked the other way, just did the opposite than the other guys did. We became close friends after that. I hang out a lot with Keith in his house in south Austin, met his mother and his grandmother was alive those days. Keith was very close to his grandmother. Behind all that bitching that happened, I think Keith was very close with his grandmother and mother. He loved them a great deal.

Keith was wearing scarfs around his knee and his head. I had never seen anybody else doing that except Jimi Hendrix. I always felt that Keith was such a good man. He certainly knew how to treat a woman.

After I first met Keith, I kind of moved around. One of my first boyfriends was Jimmie Vaughan. And this is how I got to know Keith, too, because I was staying with Jimmie.

I remember Keith was talking about Johnny Winter, and Billy Gibbons came up sometimes to his house there. Sometimes they would have parties and Billy would come. There was a really close friendship between Billy and Keith.

Lois Loeffler in the 1970s.

Courtesy of Lois Loeffler

In 1973, I married. Me and my husband moved over to California in about 1974 or 1975 and came back to Austin and divorced in 1977. That's when I kind of renewed my friendship with Keith.

If he was your friend, he was very loyal. I remember one night we talked about that I really wanted a dog. That night, he played. And the next day, he came with the money he had earned and gave it to me, and I bought a dog. Later, Keith would come over and babysit the dog for me.

One point of time, I was living in New Orleans. I was living in the French Quarter. Keith came over with The Fabulous Thunderbirds and they were playing some festival over there. Keith and Mike Buck came over to the French Quarter and got me. I packed a bag and I stayed with them where the festival was. It was about 1978.

Stevie Ray Vaughan.

Courtesy of Scott Ferris

I remember they wanted to hear some good Cajun music. You really had to go out in the country to hear the Cajun music. He loved that -- the Conjunto, the Cajun music. So somehow we got out to Cajun country. I remember the rest of the guys were not that interested, but Keith had the best time. We danced to Cajun music. Keith normally never danced.

Shortly after that, I moved back to Austin for a while, then I moved to San Antonio. But I would still come to Austin to see Keith. One night, I arrived at Austin airport; a guy named Steve was to pick me up but did not appear. So I didn't know who to call. Then I called C-Boy from the Rome Inn; I had also worked there. Keith played there that night. Keith came with Lou Ann and C-Boy to the airport to pick me up. So I stayed with Keith and Lou Ann that night. Keith always treated me like a little sister. If you offended a friend of his, especially a woman friend, he was quite evil to deal with. The next morning, that guy named Steve came and had flowers with him. Lou Ann later told me that Keith has paid him a visit that night.

This is how Keith was when you were friends. He treated you nice, defended you, didn't let people talk about you. I could call Keith at any time, day or night, and he would immediately come over. He was highly intelligent, very loving, no matter all the bad things that were around him.

I remember at a certain time, I was around with a

group called The Whorellas; it was kind like a girls group. This was late 1970s. A girl named Diane, Robin ... we used to come to all the gigs at the Rome Inn where Keith and they would play. We were terribly misbehaved. We would get drunk. I remember one night, I took of my pantyhose or what I was wearing, went to the bathroom and wet them and threw them on stage. And we were yelling, "Fuck me, Jesse," which was what Kim had instructed us to call him that time.

I remember one day Keith came over to my house and had Johnny Nicholas with him. I used to sunbath topless in my backyard. Whenever I saw Keith, I just jumped up and said, "Hi." Keith got a big kick out of that. He said Johnny was just gaga about that. "I love Texas women."

In the 1980s, I was sent to Austin for my work. I visited Keith, and this is where I met my husband, Gerard. I had originally met Gerard in 1978. This is where I remet him. Keith was very approving of the relationship. Keith always said, "If you need a best man..."

I remember when Stevie had sent a letter to Keith from his rehab. Keith sat down and read the letter and reread it and was thinking of it. I was there the day he got it. I asked him how Stevie was, and Keith said that he was fighting for his life. Keith loved Stevie, and Stevie loved Keith. I know that there were lot of people to try to get Keith into rehab, but that just wasn't for Keith.

I remember at Keith's house, he had that life size cutout of Dolly Parton. He loved Dolly Parton; he thought she just was too much.

He did tell me one story about his dad. He said that his dad and him had a fight when Keith was about 14. His dad was beating him up. Keith went off to his Hispanic friends that he was hanging out with and told them about it. And they were planning to kill his father. Keith said that he had to talk real fast to talk them out of this. I knew his father had been a musician, but Keith didn't talk much about him.

I saw a lot of a southern gentleman in Keith because of the way he treated me. He was a true gentleman in every sense of the word. He lives on in the heart and the memories.

Playing with Doug Sahm

Emma Little
Interviewed by Detlef Schmidt, October 2012

Emma worked at the Armadillo club in Austin
in the early 1970s.

I met Keith in about 1972 in front of the One Knite.
My friend wrote him all the time, and she told me,
"Emma, you should write him to move to Austin."
We started to know each other from writing letters.
And then I met him at the One Knite. We were just
like brother and sister. He didn't move to Austin until
about the middle of 1973. He had just come down
to visit a friend. I think he was playing with Black
Kangaroo in California at that time.

I was hanging out with Jimmie Vaughan and Denny
Freeman at that time. What I did was work at the
Armadillo and later hang out at the One Knite. We
also lived within a couple of blocks from each other.
I think Keith probably played with The Storm, but I
guess he was not a member of the band. I remember
Danny Galindo, Jimmie and Doyle and Lewis.

My house was the meeting place; I had to babysit all
of those guys -- The Cobras, The Sheiks and Stevie's
band. Keith also used to play with Randy Banks,
Randy and the Rockets. He played with all these
different guys, so they all lived together. It was mostly
Denny and Jimmie and then Jimmie and Keith. Alex
Napier lived there, too.

When Doug Sahm came back to Austin, he also
stayed in my house. The reason why Keith did play
with Doug is that both played all genres of music
-- Mexican music, Cajun music, roots music. Keith
loved all of that stuff. He didn't play with Doug a
whole lot of times, but he did.

Keith was my daughter's godfather. I made him go to
church.

He usually played Monday, Tuesday, Wednesday off,
then Thursday to Sunday -- not necessarily in town.
There were a lot of road gigs. They were going to New
Orleans or the Texas loop; Oklahoma, too. In 1976, I

The 1974 Doug Sahm and Freddie Fender live album, which just mentions "Keith as bass player".
© *Crazy Cajun Records*

**"Texas Tornado – The Times & Music of Doug
Sahm"**

Shawn Sahm recalls: "One time Dad had some
gigs lined up and didn't have a bass player for
the band, so he hired Keith at Soap Creek and
told him to come along. Keith was very nervous
about it, saying Dad was such a giant, such a
pro. I spouted off and gave him this inspiration-
al lecture -- 'You are just as good as anybody,
you can play with anyone.' I found out later that
he talked for years about how much that meant
to him."[6]

---

was living in Waco, and I remember the band coming and staying with us. It was the Thunderbirds and
Stevie's band. If one of the guys couldn't go on the
road, another guy would sit in for them.

Texas Sheiks

Bruce Bowland
Interview by Detlef Schmidt, 2011

Bruce met Tommy Shannon and Uncle John Turner in the summer of 1970, and moved to San Francisco to be one of the founding members of Krackerjack. It was there he met Keith Ferguson, resulting in a close, lifelong friendship. Bruce then moved back to Austin for a brief period, then went with Uncle John Turner and Roy Cox to Houston to form Rattlesnake with guitarist Benny Valerio. He decided after three months to return to Austin, where he joined Blackbird, which featured a talented local guitarist by the name of Stevie Ray Vaughan. Tommy, Uncle John, Stevie, Robin Sylar and Bruce decided to resurrect Krackerjack. The band became one of the most popular in the state.

I met Keith around 1970 in San Fransisco in an apartment of Henry Carr, who was managing Tracy Nelson of Mother Earth. Keith was kind of a homeless person at that time. He didn't have an address. He carried everything in his bass case. He had a location of people where he could stay; two or three nights at one person's, then he moved to another. He even had his clothes in the bass case.

I had moved to San Fransisco to form the band Krackerjack with Uncle John Turner and Tommy Shannon. Our guitar player flew in; we were all staying with friends of Uncle John. The guitar player decided to go back to Dallas. Keith introduced us to Jesse Taylor, another guitar player. The rest is history. We went to the warehouse district, and Keith showed me some clothes shop, and I bought some clothes only because Keith said so. Keith was a fantastic walker. We walked for a while. He looked down at me and said, "For a little guy, you walk quite good."

He was a big influence on me. He always had his watch set 15 minutes earlier, because it's bar time for the last call. He told me a lot about life philosophy.

When he moved to Austin, I was already there. Back in Austin, we had a band called The Texas Sheiks -- it was Jack Morgan, Uncle John Turner, Keith and me. Jack and I stayed with Keith. In the morning he got dressed like always, ready to play. We used to play at a club called The Lamplight. This was on the old Sixth Street. We had to catch a city bus to get to the gig; that's how broke we were. We all had very little money.

There was a Mexican record store across The Lamplight. We walked across, Keith talking to that guy in Spanish and talking about Mexican records. I was like, wow, I didn't know that he could speak Spanish that good and that he did know so much about Mexican music. The guy would dig out some album that was really old, and Keith would go, "That's it."

With The Texas Sheiks, we were playing in San Antonio; this was a concrete, flat stage. For no reason, a guy came up and showed me the index finger, and wanted to start a fight. Keith lowered his bass and stuck his headstock at the guy and looked very bad at him. The guy went away. I guess Keith actually saved my life at that day.

Interview with R.C. Banks:

Yes, I remember that Texas Sheiks lineup. Jack Morgan was great. The photo that I am in was a promo shot done in order to advertise a gig at Mother Blues in Dallas. By the time the gig came about, Keith was busy so we took Don Bennett on bass.
I also played with Uncle John, Keith and Drew Pennington at The Lamplight on Sixth Street. One Saturday night, Johnny Winter was across the street at the Ritz Theater. When Johnny's show was over, he came over to sit in with his old friends. They doubled the cover charge at the door and we had a good payday.

Diamond Joe and The Dynamo: R.C. Banks, Joe Siddons, Keith and Uncle John.

Courtesy of Jillian Bailey

Diamond Joe and The Dynamo (l to r): Diamond Joe Siddons, R.C. Banks, Uncle John Turner and Keith. R.C.: "We only had a couple of gigs, one at Mother Blues in Dallas and one at The Lamplight Saloon in Austin." *Courtesy of Jillian Bailey*

Uncle John Turner.

Courtesy of Keith Ferguson Collection

Stevie Ray Vaughan

Stevie Ray Vaughan.

Courtesy of Scott Ferris

Feb. 25, 1973
Bruce Bowland: "It was a Sunday afternoon gig, billed as Jimmie, Stevie and Friends. It was me, Jimmie, Stevie, David Frame, Mike Kindred, Uncle John Turner, Fredde Walden and Paul Henry Ray.
The day of the gig Jimmie came by -- his girlfriend had a great big El Dorado convertible -- with Keith Ferguson.

Denny Freeman: "Another time, I loaned him that song "I Tried" from Larry Davis. It was the flip side of "Texas Flood". I think Keith Ferguson had given me that record for my birthday. Stevie wanted to learn it, so he borrowed the record."

By the fall of 1973, The Nightcrawlers were Stevie, Doyle and Keith Ferguson. Bill Ham, ZZ Top's manager, got interested in The Nightcrawlers.

Doyle Bramhall: "We knew Keith didn't have a driving license because he never drove.
"We had a couple of dates somewhere else, and it ended up being a huge mess. Drew and I hitchhiked home. Stevie and Keith stayed with the truck, and someone in the Ham organization flew in to drive them back.
"We were there about three days. Keith never slept. I mean he slept, but when everybody else was sleeping, he always thought somebody had to be up. You could

wake up anytime in the night, and he would just walk, pacing the floor, looking out of the window."

The Nightcrawlers opened up for ZZ Top in Houston and for E.L.O in Atlanta and Detroit in the summer of 1973. They also opened up for J.J. Cale and Quicksilver Messenger Service in February 1974.

Keith Ferguson on his impact on Stevie's clothing sense: "I had to get him out of T-shirts. I mean, you don't want the front man to look like the roadies."

Mike Steele: "I remember The Texas Sheiks, which was Uncle John Turner on drums, Keith Ferguson on bass, Jack Morgan on guitar and Bruce Bowland on vocals.
"They played at a club on Sixth Street. They played every Sunday and Stevie would sit in."

Joe Sublett: "When Stevie was in Double Trouble, we were partying at Lou Ann and Keith Ferguson's house. They had recently gotten married, and we called them "mahdow" and "fahdow", as in mother and father. Keith decided he was going to adopt all of us and drew up a document written in Spanish in red ink and we all signed it."

Mary Beth Greenwood: "Gibbons wrote that song, 'Low Down In The Streets' --
There's Jimmie and Jojo, there's Kim and Keith, Way outside the eyes of cool."

1977
Tony Dukes: "We were at Rome Inn one night after closing. Billy Gibbons, Stevie, Keith Ferguson and Jimmie sitting at a table.
"Keith Ferguson was there one night at Rockefeller's, and we opened for them. Keith was staying with Little Junior, and I lived right next door. (Freddie Cisneros was known as Little Junior One Hand.) He said, 'Dukes, you got all weird about that sticker stuff. Let's go look at some stuff.' We found this appliqué paper, and Keith bought this roll of stuff that looked like a brick wall. He cut it out and put it on his Telecaster that night, so it looked like he was playing a brick Telecaster! Keith was always a slouch, and it really looked like he was weighted down with bricks. He took it off at the end of the night and handed it to me and said, 'Now, don't you want to use that, too?'"

Johnny Reno (sax player, Double Trouble): "There were quite a few young men interested in Lou Ann at that point. It was funny to be in a band where you had a red-hot guitar player, and most of the guys came to see Lou Ann -- the hot looking chick. She was just a big piece of work. She was like Lucy and Ethel rolled into one character and would sing her ass off. She was her own girl. One guy she hooked up with who was her equal was Keith Ferguson. He was an excellent, soulful cat and very cool -- didn't chase around."

Feb. 18, 1979
Bob Claypool interviews Lou Ann Barton for the *Lubbock Avalanche-Journal* and notes that she was engaged to Keith Ferguson, bass player from the Fabulous Thunderbirds.

Dec. 23, 1979
Stevie marries Lenny upstairs at the Rome Inn Club. In attendance at the wedding were Chris Layton, Jack Newhouse, Cutter and Peggy Brandenburg, Keith Ferguson of the Thunderbirds and Mary Beth Greenwood, among others.

Bill Ham, former manager of ZZ Top, on Stevie Ray Vaughan, Rocky Hill and Keith:

Keith Ferguson was a good guy and a great musician. I cannot recall the exact dates that Keith was with Rocky. It was off and on for several years between the mid-'60s and mid-'70s. I do know that they were great friends and jammed together off and on. The best I can remember, there was a black guy named Doby who was playing bass on Rocky's album. The album was on Virgin Records, but was never released because Rocky became ill during that time and could not tour behind the album.

I do not recall Penington playing harp on The Nightcrawlers' live album, which was recorded at the Warehouse in New Orleans in either the mid-'60s or mid-'70s. Stevie, Doyle and Keith played on these tapes, but nothing was ever done with them. That would have also been about mid-'70s.

The Nightcrawlers were a great band. Doyle was singing on the tapes as Stevie had not yet discovered that great voice of his. He later began singing, and the rest is history. As for Rocky, he was one of the best blues guitarists of anyone I had ever heard and, sadly, was virtually unknown outside of this area. As you may know, he was voted one of the top unsigned guitar players in the world by *Rolling Stone*. I so much wanted to bring that talent to surface with the Virgin album, but when he became ill and unable to travel for the European tour we booked for him, all was lost. The rest was also history. God bless their souls, all of them: Stevie, Doyle and Rocky. I hope they have found each other again and are playing the blues together.

Tony Dukes on Stevie Ray Vaughan's funeral: "The crowd at the funeral on the hillside cleared, and then it was just me and another stooped figure on that hill -- Keith Ferguson. I walked up, we hugged, said nothing for minutes. 'It's a shame,' Keith said. 'Yep,' I agreed. 'We're gonna miss him more than we think.' I remember this eerie thing, as Keith walked away in his lonesome, sad lope, clad in his usual pleated black slacks and guayabera Mexican dress shirt."

Promotional photo of Stevie Ray Vaughan in a leopard coat.

Courtesy of Billy Cross

Joe Nick Patoski:

I remember my interviews with Keith for the Stevie Ray Vaughan biography. He was very helpful and talked about The Werewolves then and how they influenced him, and how their influence regarding wearing of scarves and boas was passed on by him to Stevie. "I introduced him to wearing scarves onstage."

The strange thing about The Werewolves was, they were never considered an Austin band and were too showy or glammy for a roots scene like Austin's. Looking back, I can put them in perspective as a regional New York Dolls, but back then, very few people talked about the Dolls or followed them, unless you read *Creem* magazine.

I first saw Keith with Storm and became friends with him mainly through our mutual love of Mexican music. He knew the Texas-Mexican scene more deeply than any white boy I knew, and it wasn't just his gold-capped teeth or his Houston background. We used to go to Mexican dances out at the Rockin' M, which was the first time many locals were exposed to Flaco Jimenez, Steve Jordan, and other conjunto acts.

One of the last times we talked was when I called him to let him know The Cuatitos Cantu were playing a club on the eastside. Cuatitos were two midget twins who both had six fingers on each hand and played accordion. Well, Keith went to the gig and raved about it.

The Storm and The Nightcrawlers were the big bands at the One Knite (never a cover charge), which is where Stubb's is now. Rocky Hill was always being hyped as the Next Big Blues Rock Thing but never managed to break through or really find much interest outside of Houston. He was briefly managed by Bill Ham of ZZ Top, had a lot of support of people of influence in Houston, but couldn't make it to the next level. It was during this period that Keith played with Rocky, although Hill worked with several different bassists. John Lomax III in Nashville managed Rocky for awhile.

Keith and Stevie Ray Vaughan at a party. The girl on Stevie's leg is Lois Loeffler.
Courtesy of Keith Ferguson Collection

Postcard from Keith to Mike Steele: "I've recently learned that these swans are plastic. I was suspicious when I shot one and it didn't sink."
Courtesy of Mike Steele

Mike Steele
Interviewed by Detlef Schmidt, 2011

Keith was living with Dusty Hill when Billy was forming ZZ Top, so Billy was asking Keith. Frank Beard lived in the same apartment complex. And Keith said that he already had got a gig, but Dusty needs a gig. So he and Billy were good friends from back in Houston; that's where they met. And they stayed friends. Like I said, Billy would come by when he was in town.

I remember when Keith was in The Texas Sheiks and Johnny Winter would show up, I guess it was New Year's Eve, and sit in. It was at The Lamplight Saloon. Keith would go see him in New York.

I remember one time The Storm was playing at the One Knite. They were playing every Monday night. The One Knite was a real dive. They had junk hanging from the ceiling, old typewriters. The Storm played there every Monday night for free. I was down there with two friends and The Bandidos Motorcycle (Club) gang would show up there. There was always a bunch of Harleys parked out at the front. It was a rough place. Sometimes there were fights, but the band just kept playing.

This is what Billy Gibbons said: "Keith forever changed how blues players dressed."

Keith gave me that photo where he was together with Muddy Waters and signed it to me. "Hey Mike, I am so happy. Quack, Quack."

Back at that time, the band members were constantly changing. They'd be in only for a couple of weeks.

Above: A letter Stevie wrote to Keith from rehab, and Keith kept it on his refrigerator.

Left: Keith and Mike at Keith's 40th birthday

Courtesy of Mike Steele

Keith dancing at a party (note the record collection).
Courtesy of Mike Steele

A promo photo from Grunt Records

Courtesy Mike Steele

Keith and Mike with the Guero Caster.
Courtesy of Mike Steele

Signed by Keith to Mike: "Hey Mike, I am so happy. Quack, Quack."
Courtesy of Watt Casey, www.wattcasey.com

Angela Strehli, Keith, Jimmie Vaughan and Carmen.
Courtesy of Mike Steele

Getting into the Thunderbirds

Pat Whitefield
Interviewed by Detlef Schmidt, 2012

Pat was an original member of the legendary Antone's House Band, playing with the most celebrated blues artists -- John Lee Hooker, Jimmy Reed, Eddie Taylor, Bo Diddley and others. He was an original member of The Fabulous Thunderbirds and did extensive stints on the road with The Angela Strehli Band and Anson Funderburgh and The Rockets featuring Sam Myers. Pat lives in Austin.

Erin Jaimes, Pat Whitefield and the author in Austin's The Hole in the Wall, October 2012.

I met Keith for the first time around 1973 or '74. He was playing in a glam rock band *(most likely The Werewolves)* in Dallas and wearing make-up all the time. I was the bass player in The Storm. Then Jimmie Vaughan started the band Jimmie Vaughan and The Thunderbirds in the middle of August 1975. I remember this exactly, because both Freddie Walden's wife and my wife had their first children a month earlier. The Thunderbirds were Lou Ann, Jimmie, Kim, Freddie and me.

Keith really wanted the job as a bass player. Whenever Keith could, he would come and listen to the band. Freddie left New Year's Eve 1975. I left about Valentine's Day, February 14, 1976. I asked Jimmie if he could give me more money, and he answered if I could find a band that pays better, he would understand. So we parted as friends. Jimmie asked me which bass player he should give the job, W.C. Clark or Keith. I told him, "If W.C. wants the job, you should give it to him." W.C. had played with some bigger names like Joe Tex.

In October 1975, the Thunderbirds did a live recording. This was just a few days after Kim had moved to Austin. It was at some place on Sixth Street. Freddie and I were about 28, Lou Ann was about 20. When Keith came in the band, they redid the recording with similar songs with Lou Ann singing.

Keith's bass at that time was a silver sparkle Fender bass, the bass he played in the glam rock band. Jimmie moved to Austin around 1970; The Storm ended in 1975. Antone's opened just two weeks after the Thunderbirds were formed. At the memorial of Doyle Bramhall, Derek O'Brien and I talked about if Keith ever really played with The Storm or just was sitting in. We both couldn't tell anymore.

Danny Galindo was the other bass player of The Storm. He was born in San Antonio; I was born in Dallas; Keith in Houston. When Keith left the Thunderbirds, it was only Jimmie left who came from Texas.

Keith was one on the most sarcastic people I met. He was hilarious, extreme dry wit. Keith's father was a hi-fi freak. He loved jazz. He died at the end of the '80s. Keith and Tommy Shannon played the same way, very close intervals. I used to play more larger intervals, like 1-3-5-6. At the end of Keith's time at the Thunderbirds, Clifford Antone would pay me for the tone setting of Keith's amp. He always did the tone setting the way you couldn't hear a distinct tone. He was using a Fender Dual Showman amp with a self-made cabinet with two D140 JBL speakers.

"He always did the tone setting the way you couldn't hear a distinct tone."
-- Pat Whitefield

Nightcrawlers and early Thunderbirds

Kathy Murray and husband Bill Jones
Interview by Detlef Schmidt, October 2012

Kathy Murray is the photographer who did the classic pictures of The Fabulous Thunderbirds that were used for promotion for the band and by Keith as autograph photos. She lives in Austin and gigs with her husband, Bill, in their band, Kathy Murray and the Kilowatts.

Kathy: I met Keith first at the One Knite bar in about 1973, which has been turned into a club named Stubb's BBQ. All of these great bands were playing for tips. I literally remember the first night I saw Keith. He walked into the club, he was wearing a burgundy velvet jacket with skinny sleeves and a white shirt underneath with ruffles sticking out the sleeves. He was smiling and he was so charismatic. I was just 16 years old.

Keith loved his picture taken, and I loved taking pictures of him. So he was always really super nice to me. He had a nickname for me that my brother would tell me: "Where is sugar with the shutter."

He was protective. I think he thought I was really naïve. He was always trying to wise me up. Keith told me that he had a girlfriend who died of an overdose when they were both 18 years old. And he told me about this when I was about 18 years old. He said that he had never gotten over her and that he never would get over. I think his relationships with women were very complicated, and I think that the memory of this woman might have gotten in the way of some of his relationships. He was really upset on this one subject about the woman with the overdose. This was the only time I really saw him getting upset. And back then, because he was upset, I didn't ask him a lot of questions about this.

Keith was hilarious. If only we had a video with him just talking. He had a wicked sense of humor. He had nicknames for people. He called somebody Mr.

A picture from early Antone's that Keith used as an autograph photo.

Courtesy of Kathy Murray

Kathy Murray and Bill Jones, September 2013.

Courtesy of Mardi Wareham

The Nightcrawlers with Stevie Ray Vaughan at the Armadillo, 1973.

Courtesy of Kathy Murray

The Nightcrawlers with Keith Ferguson at the Armadillo, 1973.

Courtesy of Kathy Murray

Negavibes. So I actually wrote a song called "Mr. Negavibes", and Keith liked it. Another musician friend of his had this wife who was very domineering, and Keith just started to call her Sarge.

Keith loved music so very much, and he tried to edu-cate people about conjunto, Cajun and zydeco. T-Bone Walker style, East Louisiana style. Keith would want to educate you about Excello Records. He was the first person to tell me about Slim Harpo and Lazy Lester. I am sure the T-Birds got a lot of their music from him.

Angela Strehli with The Fabulous Thunderbirds at Antone's.

Courtesy of Kathy Murray

Early Antone's days with Keith playing through an Ampeg B-18 amp.

Courtesy of Kathy Murray

He always called me every few months, and he would say, "There are some Greek blues on Channel 9." And I knew that was him. He always wanted to educate you. He listened to a lot of conjunto music. One year, he took me out to a club called The Rockin' M. We walked in there and we were the only gringos in the place. They all danced in a circle and it's multigenerational. He wanted me to photograph Conjunto Bernard to give some pictures to Angela Strehli for her birthday. He was always thinking of people, giving them something that really meant something to them.

Playing some gigs with him and recording songs with him was wonderful. He was always very encouraging to people. Keith could be really critical about certain boyfriends. He really loved Bill, my husband.

I saw Keith after Stevie had died, and all Keith was saying was, "Poor Jimmie, poor Jimmie." You knew he was worried about Jimmie; you could see that. The way he always answered the phone was, "Bueno." And I would go, "Did I wake you up?" because he always sounded so asleep. So he wrote on this picture,

"Kathy, I am not asleep, I swear."

He did have a picture of him and Carl Perkins. He loved Carl Perkins. He had a giant Lucite thing, it had a real, dead rattlesnake in it.

I was there that night, at Antone's on Sixth Street in 1975. Muddy Waters was playing and they were upstairs in the backstage room. There was a curtain where the people from upstairs could see what was going on. Shortly after the T-Birds kicked off their opening set, that curtain flew back and Muddy and his band were looking down there. That was huge, to be embraced like that by their idol.

Bill: When I played with Keith, it was always an honor. I would always play my best because I had seen him from the Thunderbirds. And he was probably the only bass player that I knew who knew how to play the notes; that it is not the same run over and over. I called them the monkey notes, and it's very swamp. It's those kind of dark notes that happen in between. If he wasn't sure how the song would go, if it comes to change, he would play notes in be-

tween. OK, we can either go to the IV or to the V. I was always amazed of that. He always inspired me to play better. That is why we brought him into the studio. There were songs that his style of bass playing would be perfect. Keith never joined Kathy and the Kilowatts. He played some gigs with us. I never asked him to join.

> **"One thing he used to say was, 'It's a good thing that I know how to play the bass because I can't do anything else.'"**
> -- Kathy Murray

Above: A young Lou Ann Barton. Below: Kathy and the Kilowatts at The Flying Circus club, about 1984. Kathy's husband, Bill Jones, on guitar; Keith on bass; Lance Womack on drums.

Courtesy of Kathy Murray

James Cotton with Jimmie Vaughan and Keith Ferguson, around 1983.

Courtesy of Kathy Murray

Kathy: "Thunderbirds playing with Jimmy Rogers. Jimmie was just knocked out to play with Jimmy Rodgers. And there was nobody there. If there was 12 people there, I would be surprised."

Kim Wilson and Keith Ferguson (note Keith's T-shirt).

Courtesy of Kathy Murray

Taken just before the first East Coast tour and used for promotion.

Courtesy of Kathy Murray

Andy Miller on drums with Jimmie, Kim and Keith.

Courtesy of Kathy Murray

Keith playing through a Fender amp at the Armadillo World Headquarters in Austin.

Courtesy of Kathy Murray

Trying to pair people

David Murray
Interviewed by Detlef Schmidt, October 2013

David Murray is a guitarist, producer and songwriter who has deep roots in the Austin music community. Murray began his career in the 1970s at the legendary Antone's club where he learned from and performed with blues greats such as B.B. King, Buddy Guy, James Cotton, Albert Collins and Stevie Ray Vaughan. Additionally, he has performed numerous times on *Austin City Limits* and NBC's *Friday Night Lights*.

David has recorded, and or toured in the U.S. and Europe, with Austin's most respected artists. Some of these include Angela Strehli, Lou Ann Barton, Kelly Willis, Doyle Bramhall, Marcia Ball, Roscoe Beck, Monte Warden, Jimmy LaFave, Jimmie Dale Gilmore, Michael Cross, Brennen Leigh, Jo Carol Pierce and Michael Ramos.

David Murray and Scott Ferris, 2013.

I first met all of these guys through Eddie Stout, a friend of mine from school. Eddie had a motorcycle, and his neighbor was Bill Etheridge. Bill played keyboards in The Nightcrawlers. His day job was a vacuum salesman, and he won a motorcycle in a contest. He tested the motorcycle but it didn't start. My friend Eddie fixed it for Bill and this was our entre in the whole blues scene.

My sister Kathy at this time was in a photo school and used to go out to take photographs of the bands. Back in those days, there were no digital cameras, and photos were kind of a big deal. I don't specifically remember the very first time I met Keith in particular. We were just so unhampered with that whole blues scene. I was 14 years old, and those guys were like gods to us.

We used to go see triple bills at the Armadillo Headquarters. There would be Storm, Jimmie, The Nightcrawlers, Stevie and Doyle and Paul Ray. I think Keith was with The Nightcrawlers at that time. I got

to know Stevie very well. Keith used to live in that little house on the corner of Annie and South Fifth. He liked to drink, which was not a big surprise, and I wanted to be a big guy like those guys. I was a baby-faced kid, and Keith always said, "This can't be taken by you. This is too strong for you." But I will say, of all the blues guys, Keith was always the one who was consistently kind and supportive to me.

There was a guy who played at the One Knite. He plays psychedelic music and was describing to Keith his big guitar pedal board. Keith was very enthusiastic about all genres of music.

One time at Antone's on Sixth Street, Keith came up, saw me and punched me in the stomach, saying never trust anybody. You know, I was very young and obedient and this was his part of wisdom on the younger parts. Another time, he came up, punched his tongue in my ear and said, "There are Germans everywhere."

I was too young to play with the older set. I did not really perform with Keith. I offered my electronic tuner to Keith but he declined. He was very old school in that way. He did not embrace technology. His tone was so dark and full.

Keith didn't drive, so I would drive him around for

some times to have gigs whoever he was with. And one time he tried to give me some gas money and I said, "No, it's fine." He stared at me and said, "Take it, never refuse money." He was always this way with me -- big brother way, telling me how things are.

Keith had such a personality. He could size up a person or situation in a word or phrase. Keith was so good. There was a wife of a famous band member in Austin who Keith made up her name, Sarge. When I first saw Keith, he played with an Ampeg flip-top, I think a B18. I remember Keith's tone -- loping, totally hold on the bottom. He was so freaking cool.

I just remember my first band was the The Dyna-flows. The Thunderbirds were touring in the Northeast, and Keith met a black harmonica player, Keith Dunn. He told Keith Dunn all about me and told him to move here, and he moved here. We put our band together. Without Keith, that would not have happened. That's how Keith was -- always trying to pair people together and tries to lift people up.

Pat Whitefield:

When we started The Fabulous Thunderbirds in August of 1975, Keith was playing in some glam-rock band in Dallas, I think, and my wife and I had a one-month-old baby boy. As the band progressed through November, Keith was really wanting my job, showing up every week-end night he wasn't playing and trying to mess with me. Now, it is pretty difficult to mess with someone who has to deal with a three-month-old baby daily, so I just shook it off ... usually.

One night, during the break at Antone's, as I was standing at the bar drinking a Crown on the rocks, talking to Jimmie and Freddie. Keith came up to me with full makeup on and proceeded to French kiss me, leaving lipstick smeared all over my face, saying how much he loved me. Without thinking, I returned the favor, leaving Keith for the rest of the break with a stunned and confused look on his face.

One of the few existing photos from The Nightcrawlers, 1974. Doyle Bramhall on drums and Keith Ferguson on bass. Stevie Ray Vaughan is on the left but not in the picture.

Courtesy of Becky Stapleton Crissman

From San Francisco to Texas

Jillian Bailey (Jill Olsen in the 1960s-70s). She was friends with Keith since 1969 and contributed some of the greatest pictures in this book. Jillian was road manager for Krackerjack, Rocky Hill, Texas Sheiks, and several other bands in Texas and Chicago. Between 1971 and 1978, she lived with Uncle John Turner, drummer for Johnny Winter. She returned to LA in 1992 and was an A&R rep at Atlantic Records and later managed record producers and engineers. She has kept lots of photos.

Jillian with the T-Birds at Tut's in Chicago, 1981.
Photo by Paul Natkin; Courtesy of Jillian Bailey

I met Keith in San Francisco when I was 19, and we were close friends ever since. Keith was like some untamed exotic creature that everyone wanted to claim. He dressed like an English dandy, in velvet or leather jackets, lots of scarves and silver bracelets and rings, stacked heel snakeskin boots, and had the scent of gardenias about him. He was living with Henry Carr, Ellen Fritzlen and their cat Squink, when he wasn't staying with one of his many girlfriends, and playing with Benny, Cecil and the Snakes or Black Kangaroo. The night I met him, I was out with Tom Schiffour, a drummer I knew from Chicago, and they were tripping on acid. Tom had a VW van with a cat skeleton hanging from the rearview mirror, and Keith was literally clawing at the passenger window, trying to get away from it. I never saw Keith drive a car; he was famous for walking everywhere with his inimitable stride. He always had a cat, and they were all named Bob.

I met Uncle John Turner, Tommy Shannon and the rest of Krackerjack at Henry's house and moved to Austin with them in 1972. We met Stevie Vaughan at a Krackerjack gig in Ft. Worth. His friend's father owned the club, and Stevie was sleeping on the pool table. We talked to him about moving to Austin and playing with Krackerjack, which he later did. Keith showed up in Austin about a year later. There were so many great bands in Austin then, and so many great venues: The New Orleans Club and the One Knite on Red River, the Armadillo on Barton Springs, Alexan-

Henry Carr on Guerrero Street, San Francisco, 1969.
Jillian: "I met Keith at Henry's house in 1969. Henry knew everyone in the Texas music scene, and Keith stayed with him and Ellen a lot. That's also where I met Krackerjack and ended up going to Texas with them."
Courtesy of Jillian Bailey

der's in Sunset Valley, the Rome Inn on W. 29th, the first Antone's, the Lamplight, and the Ritz Theatre on Sixth Street, La Cucaracha on E. Sixth Street, and the Black Queen on W. Sixth Street. I asked Keith once how he chose which girl to go home with after a gig when there might be six or seven girls waiting for him. Keith said, "Whoever had on the brightest colors."

Keith had tremendous musical influence along with his sophisticated fashion tastes. He taught us all how to dress. Keith played in Texas Sheiks with Uncle John Turner, and also with Uncle John in Diamond Joe & the Dynamo, and with Rocky Hill, who he stayed with in Houston for a time. I met Keith's mother in the '70s after Rocky gave Keith a huge iguana, and I drove him over to Margaret's to drop it off.

At one point, Keith, Uncle John and I went to Nashville with Rocky Hill to record with Jack Clements, a legend in the music business and the producer of "Ring of Fire" for Johnny Cash. We stayed in his mostly empty mansion, and Townes Van Zandt, who was out of control, came to visit, as well as Dusty Hill (Rocky's brother) and Billy Gibbons from ZZ Top.

Rocky, Keith and Uncle John also played at Irene's Cafe in the Sixth Ward in Houston, a club from the early 1950s where Lightnin' Hopkins and other blues muscians played. Several Christmases we spent at Johnny Winter's parent's home in Beaumont, Texas. Johnny still owned every 45 rpm record he'd ever bought and played us the most amazing, obscure music. Johnny, Keith, Uncle John and I went to see Jimmy Reed play in Houston with their old friend Eddy Rodriguez on drums. Eddy was so loaded he fell backwards off the drum platform, and we all just stood there. Jimmy Reed's wife was furious and came up onstage and played drums to finish the set.

Keith didn't play with The Werewolves, but he was great friends with them. They were like The New York Dolls in Dallas in early '70s, which was pretty shocking for Texas. Uncle John's baand, Krackerjack, would have The Werewolves open for them, and they'd all sit in with each other, including Keith.

People always gave him gifts. Keith used to stay with Janette and Fain, Jimi Hendrix's girlfriends in NYC. He was embarrassed once when he showed up with them at The Scene, Steve Paul's (Johnny Winter's manager) club in NYC. Apparently Jimi Hendrix recognized some of his clothes on Keith that he'd left

The third or fourth incarnation of Krackerjack with (l to r, front) Stevie Ray Vaughan, Bruce Bowland; (back) Tommy Shannon, Robin Siler (guitar) and Uncle John Turner.

Courtesy of Jillian Bailey

at Janette and Fain's place. Uncle John told me that Jimi Hendrix was such a powerful person that when he walked into the club, even if no one could see him, everyone could feel this presence and would look around wondering what just happened.

Wherever I was living, Keith would call when he was coming to town. In Chicago, I got The T-Birds booked into Tut's in 1981. I went on a few tour dates the next time they came to Chicago and moved back to Austin in 1982, staying in the tiny apartment above Keith's house at first. In 1983, Keith and I took Johnny to get his first tattoos from Spyder Webb in New York City when I was visiting friends and went with Johnny to see The Fabulous Thunderbirds play the Lone Star Café. I saw Keith almost every week in Austin until I left in 1992, and we always found some kind of trouble to get into. We both had the same self-destructive bent.

Much later, living in Los Angeles, I tried to call him one Friday night and couldn't get through. When I called again on Sunday, I was told he'd been taken to the hospital and had passed, which just broke my heart. I've met so many amazing musicians, writers and artists in my travels, but Keith is one of the most unique, talented, funny and charismatic people I have ever met. He had a razor-sharp intelligence, a deadly sense of humor and the biggest, most generous heart. You'd rarely leave his house without him giving you one of his weird things that you had admired. I wore his afghan coat for years. If you were too cheerful at what he considered too early of an hour, he'd ask: "What? Did you eat a clown for breakfast?"

Jillian: "My favorite Keith photo -- backstage San Francisco, 1971. Tall, skinny, snakeskin boots, scarves, leather or velvet jacket."

Courtesy of Jillian Bailey

Diamond Joe and the Dynamo: Uncle John Turner, Randy Banks, Joe Siddons and Keith Ferguson.

Courtesy of Jillian Bailey

Diamond Joe and the Dynamo: Uncle John Turner, Randy Banks, Joe Siddons and Keith Ferguson. Jillian: "That photo is a really typical Keith pose."

Courtesy of Jillian Bailey

Keith and Pat Naderhoff at San Francisco's Golden Gate Park to hear a band play, 1971. Jillian: "One of his favorite photos."

Courtesy of Jillian Bailey

Krackerjack: Jesse Taylor, Uncle John Turner, Tommy Shannon, Bruce Bowland and Mike Kindred in Monte Rio, California, 1970, staying at a cabin Keith's friend Vicki told them about.

Courtesy of Jillian Bailey

Johnny Winter, Uncle John Turner and Tommy Shannon at Vulcan Gas Co. in Austin, 1969.
Courtesy of Jillian Bailey

Doyle Bramhall, Stevie Vaughan and Keith Ferguson at Armadillo World Headquarters, 1974.
Courtesy of Jillian Bailey

Drew Blood & The Blades: Drew Pennington, Stevie Vaughan, Keith and Freddie on drums at Armadillo in Austin, 1974.

Courtesy of Jillian Bailey

Doyle Bramhall, Stevie Vaughan and Keith Ferguson at Armadillo World Headquarters in Austin, 1974.
Courtesy of Jillian Bailey

Left: Keith backstage at Antone's club in Austin. His caption: "Me as a nun."

Courtesy of Jillian Bailey

> "Keith had tremendous musical influence along with his sophisticated fashion tastes. He taught us all how to dress."
>
> -- Jillian Bailey

Texas Sheiks: Keith, Uncle John and Jack Morgan at The Lamplight on Sixth Street, Austin. Jillian: "I can't remember the guy's name playing Unc's drums. Willie Purples (on Keith's T-shirt) was a jam band Keith had with Billy Gibbons. Bill Ham wouldn't let the ZZ Top guys sit in with anyone, so Billy would wear a disguise."

Courtesy of Jillian Bailey

Jillian: "Rocky Hill, Keith and Uncle John at our house in Austin, 1974."

Courtesy of Jillian Bailey

Jillian: This was Uncle John's favorite photo of himself.

Courtesy of Jillian Bailey

Keith backstage in Austin, 1975
Courtesy of Jillian Bailey

Johnny, Edgar and Roma, who was first Johnny's girlfriend and, at this time, Edgar's wife. Jillian: "She was one of Keith's favorites."
Courtesy of Jillian Bailey

Edgar (left) and Johnny Winter.
Courtesy of Jillian Bailey

Jillian: "Photos I took at Christmas at Johnny and Edgar Winter's parents' house. Johnny and Keith; Johnny dressed in his old '60s band clothes."
Courtesy of Jillian Bailey

Steve Paul, Johnny's manager and owner of The Scene, a 1960s iconic nightclub.
Courtesy of Jillian Bailey

Photos taken backstage at a Johnny Winter gig in Dallas, 1979:

(top) Keith watching Tommy Shanon tune up.
(above left) Keith and Tommy.
(above right) Keith, Johnny, Alex Napier and Tommy.
(left) Keith, Johnny and Tommy.

Courtesy of Jillian Bailey

Photos of The Werewolves. Jillian: "Keith didn't play with them but they were all dear friends."

(top left) Seab Meador, from a gig at the Abraxis Club (friends of Keith) in Waco.
(above) Cover of Buddy Magazine.
(left) Bucky Ballard and Gloria Wilkes.
(lower left) Bucky Ballard from The Werewolves and Bruce Bowland from Krackerjack at the Abraxis Club, Waco, Texas, 1974.

Courtesy of Jillian Bailey

Johnny Winter and Jillian at Keith's house in Austin, 1985

Courtesy of Jillian Bailey

117

Jillian: "I took this at the Continental Club in Austin. He was showing me his gold teeth. I think it was a Tail Gator gig."

Courtesy of Jillian Bailey

Keith with the T-Birds in Amsterdam, 1983.

Courtesy of Jillian Bailey

Keith on tour in Europe with the T-Birds.

Courtesy of Jillian Bailey

Keith with theT-Birds in Amsterdam, 1983.

Courtesy of Jillian Bailey

Jillian with the T-Birds at Tut's in Chicago, 1981.

Photo by Paul Natkin; Courtesy of Jillian Bailey

Keith at a party in Austin with Charlie Sexton (seated, left), 1982.

Courtesy of Jillian Bailey

Chapter 4

T-Birds Years

1976-1984

The Fabulous Thunderbirds

Press kit photo of the T-Birds with Jimmie Vaughan, Mike Buck, Keith Ferguson and Kim Wilson.

Chapter 4

T-Birds Years 1976-1984

Keith lived that music

Kim Wilson
Interview by Detlef Schmidt, 2014.
Kim is the frontman, singer and harmonica player of The Fabulous Thunderbirds.

When I was coming to Austin, it was Stevie and Doyle Bramhall I was playing with in sessions. I first met Keith in the One Knite. He was a very feminine looking guy. It was probably around 1973, when I first came down to Austin. Later I got a call from Jimmie, saying he wanted to come to Minnesota. I got sick of the winters. I called him up later to come to Austin. I put all my records, my amp and a few clothes in a car and drove down. Austin at that time was one big party.

Willie Dixon was my manager at that time, but he had no time. Then he took me over to Jimmy Reed's manager, but he died short after. I had a 45 out; it's very rare today. I met Mark Pollock and he told me to go to Austin. What attracted me the most was the weather.

In late 1974, we started the Thunderbirds. Pat Whitefield was bass player from the beginning. Keith was always around us. Then we took him as a bass player. He was a little older. We were 24; he was 30. He was the most experienced. I wasn't really that good at that time. I only had played for five to six years.

Keith had a very good musical taste. Johnny 'Guitar' Watson; lots of that swamp stuff; Lightnin' Slim. "She's Tuff" came through his friend Floyd Moore. Keith was real; he lived that music. Mexican music, that swamp stuff. A lot of that stuff I heard through Keith first. He was hard to record -- he had a very distorted sound, played through very small gear. He was a very cool guy, the girls liked him. He was very difficult to room with. The second you opened your eyes, he started pacing around.

We were making no money, travelling around all the time. We did not make any money out of the records, too. Austin was a cool place to be. I moved in the place where Keith's grandmother lived later on -- 3400 S. Second Street, one bedroom, 85 dollars a month.

Scott Ferris and Kim Wilson
Courtesy of Scott Ferris

Keith had substance as a bass player. He was loud as hell. He was good at what he did. He played with feeling. He probably loved the music more than anybody else who played with the Thunderbirds. He had the attitude.

Once Muddy Waters put his stamp on us -- and that we were out on the road that much -- that helped us in Austin, too. Three hundred days, 340 days were the records for being away from home. We were young, so we could take it. No time at home. We were so fucked up. Those days for me … it was a stressful life. But I enjoyed it at the beginning. Then we got the deal with CBS. Then we started getting some paychecks. I made my money with royalties for the songs that I wrote. Tuff Enuff was a million-seller. I guess it sold two million copies until today.

With the Tigerman record, my solo thing started. With the Thunderbirds at that time, we did more other things. I wanted to do more blues stuff, and that is what I am doing to day.

> **"He probably loved the music more than anybody else who played with the Thunderbirds."**
> -- Kim Wilson

Early Birds

Mike Buck

Mike Buck, the drummer on the first two Thunderbirds albums, still lives in Austin and is the co-owner of Antone's Record Shop. Mike played in serveral bands with Keith and both together were often booked as the rhythm section for recordings.

I first met Keith in about 1975. I used to come to Austin a lot just to hear music. I lived in Fort Worth. I came to Austin to live with some friends, just to check it out, thinking about moving here. I used to go down to the One Knite club. The Storm would play there, and Keith was playing with The Storm, which was Jimmie, Keith, Fredde Pharoah, Lewis Cowdrey and Mike Kindred on piano. I thought they were the best band I ever heard. So I started to hang around with them, hanging out with Jimmie and Keith. I remember I was riding around with Jimmie in his car, drinking and hanging out. "Let's go over to Keith's." Angela Strehli came to the door; Keith was still sleeping. We played some records and then he woke up. I saw them a lot. I'd go see them when they were playing in Dallas. They backed up Big Mamma Thornton.

Keith with a cup of beer and a smoke

Courtesy of Kathy Murray

Keith may also have played with the band called Krackerjack, but I'm not sure. He also played with The Werewolves, a Dallas band. They were really good. They were a crossover between the New York Dolls and The Rolling Stones. They had a little bit of glam stuff, but were also bluesy.

The Storm played in Dallas and I took Lou Ann Barton over there -- she had never seen them play -- and introduced her to Jimmie. He told her, "I'm starting a new band. Wouldn't you like to be the singer?"

He started the Thunderbirds, and she ended up moving to Austin, singing and playing with them for a while. They had a few drummers -- Andy Miller, Fran, Fredde Pharoah, Otis Lewis -- before I was in the band. Lou Ann played with them for a while, and then she started playing with Stevie. The first bass player for the Thunderbirds was Pat Whitefield.

About a year later, I got a call from Jimmie. So they were looking for drummer, and I came back to Austin and played with them. I did my first gig with them in Dallas. We had gigs in Austin, where hardly anyone came, and Dallas was the first place to open up for us. Then we started to go to New England, the first place outside of Texas, especially around Rhode Island, Providence and Boston area.

When I moved to Austin, I lived with Keith. We had a place together on Annie Street. It was a duplex, and Alex Napier and his girlfriend lived next door. The neighborhood was pretty cool. Denny Freeman lived down the street.

Keith was like a big brother. One night when I came home drunk, I played some Gene Vincent records and then fell down and fell asleep. Keith came and covered me with a blanket. He was such great guy and funny as hell, too.

He had such a great sense of humor. I remember Keith was waking up very early in the morning. He started pacing up and down the floor. As soon as he seen my eyes open, he would turn the TV on. He was a big TV watcher; he watched documentaries and educational programs. He was very well read. He knew a lot about different subjects. He loved animals, reptiles especially, snakes and lizards.

Before we did the *Girls Go Wild* album, we went to New York and did a recording with Doc Promus producing at Regent Studios. We had the Roomful of Blues horns. That sounded pretty good. It never came out. I don't even know the reason. A few people have tried to put it out since but didn't get it sorted out. Doc Promus was one of those old record guys. He did things for Atlantic Records, Big Joe Turner and wrote songs for Elvis. Then we got that other offer from Tacoma and ended up with that.

There were a couple of times when we played two times in a row and Jimmie was sick. One time Denny Freeman played, and the next day Bill Campbell

The Fabulous Thunderbirds backing Eddie Taylor.

Courtesy of Mike Buck

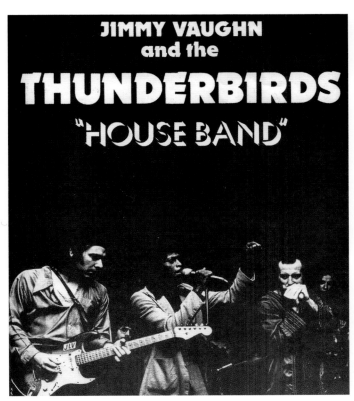

Early Antone's poster (note the misspelling of Jimmie Vaughan).

Courtesy of Mike Buck

Top right, middle and above: The T-Birds with Mike Buck at Antone's (note the Peavey amp Keith's playing).

Courtesy of Mike Buck

Antone's photo (note second bass leaning on the wall).

Courtesy of Mike Buck

played for him. All those guys sounded great with the band.

Faces, in Dallas, was a great club. One time we were there and Weather Report was in town. It was Jaco Pastorius' birthday and he was pretty fucked up. He wanted to sit in with the band. It was fun. The way he played was kind of opposite. He couldn't play Keith's bass because it was left-handed, and it took him a while to figure it out.

Keith had long hair when he joined the band. When he was married to Lou Ann he had cut it already. I left the Thunderbirds, basically because Jimmie wanted to hire Fran.

Everybody in the band had a big record collection. Keith did have a lot of cool records. As a kid he had worked for Pappy Daily. He had a label and he also had this big record distributing company in Houston. He had Starday Records; he put out George Jones and all those people. I think Keith's dad was involved, too. So he got some great records from that.

Then when I came to the band, I had a great record collection, too. There were a few songs that came from my record collection, like "Marked Deck".

Some of these older guys I used to play with in Fort Worth hung around with Frankie Lee Sounds and those Dallas blues guys. "Rich Woman" I brought, too. Keith brought in "Running Shoes". He had that record from Juke Boy Bonner.

At the big Juneteenth Festival in Houston, we went out on stage and that was sea of black faces. Everybody got really quiet and they started staring at us. We started playing and they started getting into it and going crazy. I am always hearing that the Thunderbirds changed the way the white blues bands dressed and looked.

We did a big tour in England with Rockpile, Dave Edmunds' band. Then we did a few days outside of England just by ourselves. We played Hamburg and Munich, I think, something for German TV, and we played Amsterdam.

Keith was really easy to play with; we really clicked the rhythm section. Jimmie was a big part of it, too. He had such a great rhythm style. Keith and I did a lot of other projects. Sometimes, without having the element of Jimmie there, it's not that kind of magic. He (Keith) played on the first LeRoi Brothers album. He did a pretty good job. For a while we didn't have a

Above: A promotion shot of the T-Birds
Left: A backstage shot.
Below: An old poster (note misspelling of Jimmie Vaughan)

Courtesy of Mike Buck

bass player, so he played a few gigs with us. This was when he was still with the Thunderbirds. He couldn't always do the gigs, but sometimes he did.

When Keith left the Thunderbirds, we did a lot of project bands together. We had a little Cajun band with Dan Del Santo, Ponty Bone and D'Jalma Garnier. He did a lot of pickup gigs. Everybody in Austin played in different bands.

Keith listened a lot to conjunto music. He was very well accepted in the Mexican-American community. They thought of him as one of their own. He had some very loyal friends.

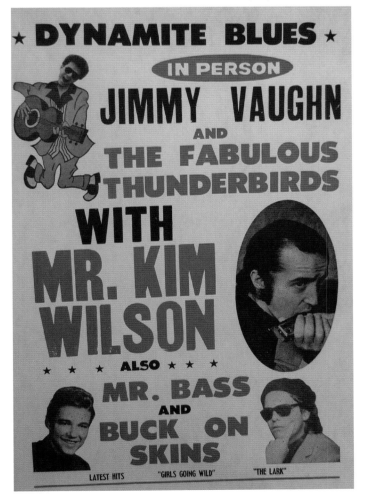

127

The first European tour

THE FABULOUS THUNDERBIRDS

FEBRUARY 18th - MARCH 4th, 1980. Inc.

SCHEDULE AT-A-GLANCE

FEBRUARY 1980.		VENUE:	HOTEL:
Monday	18th:-	Day off, London.	Kensington Hilton, Tel:- 01-603-3355.
Tuesday	19th:-	Day off, London.	Kensington Hilton, Tel:- 01-603-3355.
Wednesday	20th:-	Day off, London.	Kensington Hilton, Tel:- 01-603-3355.
Thursday	21st:-	Fly to Amsterdam. KL.132. Depart: 2pm. Arrive 4pm.	Hotel Central,AMSTERDAM Tel:- (020) 18765.
Friday	22nd:-	PARADISO CLUB, AMSTERDAM.	Hotel Central,AMSTERDAM Tel:- (020) 18765.
Saturday	23rd:-	EXIT CLUB, ROTTERDAM.	Hotel Central,AMSTERDAM Tel:- (020) 18765.
Sunday	24th:-	Fly to Munich. KL.233. Depart:12.15pm. Arr.1.35pm.	Hotel Residence,MUNICH. Tel:- (089) 399041.
Monday	25th:-	T.V. Studios, MUNICH.	Hotel Residence,MUNICH. Tel:- (089) 399041.
Tuesday	26th:-	T.V. Studios, MUNICH.	Hotel Residence,MUNICH. Tel:- (089) 399041.
Wednesday	27th:-	Fly to Hamburg. LH.796. Depart.11.20am. Arr.12.40pm UNCLE POH'S CLUB, HAMBURG.	Schaub Hotel Garni, Tel:- (040) 4603430.
Thursday	28th:-	UNCLE POH'S CLUB, HAMBURG.	Schaub Hotel Garni, Tel:- (040) 4603430.
Friday	29th:-	Fly to London. BA. 735. Depart:12.20pm.Arr.12.45pm	Kensington Hilton Hotel Tel:- 01-603-3355.

MARCH, 1980.

Saturday	1st:-	Day off, London.	Kensington Hilton, Tel:- 01-603-3355.
Sunday	2nd:-	THE VENUE, LONDON.	Kensington Hilton, Tel:- 01-603-3355.
Monday	3rd:-	THE HOPE & ANCHOR, ISLINGTON, LONDON.	Kensington Hilton, Tel:- 01-603-3355.
Tuesday	4th:-	B.B.C. T.V. Manchester. "Old Grey Whistle Test"	Kensington Hilton, Tel:- 01-603-3355.
Wednesday	5th:-	Return to U.S.A.	

Above: Keith's original tour schedule.

Courtesy of Keith Ferguson Collection

Thunderbirds . . .

Continued from page 3AA

blush. "I wouldn't want some people to hear about that. But, yeah, I've heard that from other people — that Muddy has said something similar, and . . . uh, whew! Whatsaya say about something like that, you know?"

THE NUCLEUS OF The Fabulous Thunderbirds is Wilson and Vaughan (other members are bassist Keith Ferguson and drummer Mike Buck). They teamed up some three years ago. Wilson's voyage to Austin was somewhat roundabout, from Detroit (his birthplace) through California, Minnesota, Seattle, Kansas City ("I don't like to say I'm from anywhere") and a succession of blues and blues-rock bands. Vaughan, on the other hand, spent most of his time in Dallas, working with a number of rock bands, including the well-known Chessmen. The two first met in Austin.

"What happened was that my band was playin' this rib joint when Kim came in, sat in with the band, and just tore it up! That was the beginning," Vaughan said.

It took some time for the two to join forces permanently, but the idea for such a teaming always was in the back of both men's minds.

"I got tired of playing in this turkey band I was in," Wilson recalled.

beginning to click. In addition to word-of-mouth from Muddy and Billy, plus an ever-widening circle of fans in Texas, the group has appeared at the New Orleans Jazz and Heritage Festival, have an upcoming spot on the San Francisco Blues Fest and have an album in the can (produced by the legendary Doc Pomus and Joel Dorn) that's currently being shopped around to several major labels.

"You'll definitely hear the album before long — it's just a matter of picking the proper deal," Wilson said. "We're taking our time, just trying to do it right.

"It's very hard to try and play music and take care of the business, too — sometimes it gets to be too much. But it's only the business end that gets to me, that's the only hard part. Playing the gig is the easiest part."

What would Wilson do if things didn't pan out — if the "blues rebirth" he foresees doesn't come to pass and The Fabulous Thunderbirds never make the big time?

"WELL, I'LL JUST keep playing, keep playing the blues," he replied. "As long as I can play music and make money at it, I'm OK. We're doing pretty good right now. We're not millionaires or anything, but we're doing pretty good. If big money comes, fine. If not, well, we'll just keep at it. It's

Wilson tore 'em up on vocals as well as
— Post photo by Fr

An article, most likely from a Houston newspaper, that mentions a record produced by Doc Promus that never came out.
Right: Keith and Mike Buck at the Hope&Anchor
Below: Poster from the Hamburg club Onkel Pö, and the first page of the tour schedule from 1980
Courtesy of Mike Buck

Pappy Daily/ Starday Records

The Starday Label was started in Beaumont, Texas in 1952 by Harold W. 'Pappy' Daily and Jack Starnes, Jr. The label recorded country and western, Cajun music and sacred music. Harold W. 'Pappy' Daily is one of the most beloved figures in country music recording history. Daily was born in 1902 in Yoakum, Texas and started working as an accountant in the tax department of the Southern Pacific railroad around 1920. When the Depression came, his railroad job was looking pretty shaky, so Daily started looking for other work. He started South Coast Amusements in 1932 to distribute Bally Jukeboxes. Pappy then opened up a record store and sold phonograph records. Eventually he became a wholesaler and distributed records in the southwestern U.S. In 1952, he started the Starday record label with Jack Starnes. Jack Starnes was a talent booker who owned a night club in Beaumont Texas, and who at one time managed Lefty Frizzell. The name Starday came from their two last names, 'Star' from Starnes and 'day' from Daily.

In 1954, a young ex-Marine named George Jones was playing in Starnes' club. Starnes decided to cut some records with Jones, and brought in Daily to help produce his first session. In 1955, he recorded his first hit, titled "Why Baby Why," which went to #4 on the country charts. Pappy Daily's interest in Starday was purchased by Don Pierce in 1958, and Pappy Daily left the label to be a producer at Mercury Records. While at Mercury, he also established his own independent label called D to record local Texas musicians. He soon enjoyed the biggest hit in his long career with "Chantilly Lace" by the Big Bopper which initially appeared on D but was soon transferred to Mercury Records for the distribution it needed. Pappy Daily's D label was the first to record Willie Nelson, but his recordings on D were unsuccessful. In 1961, Daily left Mercury for the A&R director's job in the country division of United Artists.

The Starday Records Story[22]
*Used with friendly permission of Mike Callahan-
http://www.bsnpubs.com/king/stardaystory.html*

The Fabulous Thunderbirds at the New Orleans Jazz Festi

"I am always h

w

Courtesy of Mike Buck

ng that the Thunderbirds changed the way the
blues bands dressed and looked."

-- Mike Buck

Above: The Thunderbirds at the San Fransisco Blues Festival (note the blue paisley Fender Telecaster bass Keith's playing.)
Below left: Keith and Mike Buck backstage.
Below right: Keith in Austin, April 25, 1976.

Courtesy of Mike Buck

> "He was one in million; not a versatile player but a bass player who exactly knew what a band and the song needed."
>
> -- Denny Freeman

Outtakes from the photo session for the *Big Guitars from Texas* album (l to r): Keith Ferguson, Don Leady, Mike Buck, Frankie Camaro, Denny Freeman and Evan Johns.

Photo by Lone Star Silver, Jeff Rowe & Scott Van Osdol; Courtesy of Mike Buck

Outtake from the photo session for the Big Guitars from Texas album. Keith's cowhide bass can be seen quite well.

Photo by Lone Star Silver, Jeff Rowe & Scott Van Osdol; Courtesy of Mike Buck

The cover of the first album

Billy Cross
Interview by Detlef Schmidt, October 2012

Billy Cross is the photographer who took the classic pictures of The Fabulous Thunderbirds that were used on the cover of their first album, and he was on tour with the Thunderbirds during their first years. He is now into radiology and lives in Port Arthur, Texas.

I first met Keith in about 1973 or 1974, before the Thunderbirds started. We were down on Sixth Street; there was a place called the Lamplighter. Some of the Port Arthur boys -- Floyd Moore, me, Herman Bennett, sometimes Walter Higgs and different drummers -- we played little gigs there. I remember the Ritz Theater being across the street. The first time I saw Keith was when he was walking over from the Ritz and he was wearing those snakeskin boots, that he probably got from England when he was over with Johnny, and this Afghan coat with the fur on the side. I think it was blue suede. He was looking pretty wild.

From him playing with Johnny Winter in Houston, he made a connection to the Golden Triangle area, Beaumont and Port Arthur. There was also a guy named Ikey Sweat (Isaac Payton Sweat) that also came from this area. Ike had played with Johnny Winter for a while as a bass player. He always had a connection to Port Arthur and Beaumont people.

He was not much on talking about San Francisco, just that he lived there and that he had a few friends over there. With the Thunderbirds, when they played there, he had a couple of friends that used to come and see him.

Not too long after that, he moved in with Hermann and Floyd in Hermann's house. When Antone's got started up, it was Port Arthur people who had a great love for blues. I remember that he played in a band named The Texas Sheiks. I don't think they were together that long. After he had moved in with Hermann and Floyd was when we all started to get to know each other.

Jimmie Vaughan, Keith and Connie Vaughan.
Courtesy of Floyd Moore

We had a battle of the bands against some guys from Houston, the Sons of the Uranium Savages. It was at the Ritz Theater; there were two bands. We were the Marsh Mongrels. It was Floyd Moore, Hermann Bennett, myself and Walter Higgs. We were all from Port Athur, and Keith played bass. They played first, then we were playing. I sang some, Hermann was singing, Keith on bass, Floyd on guitar and Butch Jarvis on drums. While the Marsh Mongrels were playing, some guy from the Sons of the Uranium Savages cut the whole power. It was a little sabotage thing. It was all fun though. Keith always had a strong relationship to Port Arthur people.

Antone's started up and was bringing in some blues acts. It was a way to see all these people we had admired for so many years. The Thunderbirds started as a house band of Antone's.

He played with Johnny (Winter) and he went to Europe, to England, with Johnny. I remember him telling me that he was back in California after that. I am not sure how long he was actually with Johnny.

Keith Ferguson, at the original Antone's on Sixth Street, playing through an Ampeg B-18.

Courtesy of Billy Cross

Mike Buck and Keith Ferguson at the Soap Creek Saloon in Austin, Texas.

Courtesy of Billy Cross

I met Johnny in New York when I was working for the Thunderbirds. Keith and I roomed a lot together. He told me, "Come on, we are going over here." We'd go down, get a cab and we get to this apartment building. We went up to the penthouse. So we went up to Johnny's place where he was living with his wife, Susan. We'd hang out there for a while. It was memorable for me; not sure if he would remember. When Keith told Johnny that I was from Port Arthur, I was OK; I was a Triangle boy.

I started driving for the Thunderbirds when they first got out to promote their *Girls Go Wild* album. This was about 1979. They would ask me if I could do some pictures for them for some album cover. I had started to do photography for Antone's when they started up. I had a little camera and started to take pictures. Then I got a 35mm camera and started learning to take some photographs with that.

So I took a few pictures that people liked, and I got a good feedback on that. I took some pictures of them when they were playing as a house band at Antone's. They asked me to do some pictures for their album cover. I was by no means a professional photographer; it was just something I got in to.

Jimmie had that old poster of Bobby Blue Bland that he had in his house. Back in the '50s and '60s they were doing these flashy dayglow colors of all these R&B and soul acts. That was what it was. It had the star in the middle. It may even had that "Girls go wild" on it. That's where the layout for that cover came from, and Jimmie really liked that poster. They wanted it to be kind of like that.

So we went down on Sixth Street. There were a couple of boys from Nederland area that had a record store there. It was called OK Records. So we went into the backroom of the record store; that's where we made those photographs. I did some pictures of each one of them and it was just a kind of "do what you want", and then I did a couple of them all together as a group.

They picked out the pictures that they wanted for the album. Each one picked out their individual pictures. Kim did bring that big harmonica. Jimmie had brought a Telecaster. I don't even remember if he brought a Stratocaster. He mostly played Strats, but the Tele ended up on the cover. Keith was always doing something to his basses. This one

Above: Keith Ferguson, Andy Miller and Jimmie Vaughan at the old Antone's. Below: Jimmie Vaughan, Kim Wilson and Keith Ferguson at the old Antone's on Sixth Street.

Courtesy of Billy Cross

had leopard skin on the back. He liked to do things like that.

Then when the album came out, they had a Plymouth van they were travelling in. So they decided that they were going to do this little tour to promote their record. They asked me to come with them on the tour and drive so they didn't have to do the driving and could sleep. I did this no less than two years. It was always wild. It was '79, '80, '81.

Keith and I roomed together a lot on the road. We got along fine. Keith always had a lot of knives and stuff like that. He also had some throwing stars. I remember a few times when we had nothing to do, we were throwing those stars in the motel room.

I remember when we were in New York, we got to Manny's (famous New York music store). I think that's where he bought the bass with #0172. He freaked out; he had to have it. He had a lot of Fender Precision basses over the years.

Keith was always known for his postcards from the road. He was really good in doing that. On the road back then, it was the only way to communicate. So when we were on the road, we were always looking out for postcards. He was always looking for classic postcards, like '40s pinups and stuff. Sometimes he would put little stickers on them.

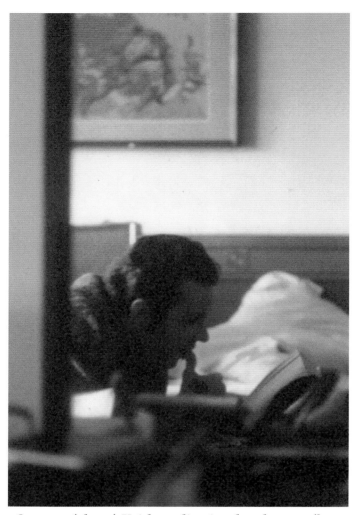

On tour: (above) Keith reading in a hotel room; (below) Keith sleeping on the road in the T-Birds van.

Courtesy of Billy Cross

Outtakes from the 1979 photo session for the *Girls Go Wild* album.

Courtesy of Billy Cross

Keith and I were at this place in south Austin called the Alamo. Kim Wilson came in with this guy from Elvis Costello's band. And there were all these Mexicanos there, and one of them goes to us and said, "Who are you?" And the guy answered "I play bass for Elvis." And the Mexican guy answered, "Elvis is dead, man." The guy just didn't know who Elvis Costello was and that he was playing in town.

Not too long after touring with the Thunderbirds, I went back to Port Arthur. So when they came down to play in Beaumont or Houston, I went to see them. I then moved back to Austin about 1986.

On my 35th birthday, I had a crawfish boil. Everybody liked it, so we made it an annual thing. Keith would always come out. Even when I came down to Port Arthur again at the end of 1991, we continued to have that little annual crawfish boil. I didn't see Keith for a good while. Some people came down from Austin. I got a call in the morning from Mike Steele. He said he was in Beaumont and Keith was with him. Keith wanted to come for this crawfish boil. This was at the time shortly before he passed away and didn't want to travel anymore; didn't want to leave Austin and his house. This really blew me away. I was surprised knowing that he didn't travel.

We had a pet deer at that time. She walked around the yard like a dog. She was about one year old. Keith was so much into animals. Animals and music, he knew everything about. Keith really liked it. The deer was running around, the dogs were running around and the chickens. I guess he really had a good time. That was the last time I saw him.

Left/above: Other outtakes from the *Girls Go Wild* session. Below/above: T-Birds at the Rome Inn, Austin.

Courtesy of Billy Cross

He had this unreal record collection. As soon as he would know what kind of music you were into, he would be pull out record and playing stuff to you. If it was just him and me hanging out in the middle of the night, he would start pulling out all this obscure Cajun music because that's what we grew up with here in this area. He would play rhythm and blues and what you call 'swamp rock'. He liked all kinds of music.

"Keith was always doing something to his basses. This one had leopard skin on the back. He liked to do things like that."
-- Billy Cross

The Keith Walk in Port Aransas.

Courtesy of Floyd Moore

At Keith's birthday party, holding his godson, Jason Jarvis, 1979.

Courtesy of Billy Cross

Floyd Moore, Billy Cross and Keith in Lake Travis.

Courtesy of Floyd Moore

Amazing Records

Jim Yanaway
interviewed by Detlef Schmidt, October 2011

Jim was a radio deejay and had a record company named Amazing Records. He was around The Fabulous Thunderbirds during their early days. He recorded the Thunderbirds prior to their record releases, but they were never issued. He also put out the first LeRoi Brothers album.

I met Keith for the first time in the early '70s, but really got to know him through Mike Buck. That would have been about 1976. I remember talking with Mike when he first got the invitation to join the Thunderbirds. He came down to Austin from Fort Worth. Lou Ann Barton was also doing something with the Thunderbirds at that time. And, of course, she knew Mike from Fort Worth and she got Mike to come down to Austin.

The band I remember Keith performing with pre-Thunderbirds was Krackerjack. That was more rock, a glam-type thing; the members of the band dressed up with a lot of scarves and feathered boas and eye make-up! That was definitely NOT my thing!

I was with the Thunderbirds when they did their first out-of-town performance in Houston. It was at the Juneteenth Festival, I think in 1978. That had all the great living blues giants then including Muddy Waters, Lightnin' Hopkins, Big Mama Thornton, Clifton Chenier, John Lee Hooker among many others. That was also Juke Boy Bonner's last performance; he died within a week. The Thunderbirds came out and opened up the whole celebration on June 18 at noon. They got out there and the crowd, which was mostly black -- it was at the Miller Amphitheater in Hermann Park in Houston, and Juneteenth is sort of an unofficial holiday for all black Texans -- was kind of skeptical about this young, white band. Keith was the oldest; he might have been 30 then. The rest of the band were 26 or 27. At the very beginning, there were people shouting, "Get off the stage!" The Thunderbirds played a few more tunes and the people

Keith with the newer sticker on his 1952 Fender Precision bass.

Courtesy of Becky Stapleton Crissman

then realized how incredibly solid they were. I have a recording of this, and you can hear them winning the crowd over. Whistling. Alex Moore, the old boogie piano player that recorded 78s in the 1920s, and was in his mid-80s at that time, was standing right next to me. He was whooping and hollering and whistling -- excited because he hadn't heard solid blues like that in years. That was the Thunderbirds first performance out of Austin, and they just nailed it. All the great performers that were on that festival were won over by the Thunderbirds, and that opened many doors for the band.

I did a radio show for KCHU in Dallas for several years, and played recordings I made of The Thunderbirds on air. A lot of people found out about The Thunderbirds because of this, and came out to their shows and found out how great they were.

I started my record company in 1980. I had recorded the Thunderbirds at Gene Huddleston's studio in Garland, Texas. I had talked to the Thunderbirds for a while about recording as I had been working with another company named Flying High Records. I also talked with Stevie Vaughan for more than five years about recording his first record.

I got the Thunderbirds in the studio, but they had a show at a college in Dallas at mid-day and they had performed the night before in Austin. We were scheduled to get in the studio at about eight at night. By the time we had gotten into the studio, they weren't as sharp as they would ordinarily be. And

being in a studio was a bit different atmosphere than doing a live show. We didn't come out with as good of a recording as any of us knew we could get, and I agreed not to put out those recordings.

They recorded largely the same tunes that later came out on the *Girls Go Wild* album, and pretty much did the same set when they went in the Sumet-Burnet Studio for that album. Mike Buck probably brought most of the material that came out on this recording, because he had the record collection that had all the good Louisiana music and records from Vee Jay and Cobra. The recording I did was with a 16-track machine on one-inch tape. I never thought of releasing it -- I didn't want to bring anything out that was inferior

Before we did those recordings, Keith and I were sitting around at Lucas B&B Deli in Dallas. I didn't yet have a name for the record company. We were talking about this, and somehow it came up that if the Thunderbirds record sells it would be a miracle. And I said, "If it's a hit, it's amazing." So that's how I came up with the name for Amazing Records.

At some point, when he was kicked out of the Thunderbirds, that was in large part … he didn't want to travel. He said he didn't like to get cold, among other concerns, and he maybe was complaining too much.

I put out the first LeRoi Brothers album, *Check This Action*. It was later reissued on Jungle. I got the LeRois in the studio, and Alex Napier was the orig-

The cover (top) of *Check This Action,* and the back showing Keith (far right) with a switchblade.

© *Jungle Records*

inal bass player. We recorded at Lone Star Studio in Austin, and Alex left the band shortly after they started recording. The LeRois needed a bass player, and Keith came in.

Then, next joining Don Leady's Tail Gators was a natural progression for Keith. Don had also been in The LeRoi Brothers, and The Tail Gators were pretty authentic, straight ahead, low-down, uncompromising. They were playing more swamp rock.

Going back to the days when Keith grew up in Houston, his father had a record store there. He sold records to the Mexican-American and black community there. They had real Mexican 78s, and he also sold blues records and zydeco. I don't think blues was Keith's first love; it was Mexican music and maybe zydeco. So Keith grew up in Houston with those influences. He also picked up speaking Spanish from the people that were around there and was very fluent. Among others, he became good friends with the guys from Los Lobos, particularly César Rosas, in part because he also played guitar left-handed like Keith did.

Keith was well-respected among many fine musicians around the world. One time, the Thunderbirds were doing a show at a club called Faces in Dallas. Another bass player showed up and wanted to sit in. Keith generally didn't let anybody sit in, and being left-handed and all set up for that, but Keith just wanted to see how the guy did with his bass. The guy went on, started playing left-handed and halfway through the song he flipped the bass over and started playing right-handed. As it turns out, the bass player was Jaco Pastorius. He had come to The Thunderbirds gig because of Keith. Jaco was pretty impressed by Keith's playing and Keith was impressed by Jaco's playing, especially flipping the bass over and playing it upside down.

The Thunderbirds were hugely influential in the late '70s. They had a whole different stage presence, looking pretty sharp-dressed and all that influenced a lot of California bands. Keith had his own style, including the way he dressed and played bass on stage -- the whole persona. Keith did popularize those see-through shirts. He always had a pack of Kool cigarettes in the pocket you could easily see, and that was kind of a Keith Ferguson look.

There were mice at Keith's house, and he heard of giant gecko lizards that ate mice. So he went to a pet

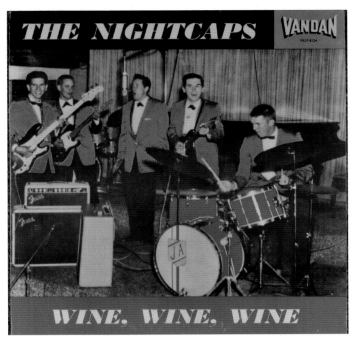

"Thunderbird" was the first song that Stevie Ray Vaughan sang.   © *Vandan Records*

Omar Dykes (left) still lives in Austin and made an album with Jimmie Vaughan, *Jimmy Reed Highway*, and did an album with Howlin' Wolf tunes.
© *Austin Records*

store and bought a bunch of them and let them loose under his house. The big Madagascar geckos are still around. He has now gotten the whole neighborhood full of giant geckos!

Keith was very bright and surprisingly informed about many subjects, and he was fairly eccentric, too! One of my best friends.

Managing the Thunderbirds

I had just began life as a personal manager with Lisa Kindred, a blues singer with two albums on Vanguard, whose first booking was opening for Magic Sam from Chicago. Sam was such a great singer and futurist, and it was a little intimidating to make small talk in the communal dressing room. He popped a can of Bud and asked me what I knew about show business. He said he needed a damn manager that cared about him and could get his career moving. We shook hands and for the next two years I managed him (untill his untimely death in November 1969 at age 32). During this time I also managed Albert Collins, Earl Hooker, George 'Harmonica' Smith and Sunnyland Slim. Nobody could be expected to fill the void left by Magic Sam, but the collective spirit of the original Fabulous Thunderbirds comes from the same place.

During the middle-70's I was managing and producing Leo Kottke, John Fahey, T-Bone Burnett, Albert Lee and Jack Nitzsche. A close friend, Dan Bourgeoise, was leaving U.A. Records to start a publishing company called Bug Music. He called and asked if I wanted to share an office and the secretary. He had found a "Nathanael West-bungalow walking distance from Frederick's of Hollywood". Dan had signed Asleep at the Wheel to U.A. and was friends with Ray Benson, the band's leader. Ray placed his publishing company with Bug and would hang out in the office when he was in town. Ray lived in Austin and told me there were some good R&B bands there, one in particular, that I should come with him and check 'em out.

I went to London in 1977 to make a production deal with Dan's counterpart at U.A., Andrew Lauder. He said if I could hold off for a while he was starting up

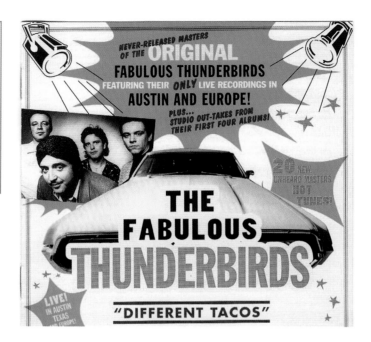

© *Benchmark Records*

an exciting indie, and I'd have the third release. The new label was *Radar* with Elvis Costello as the first act. Eventually Andrew and Jake Riviera, the manager of Elvis and Nick Lowe, formed Demon Records. Punk rock was getting huge here, making it almost seem impossible that in less than two years the Fabulous Thunderbirds would be the cover of a huge spread in Melody Maker, duly christened "The Wild Bunch".

Los Angeles was feeling the effects of the Sex Pistols with bands like "X" packing the clubs. Ray asked me if I had ever been to Austin, and the answer was no. He described the scene as being fertile grounds for musicians. Joints to play, cheap rents and food. My gut feeling was I didn't need to hear "I got my Mojo working" by white guys. He said, "Please call Jimmie, they are lot cooler than that."

Jimmie Vaughan started chuckling when I asked if all the guys in the band had beards, wore denin work shirts and wire-rimmed glasses. It got better with the "Mojo" question.

He very softly said, "We're an encyclopedia of all the good shit from the Gulf Coast, you know, Lightnin' Slim, Lazy Lester, Excello, Texas shuffles, rockin' cajun. Muddy Waters helped get us a gig in Boston when he said Kim, our harp player, is the best he has heard since Little Walter. Our bass player did a gig with Johnny Winter then went across town to play bass in a chicano show band where he had to dance the side-ways pony with a tambourine on his hip. To answer your other question we are all 27, handsome motherfuckers that dress cool and our music drives girls wild." While wondering who Lazy Lester is I tell Jimmie I'm on my way.

Ray picked me up at the airport in his big black Caddy and took me to the Driskill Hotel. Their gig that night was across Sixth Street at the original Antone's, backing Hubert Sumlin and doing two or three sets of their own. Jimmie Vaughan and Kim Wilson came by the hotel with Ray to say hello, and I took a picture of the three leaning on Ray's Caddy. It was June, 1978.

Sauntering into the club came Mike Buck to say hello. We had met in Ft. Worth through T-Bone several years earlier. Mike was drumming with Robert Ealey and the Five Careless Lovers at the New Bluebird. He is extremely knowledgeable about records, especially Rockabilly and r & b.

Jimmie and another guy joined us at the bar. After five minutes of talking it dawned on me that the other guy, wearing a turban, was Kim. I thought Chuck Willis ("King of the Stroll") might be his inspiration, but he rattled off

Barbara during his formative years and would catch George in places like Oxnard. George was as gracious as he was talented, and Kim learned a lot from this master. We agreed George was a genius, especially his work on the chromatic harp of "Hawaii-Five-O".

Keith Ferguson said we met in '69 at the Ash Grove when his band with Angela Strehli opened for Albert Collins. He had been in all kinds of bands, has backed virtually everybody. He was curious if I'd heard of a black transvestite in L.A. that played like Hendrix in a band called "Queen"? I admitted that my curiosity had led me to attend a rehearsal where three guys wearing dresses and make-up were pretty wild. The bass player was Nick St. Nicholas, ex-Steppenwolf. Keith smiled and said, "He took my place." Through Keith's see-through rayon shirt I noticed a pack of Kools and interesting pachuko tattoos of various birds, Madonnas, and the Sistine Chapel. One hour into meeting these guys, after smoking Ray's pot and having a tequila or two, not seeing Waylon or Willie, I felt Austin is ready for whole new thing.

The band finally took the stage and blasted off with "Scratch My Back". From Kim's rich harmonica tone to Jimmie's Fender amp vibrato, this was something absolutely, knock-your-socks-off special. Kim sang better than I ever could have anticipated and proved an excellent front man. Jimmy was the glue, with his unselfish ensemble playing. Many of the songs in the first set were unfa-

R&B groups from Louisiana where all the members wore turbans. He surprised me by saying he had hung out with George "Harmonica" Smith all over funky parts of California. Kim lived in Santa

Producer Denny Bruce, 1973.
Photo by John Van Hamersveld; Courtesy Denny Bruce

147

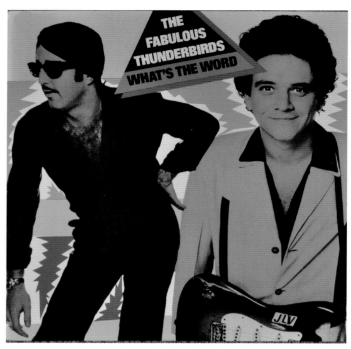

miliar to me and I was elated to find out how many had been originals.

We decided the only way to record was to be real and raw. Ray suggested a studio in Dallas and Jimmie checked it out. The engineer was Bob Sullivan, from Shreveport, where he was engineer for the Louisiana Hayride. I called him and he said, "Yeah, I did Elvis a few times on the Hayride." He asked if I had heard of a cat out of Shreveport named Dale Hawkins? I sang "Suzie-Q, baby I love you" and he said "I did that crazy son of a bitch, too".

The first album was pretty much cut the first two

nights. I had asked Bob for a studio set-up like it was a live gig or the way he'd set it up to get a "Suzie-Q" sound. He smiled and said, "It's the same thing, anyhow." After rightly twenty minutes, the balances felt right and everybody could hear each other. Never was a band so ready to record. After several rolls of tape were used, I split to requisition some liquid refreshments. The band wanted to keep rolling but it was time to cool out and listen to what we had. Bob was enjoying himself, telling some good stories. I asked him who was absolutely the worst act he ever had to record? Without any hesitation, he replied, "The 13th Floor Elevators." Jimmie has just taken a gulp of VO and spewed it on me in a cloud of spray,

rolled on the floor in stitches, looked at me, pointed at Bob and blurted out, "This poor bastard had to put up with all that acid horseshit." As Bob gravely recounted how the police had to get "the Elevators" down from the trees outside the studio, we called it a very good night. At the third evening's session we ate bar-b-que, listening back to everything, and felt we had an album, but we returned one more time to do instrumentals and some obscure cover songs.

The band always delighted in wild posters to advertise their gigs. The wilder the colors or pictures, the better. They used a printer in Houston who did all the chitlin-circuit stars' posters you see on poles in the ghetto. We wanted to retain this style of artwork for the first album cover, but a little streamlined in production because a few people thought it looked like "an old LP."

The album was released without any hype, but quickly garnered rave reviews and good alternative radio play. The decision was made to release a second album quickly, to build momentum instead of touring for a year, recording, and starting all over again with the media. Kim already had nine or ten originals and Jimmie had some tricks up his sleeve, too. Bob Sullivan was ready at Sumet-Bernet Sound Studios. After starting with some down and dirty grooves ("Low-

149

Down Woman", "Runnin' Shoes"), Jimmie wanted to turn the heat up a notch. "Extra Jimmies" had a classic Texas shuffle that required a different drummer. Fran Christina had played with the T-Birds early in their career when they gigged in Canada. He hailed from Rhode Island, home of the band's good friends, Roomful of Blues, and now lived in Austin, playing with Asleep at the Wheel. Both Mike Buck and Fran are on the second album. Fran gave his notice with the Wheel" and came on board. He truly was "the joker in the deck." I've always admired a guy who can hear any song and start singing along with dirty lyrics that are perfect. He's always up, crackin' jokes, which is a big plus to a band that plays one-nighters, parties, and has to leave town at the crack of dawn. He even drove the bus if the bus driver was tired.

Roger Forrester, Eric Clapton's manager, called to inquire on Albert Lee's touring status. Eric wanted another guitarist who sang for his upcoming tour. Albert would get to do several songs from this new album, *Hiding*, so we accepted. I went along for the first part of the tour, which included Austin. Muddy Waters was the support act. After the show, the T-Birds came backstage and drank champagne with Muddy. Eric met the band and the talk was thick with the Texas music that he loved and had influenced him. The T-Birds opened his next two U.S. tours.

The first thoughts for the third album was to do an instrumental/comedy album. Seriously. After touring with the Roomful of Blues, we scheduled time in L.A. and brought out Al Copley, piano, Greg Piccolo, tenor sax, and Doug James, baritone sax. The album covered flat-out rockers, ballads, cha-cha instrumentals, bayou swamp rock, you name it.

I first met Dave Edmunds in the mid-'70s over lunch

in L.A. An RCA artist in the U.K., he was seeking U.S. representation. He produced himself and was a consistent hitmaker. He had produced the first Foghat album, which had done rather well. I suggested he get a band and tour if he wanted to sell records here. He replied touring was out of the question. A few years pass and Dave Edmunds and Nick Lowe form Rockpile, with Jake Rivera as manager. I arranged with Jake for the T-Birds to be the support act on a two month tour of the U.K. After the first show, Dave smiled and said, "I think you're right about touring."

I mention this because I thought Dave would know how to produce the band. We were at work on the fourth album, trying a more state-of the-art studio in Dallas. A good friend of the band, Johnny Nicholas, played piano and sang back-ground on two tracks. We cut a third song. "You're Humbugging Me" and I returned to L.A. to "live" with the songs and the studio's sound. I liked all three but questioned if we were making the same record again? We talked over "new blood" if the guy fit in like a band member. There were two producers everyone liked: Nick Lowe and Dave Edmunds.

Kim had already spent time with Nick in London, co-writing ("One's Too Many") and cutting several demos. Nick's humor and night owl habits were a perfect match. He was available and Dave wasn't. Nick rented a house in Austin and started the album fresh, doing new versions of the three we cut at Goodnight, Dallas. The band definitely had a ball, embracing Nick like he was another guitar player in the band. Nick brought along Colin Fairley to engineer. New areas of sound opened up the band experimented, "The Monkey" being a good example.

This was the last of the recordings of the original

Above and right: Advertisements from English newspapers.

unit, as Keith Ferguson was to leave before they made their next album (produced by Dave Edmunds)

P.S. When I became the band's manager, they hounded me about wanting to tour and get out on the road. Eventually, the bookings came and "away they went." Jimmie and I were the phone guys, talking every day. Kim or Fran would call with the "why aren't we getting more bread for this gig" or "don't we have a rider?" I never heard a peep from Keith.

I flew out to be with the band somewhere and made it a point to ask Keith how the tour was going from his perspective. He was dinking a 12-oz. Miller draft, smoking a Kool, and watching *Benny Hill*. He was making fun of my shirt, said I looked like a professional golfer. I asked, "How do you like being out on the road?" He frowned and said, "It's just different tacos."

For the fans
Denny Bruce, 1996

" ... we are all 27, handsome mother-fuckers that dress cool and our music drives girls wild."
-- Jimmie Vaughan

Advertisement poster for *Butt Rockin'*.

151

In the band with Keith

Fran Christina
Interview by Craig Higgins, 2008

Fran Christina had played with The Fabulous Thunderbirds prior to becoming their drummer in 1980.

Although I have been banging the tubs since the ripe old age of 11, my first real professional band, which was formed when I was 16, was called Roomful of Blues. It was me, Duke Robillard guitar, Al Copley piano and bass player Larry Pedruzzi. The year was 1967. Since then, until the first gigs with the T-Birds in 1975, I've worked with Big Walter 'Shakey' Horton, Johnny Shines, Boogie Woogie Red, Mighty Joe Young, The Boogie Brothers, Koko Taylor and other Chicago and Detroit blues artists. So, the transition to the T-Birds was a natural.

At that time, the band actually had about three or four drummers they worked with around the west -- Freddie Pharoah, Mike Buck and Joey Scattino -- but none of them really wanted to tour, so they wanted me to work with them full time. As much as I loved the band, I didn't want to move to Texas at the time because I had just moved to Nova Scotia. They said, "Well, if you ever want to move and come down and start playing, we're ready. We want you to join the band." I said, "OK."

I did the road tours over the next couple of years then decided I was ready to get back into it full time. I called them up and said, "I'm coming to Texas!" They were like, "Oh, you know, OK, but ... " Nobody was ready to fire the drummer they had. So I said, "Well, whenever you guys are ready. In the meantime I'm going to go play with Ray Benson's western swing band, Asleep At The Wheel, because he's asked me if I'll play for him." So I moved to Texas and did about 18 months of touring and recording with the Wheel until I hooked back up with the T-Birds in the studio to record *What's The Word*.

When I first met Keith, it was pretty funny. I had shown up at my first gig and was sitting across the street from the club on a bench in London, Ontario,

Fran Christina and Keith at a gig in Houston.
Courtesy of Tracy Hart / The Heights Gallery

waiting for the band to show after having hitch-hiked from Nova Scotia where I'd been living in the woods for a few years. I looked like a lost lumberjack. Along comes Keith out of the van. He's got shoulder-length hair, blue python boots up above his knees, smelling of Jungle Gardenia and a mouth full of gold. I guess he was a little ahead of the curve at that point. He had a mass of body ink. Tattoos weren't as common as they are today. Back then, it was really something that not everyone had, give or take some sailors, bikers and a few creatures with bars in front of their faces and numbers on their chests. We looked at each other like we from different galaxies. He had some great tats. We had friends in Amsterdam that, when we were touring, Keith would go in -- well, we would all go in there -- to the tattoo parlor below the Hell's

Angels bar. It was more than just a tattoo parlor. It was a tattoo museum run by the main man, Hanky Panky, a great tattoo artist who is pretty well known with all the rock 'n rollers. He was shootin' ink, and Keith always came out with a new scene on his booty.

We were always on the road. From the minute I joined the T-Birds, they really started going on the road I think in '76, '77. We were a working band. It was over 225 days a year, sometimes 315. I mean, we toured a lot. We toured all the time. We were just gone. When I first moved to Austin, there were a couple of times I was gone so long I didn't know where I lived. I was on the road so much I would have to call up my wife and go, "Hey, where do we live?" It's a grind when you're on a bus day after day. But back then, in the early days of the T-Birds, we were travelling in a van. All of us and all of the equipment in one van, sleeping sitting up, no room to get horizontal. A lot of times I was doing the driving because I was the only one fit to drive … almost.

T-Bird Rhythm I think was my favorite album to record. It was a gas. With Nick Lowe, it just seemed to come out real easy. We got in the studio and had so much stuff we wanted to put down. It was just like, you go in the cutting room and have a party and then go into the control room. "Hey, let's try this one!" And we'd play it three times -- and if we didn't get it in three takes, we just junked it. We just tossed it out. It was all live. It wasn't like we spent hours and days and weeks and months on any one song. Nick's brilliant. He's a great songwriter. He can play just about any instrument. He's a great producer and director. He has fantastic ideas, knows how to throw a great party!

During the recording of *Butt Rockin'* and after, Keith started becoming testy (laughs). He wasn't getting it. He wasn't willing to compromise any-thing, which may or may not be good. You listen to those things now and you go, "That's great!" But if you listen closer, you hear some distortion or something like that and you go, "Whoa." The pro-

The T-Birds backstage in Houston with Rosana (Cullivan) Sherrill and her husband, Douglas. Keith's gold tooth is clear to see.

Courtesy of Tracy Hart / The Heights Gallery

Keith, playing through a Mesa Boogie amplifier, has both pickup and bridge covers on his Precision bass.

Courtesy of Tracy Hart / The Heights Gallery

ducer would moan, "Shit, we could get a much better sound on the bass than that!" But you can't unless the bass player wants to try to get a better sound. He was just concerned with the sound that he was hearing in the room and not what was going on the recording. We had the hardest time trying to convince him to change. We'd be saying, "Keith, you're only hearing it right there where you're playing. That's not the way it's coming out on the record because you're not hearing it in the control room with everything else. You're hearing it out there."

His thing was for him to play right, the way he liked it, to have his settings the way he liked it. I understand that; everybody understands that. But when you're in a recording situation, you have to take into account what the microphones are picking up. And that's got to do with what the acoustics of the room are, how good your mics are, where it is in location to everything else. You have to tweak things so it sounds on the record like it does when you're playing

it. That's the object. But he didn't understand that! He wouldn't listen to any of it. All of us sat there and just threw our hands up like, "Well, what the hell are we going do? We can't talk him into this, cooperating with the producer, and he's not going change. He's just going fight, so it's not worth it so we'll record it like this." Of course, you bring it to a record company and they go, "We can't play this on the radio. It sounded like it was recorded in a garage." And that's it. Over the years, I look back and I think that's some of the charm of the records -- that it's got that nastiness. We called it motorboat bass.

Keith had beautiful tone live. He had beautiful tone. He had a great round sound. His notes were big, fat, round -- sound like an upright bass. It recorded well in the right room. He had that fantastic tone, and that's why I loved playing with him. His bass playing was just like another percussion instrument. He whacked the strings. It was like you're hitting a drum that was tuned to pitch, always right there. He was another percussion instrument. We didn't have to look at each other, we didn't have to think about each other. He was always there for me; I was always there for him. It was like your left hand and your right hand working together. That was the great thing about playing with Keith. It was one of the best musical experiences of my life.

Keith was a genius, in a lot of ways, you know? He was the kind of guy who couldn't tie his shoelaces but could rattle off the names of every reptile and tell you anything about Mexican or American roots music and was really well read. He was really an interesting guy.

We played at places like chitlin' circuit clubs and places like Jay's Cockpit and Lounge in Cankton or Lafayette, Louisiana. The audiences were great at these joints. We would play note one and the entire audience -- young, old, black, white, everybody in the audience -- was up dancing. And when they danced, it was all in time to the music. A lot of people don't understand what that's like now because it

doesn't happen much anymore. But when that's going on, it's back and forth. It's like the audience is as powerful as the band is. It's like Ping-pong. The audience feeds the band, the band feeds the audience. And by the time you're done, you haven't got anything left. It's like a big orgasm.

Lou Ann Barton was one of the first singers for the T-Birds. She was actually a Thunderbird (who back then hadn't yet acquired the "Fabulous" prefix yet). We recorded a demo with Lou, produced by Jerry Wexler of Atlantic Records fame. I think that thing is still floating around somewhere. Jerry loved that record, and he wanted to put it out the way it was -- the T-Birds and Lou Ann. But he had to go use the Muscle Shoals guys, who smoke, too. That's what the record company wanted. But that demo kicks ass! It was recorded at Third Coast in Austin. Yeah, it was good. Half the time that Lou Ann was singing, she was lying down on the couch. That was a good session.

Keith didn't like touring at all. And the more time

Keith and Kim Wilson on a gig (note the cigarette in the strings in the headstock of Keith's bass).
Courtesy of Tracy Hart / The Heights Gallery

that went on, the less he liked touring, for a number of reasons. It was getting tougher and tougher to tour with Keith because he basically was unhappy. We were friends. We were like brothers. I loved Keith. I spent more time with him than I did my real brothers. So it was like, "Hey, man, you're unhappy. Why don't you just quit so we don't have to fire you because we got shit to do." He agreed, and everything was all well and good. We parted in good company. We were a Texas cult band, right? And Keith was … he was one of the real Texans (laughs). People knew him from Houston to Dallas and all around, for a long time, including us. We talked about, "Maybe we should just break up the band," after he left. But we had lots of stuff that we wanted to do. "We're gonna rock the world," as Jimmie Lee would say.

We knew we could get a bass player that would fit the bill. So, of course, now you've got the hometown guy and then you replace him with somebody from out of town. And everybody was like, "Ah, we want Keith. We want Keith!" -- until they heard Preston (Hubbard). Then they were like, "Well, you know, he's … he's pretty good!' (laughs).

Keith left the band in '84. That was an interesting time because we got a record deal from a new and upcoming record label, and we went to London to record. The deal was they were going to send us money to pay the producer and the studio. Every week, they'd send us so much for expenses. So, we went and basically lived in London for a month and a half, two months, and worked our asses off on the record. We were in the studio, and then the record company stopped sending the checks! So we're stuck over there. We're just about finished with the record and we needed more money, and the record company studio says, "Hey! You owe us umpteen thousand dollars. We're not giving you your masters until we get paid," which is understandable. So we had a decision to make. "Well, are we just going to forget this record, or are we going to go try to find the money someplace else?" We really liked the record a lot and didn't want to just trash it.

So our road manager put a tour together of Europe and Scandinavia in the middle of winter, which was interesting. We pretty much didn't pay ourselves but put all the money back into getting the record out of hock, and then went through a process of going back

Jimmie Vaughan and Keith smoking cigarettes on stage.

Courtesy of Tracy Hart / The Heights Gallery

Keith with his beloved Fender Dual Showman amp and the 1956 Fender Precision bass -- the cowhide bass -- he used at the end of the Thunderbirds and in The Tail Gators.

Courtesy of Tracy Hart / The Heights Gallery

to several record companies two or three times. "You want this record? It's all finished and it's great!" Finally, after I think the second or third time, we went to CBS. There was one guy there that really liked it, and he happened to be in a good position to do something about it. That was Mr. Tony Martell. He loved it. So he said, "I'll take it!"

We basically gave them the whole package. We had cover design, everything laid out. They didn't have to do anything but say, "OK." And they did. They ran with it. That (*Tuff Enuff*) was a million-plus, platinum-selling record. But I was surprised. I always thought, "Geez, if I ever got a gold record, I'd be like shittin' in high cotton!" Now I'm surprised at how much money you don't make on a gold record, you know what I mean? That's why when Keith started suing us, it was kind of a joke because the band only had ... I think it was $17,000 we had in the bank. That was it. A couple of lawyers had apparently talked him into suing. Whatever their motivations were, they figured we owed Keith something because he'd been in the band and now we had enough money to pay him off. We got sued twice for *Tuff Enuff*. They lost both times, but it still cost ... hell, just fighting Keith!

We offered him a settlement early on. We said, "Hey, you know, we don't owe you anything. I don't know where you get this from. But listen, we'll give you so much money if you'll just drop it." And I think Keith might've, but his attorney didn't want to settle. They thought there was more there. And they just didn't want to give in because they would see us on *Johnny Carson* and all that -- opening for The Rolling Stones and Eric Clapton -- and they were thinking that we were making huge bucks.

Keith sued everybody in the band individually. The way he had it set up, it wasn't as if he was suing the record company or the band as a corporation. That would've been something else. The individuals would be protected. And if he'd won, he'd win the band's money, whatever that was. But it wouldn't be attacking our personal assets. Basically, that means he'd take my house and my car (laughs). I was completely surprised that he would do such a thing, especially since the last time we saw him we were great friends! The way it worked out was we went to court after a while, months and years of taking depositions, all that crap -- getting up, putting on a suit and tie and going to court. We got in there the first time and the

Fran Christina on drums with Keith.

Courtesy of Angela Strehli

judge basically called the trial off because it was too ridiculous! He said, "Look, there's nothing there. No evidence that the band owes him anything. It's obvious. You (Keith) yourself said that there's nothing that the band owes you. So there's absolutely no reason for being here, right?" And then his attorney appeals it and wins the appeal. Now we have to go through all of this stuff all over again. Then that goes on for another year and a half or something, and we're spending more money for attorney fees and stuff like that -- until the night before we were supposed to go to court again. I get a call from our attorney. He says, "Keith decided he doesn't want to go in any further. He's calling it off."

I never spoke to Keith again. I think Jimmie did. Jimmie went to see him on his deathbed. That's good. I'm glad he did. Jimmie's a bigger man than I am because (laughs) I couldn't. I don't know, must be the Sicilian in me, but I just couldn't go see him. I suppose I should've forgiven him, but he didn't ask me for forgiveness. I prefer to remember Keith in the good times (laughs)! But I'm not going to lie and say that I loved him at the end. As a musician, I loved my time with Keith. He was like a brother to me. I

Information on the trial

Casey Monahan
AUSTIN AMERICAN-STATESMAN
DATE: November 4, 1989

SOMEBODY LOSES, SOMEBODY WINS: The long trial of former Fabulous Thunderbirds bassist Keith Ferguson vs. his old bandmates concluded Wednesday in Judge Paul Davis' 200th State District Court, with Ferguson unsuccessfully attempting to collect money from his former band. T-Bird attorney John McLish told the beat that Davis determined Ferguson "was not entitled to recover anything from his lawsuit," he said. "Ferguson claimed that during the time he was a member, he established a business relationship that made him one of the owners of the band. The band's position was always that he was just an employee. Ferguson was claiming that his ownership was continuing, and he wanted an order from the court for the band to continue to pay him in the future. The band argued that since he was gone, he wasn't entitled to anything.
"The judge issued a directed verdict," said McLish. "At the end of Keith's testimony, the judge concluded that the case could not be continued in the face of Ferguson's testimony."[23]

Peter Blackstock
AUSTIN AMERICAN-STATESMAN
DATE: January 31, 1991

SUIT GOES ON: The 3rd Court of Appeals this week gave Keith Ferguson, former bass player for the Fabulous Thunderbirds, another chance at a trial against the T-Birds. Ferguson played with the group from 1975 to 1984. He later sued the band, saying he owned 25 percent of the group. While acknowledging Ferguson had made statements "very damaging" to his case, the appeal court overturned a directed verdict against him and said he should be given a new trial. Ferguson, when informed of the ruling Wednesday, said he'll keep pushing the case.[24]

don't think there were many other musicians I've ever played with that I was as locked in musically more than I was with Keith -- or he was at least one of the top five.

Keith playing the 1952 Fender Precision #0171.

Courtesy of Tracy Hart / The Heights Gallery

Keith had beautiful tone live. He had beautiful tone. He had a great round sound. His notes were big, fat, round -- sound like an upright bass. It recorded well in the right room. He had that fantastic tone, and that's why I loved playing with him. His bass playing was just like another percussion instrument. He whacked the strings. It was like you're hitting a drum that was tuned to pitch, always right there. He was another percussion instrument. We didn't have to look at each other, we didn't have to think about each other. He was always there for me; I was always there for him. It was like your left hand and your right hand working together. That was the great thing about playing with Keith. It was one of the best musical experiences of my life.

-- Fran Christina

This photo, used in a 1986 *Guitar Player* magazine article about Keith, shows him playing the 1952 Fender Precision #0172.

Courtesy of Tracy Hart / The Heights Gallery

On the road with the T-Birds

Dave Gardner
Interviewed by Craig Higgins, 2008

Dave Gardner was the tour and sound manager for the T-Birds from around 1978 to 1984. He lives in Austin and works for Pauline Reese.

Photos courtesy of Dave Gardner except as noted.

Most of his friends were Mexican, either musicians or just regular buddies. That was just Keith. He hated the road, and we would play like 250-300 nights a year out on the road. And he would hate it -- he would bitch about it, on and on, when we were out there.

We were doing tours with really big people, too, sometimes, but they did their own thing and got paid great -- get paid real good out on the road. But he just hated it. And then once he got home, he'd bitch about not having any money. But that was just Keith. He was just about the nicest guy in the world. He was so mild-mannered. If he got mad, he would just go off by himself. He didn't have a bad temper, nothing like that. He'd bitch a lot out on the road, but no hot-tempered guy or nothing like that, no fights. I never saw the guy want to hit somebody, anything like that.

Keith would wake up in the morning and drink beer, in the bus. I'd wake up and there'd be Keith walking -- and he'd wake up real early -- and he'd have a beer in his hand. He'd drink beer constantly, all day long. But the rest of them, they didn't drink much until at the gig. I never saw Keith get fucked up or fuck up a gig. What he did, he did it on his own, and it never got to where it interfered with his gigs.

I used to go out with Keith. Keith never had a driver's license, I don't think, in his life. He might have, but as long as I knew him he never had one. He'd call me up and say, "Let's go over here! This place I know... ," when we were off here in Austin. I'd say, "OK." We'd end up over on E. Seventh Street. In some of these places we'd go into -- I wouldn't, but with him I'd walk in there with a cowboy hat on, boots and shit, that's just the way I am -- and I'm following Keith with his doo-rag. We'd go in these places, and I was afraid I wouldn't walk out. And I ain't scared of too much. And everybody knew him because he was going to see this band that was playing or he was meeting a buddy. I mean some of these places, you'd be scared to death to go in. We went in there, have a good time all night. Drink free beer. It was fun!

I grew up down in the Valley, so I been around Mexican music all my life, and I like it. We'd go listen to these bands -- and it might be a mariachi, might be just an electric Mexican band, whatever -- just friends of his. Lot of times I'd take him over there and we'd go in these places. But he amazed me the first time I went. I was scared to death. But Keith would say, "Hey, don't worry about it!" He belonged there, period! He was one of those guys. All of his friends were Mexican, except for maybe Johnny Winter. Johnny Winter was a good friend of his. We used to go to his house in New York City. He had a penthouse up in New York. Me and Keith were the only ones who'd go because they had something in common.

Keith never went anywhere on the road unless it was to see a buddy, or a band if we had time, or to Army surplus stores. He knew where they all were in the towns we'd be in. He liked to go in those places and get stuff. You could find stuff like clothes and boots -- not army boots, but just regular stuff; just all kinds of crap. You could get like old stuff that he liked, patches and all kinds of stuff; just weird stuff. Or pawn shops. Both -- pawn shops and army surplus stores.

They would find instruments that they wanted. Jimmie used to go in all the time. He'd find these lap steels; he loved lap steels. He'd find him all those Fender lap steels. On the road Jimmie used to play that song "The Monkey Speaks" with a lap steel. Only it wasn't a lap steel, it was a stand-up. (Shows a picture of a guitar stand with several Strats, Keith's Precision, and a lap steel set up on a stand). That is the old '52 Precision that he used, one of them that he lost. He lost it on an airplane. I don't know if he ever got that back. I think it was in Florida. The crew was either driving the bus down to pick them up or we were leaving and they (the band) were flying. They put the guitar on the plane and it never got to the next place. I don't think it was that one. I think it was another one. He had like a '52 and a '51 or something. One was a Precision; one was a Tele.

They did a lot of touring in Europe. They were big, big over there. People would come, like Robert Plant and Jimmy Page, to gigs. One of the tours I went over there, and we started in England. One night, I just flew there that day and got in; they flew ahead of me. I flew there that night and got in and we were playing at this place called Dingwalls. We did like 14, 15 shows all over England, different towns, before we went up to other countries. And every night of the gig, Robert Plant and Jimmy Page would come to the gig.

The first night, this guy walks up to me, and it was in this little place and it was crowded as shit. And this guy comes up, and I'm having a bad night -- I'm not in a good mood at all -- and this guy says, "Don't you ever put any echo in?" in this English accent. "Don't you ever put any echo on the vocals?" And I said, "Get the fuck out of here!" The next night – well, I think several nights later -- me and the guy we hired to do our guitar stuff over there, we're in another place, and we're laying on some benches at the club waiting for the guys to get there for the sound check. I look over there, saying, "Well, who're these guys?" Mick says, "You know who that is?" "No", I said. "That's Robert Plant and Jimmy Page. They've been to the gigs every night." I said, "Oh, really? Oh no, you know I told the guy (Plant) to fuck off the other night!"

So Plant came up in a little while, and I had this shirt on -- said "Los Fabulosos Thunderbirds" on the front

Kim and Jimmie.
Courtesy of Tracy Hart / The Heights Gallery

Note the lap steel on the stand and the red bass that Keith used as a substitute.

Hanging out at an aftershow party.
Courtesy of Tracy Hart / The Heights Gallery

and says "Butt Rockin'" on the back. It was a big shirt; those guys used to sell tons of them. He came up and said, "Hey, I was at Dingwall's the other night!" I said, "Man, I'm sorry what I said to you." He said, "Ah, don't worry about it. I know how that is. You know what? Can I get one of those shirts?" I said, "Well, we just sold the last one last night; we're out of them." He said, "Oh, man." I said, "I'll tell you what. If you don't mind, you can have this one. You can take it home and wash it." I always get extra-larges; I'm a pretty big guy. He said, "That'd be great!" I said, "The problem is, I got nothing with me except at the hotel." He said, "Well, you can have mine. I'll trade with you." He had some T-shirt on. And he gave me his shirt, I gave him mine. And he said, "Thank you." They came to a bunch more gigs. Later on he said, "Well, we're doing a tour called Principle of Moments next year, over in the U.S. We want y'all to come to it." So I gave him my address and phone number.

Months later, phone rings; the telephone voice says, "Hey, Dave!" in this English accent. I said to myself, "What's this shit? Somebody's fuckin' with me." So I say, "What?" "This is Robert Plant." "Yeah, right!" And then I hung up. I didn't even think about that. So he calls back three times: all of them -- hang up, hang up. The third time, he says, "No, no, no, no. This is really Robert Plant! We're playing tonight at the Erwin Center." And I thought, "Well, I saw that in the paper." He said, "I want y'all to come down." Came down, all sitting around after the gig in the dressing room, and he said, "You know, someone stole that shirt you gave me. You got any more of those?" And Mark Proct said, "Yeah, man, I got a whole box full in the car. You can have one." And he gave him the whole thing. And they were happy. But a lot of big-time people used to come. We did tours with Eric Clapton and opening-band stuff.

When we'd go to Europe, we could generally only take one guy. Well, me doing sound and Mark being the road manager, and then we had James Arnold, the guitar tech. We could only afford to take two guys on crew all the time, and then we would hire a guy over there (Europe) to be the guitar tech. And that would be Mick.

We would bring the guitars, and the drums would be -- of course, the power is different over there, so I think Jimmie would take his amp -- we would rent the drums. Of course, the PA was always provided. We would rent drums, and later on when they got bigger they could take their stuff. But, just to save money and stuff, we would leave the drums here and rent ... the first time. Most of the time, Jimmie would take his amp and that was it. The bass and the drums would be rented over there.

When we would play in New York City, we used to play there quite a bit, different places. We would go to Johnny Winters'. He had this penthouse up on top, the very top on the roof -- some big-ass building there; overlooked the East River or the Hudson River. I forget which river, but it was a good view. Keith would say, "You wanna go? We're going to have a barbeque!" And it was just me and Keith. The rest of the band wasn't even invited.

Johnny would go out there, and he'd have this little old barbeque pit, little square thing, and it stood up about waist-high -- one of those black-top, you take the top off. He'd fill it full of charcoal -- and he can't see worth shit -- and he'd squirt it all full of stuff. He'd get down there that far away from those coals. And I thought, "Oh my god, he's going to light himself on fire. I just know he is!" And he'd get those matches out, and he'd get right down there and start throwing those matches in there. But he lit it away from there, alright! But we'd eat, and I'd sit out there -- after we'd eat and everything -- I'd sit out there and talk to his wife. Him and Keith would go off for a while.

Keith would be drinking beer from the morning he got up. He'd put 'em in the sink, fill up the sink with ice, fill it up with beer from the night before from the bus or whatever was left over. Or he'd get his own, but he wanted beer in the morning. He'd drink beer all day long, all night long. Never bother him a bit. I never saw Keith drunk. It seemed like he'd drink some kind of other alcohol, but I don't think very much. Seemed like he'd drink tequila or something -- I don't know what, but not very much of it. It was always beer. Never saw him fuck up a gig, never saw him drunk. For somebody that drank all day long, it was amazing. And still sit there and play like … I mean, you couldn't even tell. I don't care what he was drinking -- he was always the same.

He'd sleep three to four hours a night; that was about it. He was always on the road; we were always on the road, you know? You figure at least 250 to 350 days a year. And I'm not talking about straight days. You might do two or three months and then come home for a week or two, and then do it again. I can't re-member having more than a couple weeks off at one time when I worked for them. Maybe two weeks at

Dave Gardner in England.

the most. Any longer than that, I don't think so. *T-Bird Rhythm*, the fourth record, I don't think that one took over a month. It was this studio right off 35 up there. I don't even know if it's still there anymore. It was like a block or two south of Sixth Street; right on 35. It was right on the access road, big old stone building. Nice studio! Forget the name of it. That was Nick Lowe producing it. They were buddies. They knew Nick from across the creek (Europe), being over there ... because all these people used to come see them. They thought the Thunderbirds, over in Europe, all these famous musicians thought the Thunderbirds were the biggest thing in the world! They loved them! I mean, big time. Big time. Pete Townsend, all these kinds of people. It was top notch. And they were admired by some amazing people. It was really cool.

They'd open up for people and blow them off the stage! We got fired. We were on the tour with Tom Petty and he fired us! We were sitting on the bus one night talking to Petty's bus driver -- me and somebody, I forget who, one of the band's -- and he said, "Y'all are gonna get fired in a day or two." "Why?" "Petty says you're killing him. Y'all are getting better responses than he is." And we did. Like for the Stray Cats -- we did a bunch of opening shows for them. Just blew them off the fucking stage. We got a better response from the crowd.

We did a couple tours with Eric Clapton and Muddy Waters, but everybody loved that. Clapton liked Jimmie, and everybody was good. It was a good thing. Nobody said they were getting blown off the stage or none of that kind of crap going on. They played some shows with The Rolling Stones, the 1981 Stones tour -- two days at the Cotton Bowl, two days in Dallas. Well this was just four shows. This was two days at the Astrodome in Houston -- the T-Birds, ZZ Top, The Rolling Stones -- and two days at the Cotton Bowl; same bands. And that was good, too. I don't know how we got this. We did a bunch of shows where we opened for the Beach Boys. I'll never understand that one. They got in fist fights with each other on stage, the Beach Boys.

We opened a lot of shows for a lot of weird people. It was fun. Keith was always there, right there, right on -- all the time, you know? He had the strangest damn sound, though. I guess nobody really bothered to work with him on his bass amplified sound. When I first started working with them, I said, "Man, this guy's really boomy." It was like a roar, with no clarity, you know what I mean? There was no definition to it. I thought, "I've got to do something about that." Finally I worked with him enough to where I could get him to just take some bottom end off. He had the low end cranked up all the way on that old Fender Bassman. There was two 15s -- big old box about so high; a Fender. It had a silver screen at one time, but he made it leopard (refering to what appears to be in photos of the T-birds actually a snake-skin print covering the Bassman head he used in concert) – 150-watt amp or something. No power; it didn't have enough power for one thing. But he would take and crank everything wide open on it. That's all he ever used. I mean, that's ALL he would ever use. Clubs, concerts, anything, it was all he ever used -- that two 15s.

You get a PA, you don't need all those double stack and Marshalls and shit. That's all 'look' stuff, where people do that; that's a look thing. Most of the time, all that shit's not plugged in. You put a microphone in one speaker, the PA's going to make the sound. As long as the guy can hear himself and the other guy (the drummer) can hear that, you can put it in the monitors and switch mixes and all that. This guy can hear that guy and that guy can hear that guy. Most of that other crap is just for looks. But Keith, I never saw him use anything different except maybe when he had that different one (amp) in Europe … it was probably pretty close to that, two 15s and an amp top.

His dad always came to the gigs in Houston. They got along really good. To me, him and his dad were a lot alike, in their personalities, because they were both real quiet and laid back. Keith was not a loudmouth guy. You know how you're in a bar with somebody and say three guys sitting at a table, and you can hear this one guy spoutin' off and all that shit? Or there's a group of people, and you hear people laughing, and one guy's always ... Keith was always the quietest person anywhere. He'd be over there talking, and they'd be over there huddled, talking about shit. Other than that, he'd be sitting down there in the dressing room, and all of a sudden there'd be people milling around and he'd be talking to his buddy or his dad or somebody, and it'd be a quiet conversation. He was not a loudmouth, attention-seeking person.

His dad -- as a matter of fact, I think you'll find his dad in one of these pictures, this white-haired guy with glasses on -- would come to the shows in Houston every time. His dad was the nicest guy in the world. He was real polite, kind of a shy-type guy. I got along real good with him. We spent a lot of time talking about music and stuff -- old people like the Bing Crosby era of musicians, stuff like that, jazz, classical -- and I think he even had a lot of the 78s stuff.

Keith had a lot of stuff. A lot of it was Mexican. Keith knew every goddamn Mexican band in the world and even like the old, old ones that I'd never even heard of -- and I grew up down in the Valley on the border, and I've heard conjuntos all my life and knew a lot of the older ones, But Keith, he could rattle 'em off ... and he even knew them, the people.

In Amsterdam, we'd spent three or four days over there that tour. We played at this place called the Paradisio, this old church had a neon cross that did like this all day and night long -- blue neon cross, and it would lay down on top of the roof, then it would stand up, then it would lay down. Link Wray, he would open for us then he would come out and jam with us. Two days I think we played there.

Generally, on a tour like that, you're on the bus, and you get there ... back then, unfortunately a lot of these tours ... it was like somebody would throw a handful of darts at the map. Some nights there'd be like a 600- or 700-mile drive overnight. Say, like you'd (points as though there was a map in front of him and he was picking different places not close together) ... and then come back when you could've went here and then there.

So a lot of times you would get there, just in time, you would stay on that bus for days sometimes, without a hotel room. You could shower at the gig because there'd be these big coliseums and shit like that. But, most of the time you would drive, get to a gig, do a sound check if it was for a big show. Now, if it was for the T-Birds, we never did a sound check. If it was the T-Birds' tour, we'd generally have hotel rooms. But sometimes the drives were still long as hell.

Keith did good (made a lot of money), except he bitched a lot. I said, "Keith, what are you bitchin' about?" He says, "Well, goddamn it, we're always on a tour." I said, "Well, you ain't gonna have no money if you stay home, if you don't do it." He said, "Well, I know, but goddamn it!" And then he'd get home and say, "Goddamn, I need some money! I need to go again." But I kind of think it must have got worse or something after I left because that's all James told me. I said, "Why did they fire Keith?" "Well, Jimmie didn't think he wanted to be on the road anymore because he was always bitching."

Above; Keith's dad (with white hair and glasses).
Below: Keith posing roadside.

165

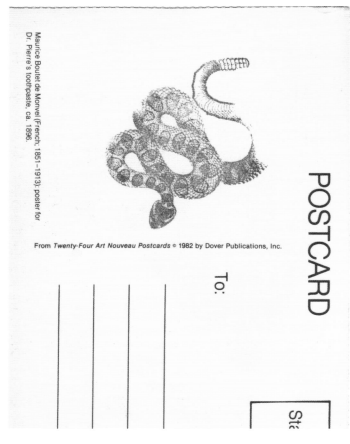

Maurice Boutet de Monvel (French; 1851–1913); poster for Dr. Pierre's toothpaste, ca. 1896.

From *Twenty-Four Art Nouveau Postcards* © 1982 by Dover Publications, Inc.

POSTCARD

To:

St

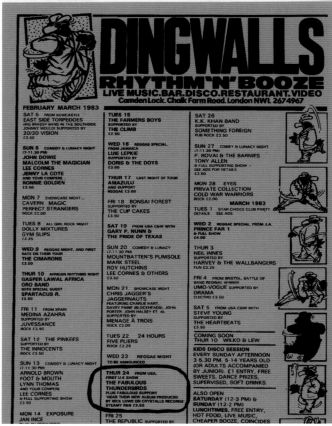

There's a guy named Spider Web, out in New York, he was a tattoo guy. I think he was in the porn business. I think he was an actual actor. He introduced us to a bunch of porn chicks, porn stars and shit. And he had a little tattoo parlor up in his apartment. Keith would always go over there, not every time, but two or three times when I went over there with him he went over there and got a tattoo. And in Amsterdam they'd always go over there, him and Jimmie, would go to Hanky Panky -- the guy with the shop below the Hell"s Angels -- and get a tattoo. Jimmie got one on his leg and Keith got something somewhere, I don't remember where.

Keith was into snakes. I'll show you something (pulls out a stack of pictures to produce a postcard with a coiled snake ink stamp on the back). Keith had these cards ... Keith would like to get postcards -- and he would send them to his people over here, his friends -- where he was touring in Europe. The postcards, instead of signing them, he had a rubber stamp, so that's how you knew it was from Keith. He would write a little message and put that on it, and that was Keith. You'd be over here and with a buddy and say, "Ah, Keith sent me a card!" You'd see that snake, you knew. Any hotel we were in, I don't care where it was in the world, Keith would take a Bible -- there was always a Bible in the hotel room – so on the very back page, he would put that stamp on it. After I left the Thunderbirds, and I'd be out on the road with somebody, I'd always look in the Bible in the room to see if there was a snake on it. He had a lot of snake tattoos. He had a couple of lamps in his house that he had shaped like cobras or something.

Cats -- he had this female cat named Bob. Bob the cat. And he used to feed it cheese. "Cheese food," he called it. I said, "What the hell you doing giving it cheese?" I was over there one day and hanging around. He had a pile of cheese. I said, "What the hell you doing with all that cheese?" "Feedin' it to the cat." You know, sliced cheese. He said, "It's not real cheese anyway." "So what is it?" "It's cheese food." He's throwing it to that damn cat!

" ... we would play like 250-300 nights a year out on the road. And he would hate it -- he would bitch about it, on and on, when we were out there."
-- Dave Gardner

Keith and Marc Proct, the road manager of the Thunderbirds.

Connie Vaughan and Dave Gardner.

BACKSTAGE PASS

T-BIRDS

1-29-83

PG
PARENTEAU GUIDANCE
CONCERT PRODUCTIONS

Rockpalast Germany

German Television, May 23, 1980
Rhein-Main Halle Wiesbaden

On the 1980 tour, The Fabulous Thunderbirds were recorded by German Television. I succeeded in finding the photographer, who did the official photos back then.

They were wrongly announced as a blues group from California on a poster in front of the Rhein-Main-Halle. Jimmie Vaughan had a cast because he broke his leg.

The photographers task was to take a photo of every single musician, because the photos were broadcasted in front of the concert. The result was some great photos that are shown here for the first time.

Photos by Manfred Becker

Fran Christina:

"Those first concerts in Germany were very exciting as it was all new. It's always great to play for a new audience -- especially those in foreign countries that most likely have no preconceptions of what they are about to hear and it's twice as exciting when they dig what's goin' down. The *Rockpalast* and the Blues and Jazz Festival at the Berlin Philharmonic gigs in particular stick out in my mind. At the *Rockpalast* show, I was having almost as much fun in the audience as I did on stage. It was great meeting and hearing Rockin' Dopsie. In Berlin, the atmosphere was a bit formal and no one knew what to expect. One-third of the audience got up and left after the second song, but the other two-thirds that stayed had a rockin' time. I heard it was the first time in the Berlin Philharmonics history that the audience got up and started dancing on their chairs. Quite a compliment. Thank you, Germany."

Friends, lovers, marriage

Lou Ann Barton
Interviewed by Detlef Schmidt, 2012

Lou Ann and Keith were married from March 20, 1980 until June 1, 1981. She was 27 and he was 35 when they divorced. Lou Ann still tours with Jimmie Vaughan.

I met Keith from Jimmie when I joined the Thunderbirds in 1975. Also I met Jimmie in 1974 in Dallas when I sat in with The Storm. He flipped out and said, "I want to put you in my new band." He also asked me to marry him that night. We were all very drunk. But a few months later he called and I moved back to Austin and we started the Thunderbirds.

I only stayed there for a short while and left the band before Keith joined the Thunderbirds. Then I got to know Keith. We were very good friends and lovers from about 1975 to 1976, then we fell deeply in love and moved in together. We were together for four years, and then I decided to divorce him due to his personal problems.

Most of the things I can tell you about Keith would be personal. I don't know anything about guitars and that aspect of his life -- just the fun and sometimes sad times we spent together as friends then lovers to marriage.

I have many wonderful stories, too. I will say we laughed all the time and it was wonderful until the dope ruined it. I treasure my good times with Keith and still have dozens of incredible and very touching love letters from him. He was an incredibly gifted guy. Everybody loved Keith. Hell, I did and do, too, but I just thought more of myself than to put up with the drugs and a possibility of being busted by the cops due to his addiction.

Nobody knew him better than I did because I was the love of his life and he was mine, too. But dope was all he lived for and who he was. Drugs were more important than me. That's why I left him, and my leaving him was the cause of him spiraling downhill, doing even more dope -- also the reason he hated the

Above: A wedding photo from 1980.
Courtesy Ralph Ritchie
Below: Lou Ann's album *Old Enough.*
© Asylum Records

Thunderbirds and having to go on the road. You see, he just wanted to stay home, do dope and always be close to his dealer.

When I left him, he didn't talk to me anymore. I guess he was really hurt, and I think it made him go deeper into drugs. We didn't talk until the mid-'90s, when Hector Watt played with me and brought us together again.

Dos Guardenias

Conni Hancock
Interviewed by Craig Higgins, 2008

A musician herself, "la Conni" was Keith's girlfriend from 1981 until 1984.

Daddy started a band in the '40s and my mom joined it in the '50s. We became a family band in the '70s. We were on the road a lot. John Reed and Jesse Taylor told us we should play in Austin. When we were first passin' through, we played the Armadillo, Soap Creek and other legendary places. Having met Marcia Ball, Stevie Ray Vaughan and other people on that trip, we felt comfortable and welcomed in Austin and decided to move back here for the winter. We stayed. This was round the end of '80 to the middle of 1981.

In the late '60s, early '70s, long before we moved to Austin, Jesse Taylor, a guitar player from Lubbock, was in a band called Krackerjack. Krackerjack was a band based in Austin. It was Bruce Bowland, Uncle John Turner, Tommy Shannon and Keith played with them for a bit, too. Years later, when Keith found out that I knew Jesse Taylor, he started laughing and said, "How many tattoos does he have now?" He and Jesse would compare tattoos every time they'd see each other. Back then they were rare. Not many people had tattoos.

Jesse Taylor said I should go to Austin and meet people like Clifford Antone, Angela Strehli and Keith Ferguson. When I finally moved to Austin, it was Denny Freeman who told me I should meet Keith, saying he was "the only person he knew who was embarrassed that he was not born Mexican". Our band played Mexican music that my sister, Traci, had learned when we lived in New Mexico. We all just loved the culture.

It was at a party, and I think it was Angela Strehli who introduced Keith and me to each other. We talked about music the whole night. By the end of the evening, he'd invited me to his house to hear some records. The whole house was pretty empty besides

The cover of Conni's record with Keith playing bass on the song "Powder & Paint".

a record player and his record collection. I came to find out that he and Lou Ann Barton whom I didn't know had just split up. We started dating each other. Keith travelled a lot when we were together, so when he played as close as Houston, I would go and see the shows. This is where I met his dad. His dad would come to those shows and would come backstage. He was always very nice to me, and it was obvious that the guys in the band did like Keith's dad. I liked John.

One of my favorite memories was the time I went with the Thunderbirds to a music festival in New Orleans where they played on a Riverboat on the Mississippi River. The show was the Thunderbirds, Taj Mahal and Etta James. It was a thrill to get to meet Etta James. She and Keith had a great conversation and clearly liked each other.

Keith went to my dad, Tommy Hancock, at one point in a very old-school, old-fashioned way, for a man-to-man conversation asking for his blessings. I don't know what exactly they talked about, my dad said, "You're not going to have any problems with me, but you are going to have some problems with Conni," probably referring to drugs and alcohol. Keith enjoyed my parent's musical history. He had their pictures up in his living room. He loved that his mother-in-law, my mother Charlene, was a left-handed bass player as was he.

It bothered Keith that the Thunderbirds were going to cold countries during the cold time of the year. He hated spending winters up in the Northeast. That was the first complaint that I heard from him: "Why do we always have to go in the winter? Why can't we go when it's August here?" Plus, he was concerned that he was gone so often and that I might lose interest in him. So I would get lots of postcards. He was really good at courting me at long distance. He would do all kinds of artistic things on a postcard. He customized anything and everything, whether it be postcards, his bunk in the bus … his arms!

When the T-Birds would travel, he would have gardenias delivered to me. The telegram would say, "Wear these in your hair, and when you smell the fragrance remember me." He told me that the idea to do that was based on a Mexican song, "Dos Gardenias" which I heard in the movie Buena Vista Social Club after Keith had passed.

I recall when I was first aware of things getting tense with the Thunderbirds. They were doing a recording session with Nick Lowe. I was sitting with Keith, actually in the room where he was doing a part by himself. The rest of the guys and Nick were in the control room. Nick came in and he changed the tones on Keith's amp. The second when he turned his back and went out the door, Keith turned it back to where it was. That happened like three times. By the time we left, Keith was really angry. Keith wasn't comfortable with the direction the Thunderbirds were going. They were trying to be more commercial and he just wanted them to continue doing what they had done. I think Keith was ready for a change anyway. It was just kind of sad, the way it was.

Keith and Jimmie were very, very close. Keith considered Jimmie one of his best friends, like a brother. He loved him, and Jimmie loved Keith … still does from what I can tell.

I think it was about 1984 when Keith's mom, Margaret, moved to Austin. She had already bought that corner lot that had Keith's house on it. There was a bunch of bamboo around; the lot was almost covered with bamboo. Then she had a house

Below: The T-Birds, Conni and Jerry Lee Lewis.

Courtesy of Keith Ferguson Collection

Conni, Keith and Conni's sister, Charlene Hancock.
Courtesy of Daniel Schaefer

Conni and Keith.
Courtesy of Keith Ferguson Collection

moved to the property. It was a beautiful, old house. Keith really loved to have flowers, and he was very thankful for his home.

Whenever someone would come to his house, he would never let them leave the house empty handed. Quite often when someone visited, they would leave with a shirt, or a pair of shoes, or a scarf. He'd just love to give and make sure that people had something when they were leaving. It was a tradition for him. He said he learned it from the Hispanic culture. He was in on so much of the action going on in the '60s -- Summer of Love, travelling to London with Johnny Winter -- that by the time Margaret bought that house, he was ready to just be at that house. He did not like being cold. He didn't like to be away from home in the winter time. He really loved that house a lot.

Keith would call Johnny Winter every time he was in New York. Keith said, "I keep telling Johnny he needs lots of tattoos. He has got the perfect skin for tattoos. People with brown skin look like western belts when they get tattoos."

After the T-Birds and after I'd moved out, we did a few gigs together and had a great time. D'Jalma Garnier was the bandleader and on the fiddle, Dan Del Santo on guitar, Ponty Bone on the accordion, Keith on bass and me on the steel guitar. Keith also played on my record produced by Lonnie Mack round '84. Keith was especially enthusiastic about The Tail Gators, led by Don Leady. He listened to that Louisiana-influenced music a lot at home.

Keith was so smart. He knew many things. He read a lot. Yes, he had a gold tooth with a star and he could talk to just about anyone about anything. Jimmie Vaughan said at the memorial service, "Keith taught all us guys how to dress like men."

He was a Renaissance Man of sorts, a brilliantly unique and precious flaming star. He considered fans as friends. His friends were and are fans.

Though my time with him was short, I've realized that one never gets enough of a truly good thing.

> **John Conquest,** *3rd Coast Music*:
> One story that Keith told me himself. He was over in Van Zandt County, East Texas, and decided to stop by Link Davis' home. So he pulls up outside it and Link Davis Jr. was outside, chopping wood. He sees Keith coming down the path and says, "What do you want, square?" When Conni was living with him, she looked out the front window and said, "Keith, there's a car full of guys outside who look like Mexican gangsters." So Keith comes to the window, looks out, and says, "Well, honey, that's because they are Mexican gangsters."

Tuff Enough

Preston Hubbard
Interviewed by Craig Higgins, 2008

Preston 'Prez' (or 'Pinky') Hubbard was the bassist for Roomful of Blues when he was called up in 1984 by his old friends in The Fabulous Thunderbirds about taking over for Keith Ferguson. Prez is a man who went from dining at Eric Clapton's mansion to living in flea-bag motels in Austin, on the run from the Austin Police for distributing heroin and cocaine. A stretch in the pen helped him to stay off junk for good, and he now plays with Los Carnales, a blues band in St. Louis, Missouri.

Preston Hubbard and Keith.
Courtesy of Preston Hubbard

Well, what happened was Muddy Waters was a mutual friend of both bands, and he told us about them. He said, "There's this great band out of Austin. You would love 'em." And he told them about us. So we knew who each other were. One night we were playing up in Boston, and they were up in Boston, and we finally all met, and it was like instant, you know, we were like instant friends. We started bringing them up to the Northeast doing gigs and they started bringing us down to Texas. That was around '78, I think. It was like family immediately, all of us. It was that affinity. We were out there in the face of disco and corporate rock and all that crap and we were keeping it real, both bands. We just bonded immediately.

We were a big, slick, horn band. We wore the three-piece shoes and Italian shoes and all that shit. The first night we met them, I think Keith had a dashiki on or something and Jimmie had like an orange jumpsuit or something. And Keith had like, women's perfume. It wasn't cologne, it was like women's. We were all like, "Goddamn, these guys are fuckin' crazy!" It was like instant, instant bonding. It was great.

I joined in August of '84, and immediately I moved down there with my wife. Immediately we went on the road, and *Tuff Enuff* came out in '86. We paid for it ourselves because the record label tanked on us that had signed us. We ended up doing every-

thing ourselves and CBS picked it up. And we never thought in a million years it would be mult-platinum!

It was hard for Jimmie, because he and Keith were very close. That was a hard thing for Jimmie, to go over and fire him, but Keith and I were both junkies. They knew I was a junkie, and I would go back and forth to keeping my shit together. But Keith's dope habit was interfering with the band, with his playing. He didn't want to go on the road, he didn't want to rehearse, he didn't want to learn anything outside of straight blues changes. They wanted to bring me in because I could play ... they wanted to branch out a little, and I could play the upright, of course. That was a big thing. I guess Keith was just not there for them, and so Jimmie finally made the call. The funny part is, too, Jimmie and I both said, "OK, on the same day I'll give Roomful notice and you will fire Keith." When we got on the bus for our gig that night, I said, "I gotta talk to you guys about something. They already knew (laughs). The pipeline between Providence and Austin. They said, "Yeah, yeah, you're joining the Thunderbirds."

I'd go over to Keith's house and hang out and stuff,

but not as much as the earlier days when both bands would be playing together and stuff. When I got with the T-Birds, we were just on the road constantly. But I'd go over to his house and hang out sometimes.

Keith filed some legal action against the Thunderbirds. That was a couple of lawyers because Keith wasn't that type of person. Now here's one of the things with the manager at that time. When I joined and they fired Keith, I told him, "Get Keith to sign legal papers, sign off whatever part of the band he had." And he pushed me out. He was afraid to go to Keith with legal papers.

That bit us in the ass later because these two lawyers got Keith, said, "Hey, man, we can really screw these guys and get you a lot of money." And Keith went for it. He was strung out and all that. They went to court, and I told the guys, "Just offer Keith like 10 grand or something and he'll probably take it." They wanted to fight it, and it cost us a bunch of money.

Keith and I were still fine because he took it for what it was. So we never really had animosity, but I saw less and less of him all the time.

Keith was such a sweetheart. He was such a great guy and everyone loved him. Whatever personal things were, the dope addiction and stuff, didn't change who he was. It's the same thing with me. When I got out of prison, all my friends came back to me, welcomed me back with open arms.

Keith clowing around at Western Photos.

Courtesy of Becky Stapleton Crissman

"The first night we met them ... We were all like, 'Goddamn, these guys are fuckin' crazy!' It was like instant, instant bonding. It was great."
-- Preston Hubbard

Working on Keith's basses

Freddie Cisneros
Interviewed by Detlef Schmidt, October 2012

Freddie is a Texas guitar player also known as Little Jr. One Hand. He worked for the Houston guitar store Rockin' Robin. When Keith played in Houston, he always stayed at Freddie's house. Freddy had worked on most of Keith's basses.

I first met Keith when me, Mike Buck, Jackie Newhouse and Lou Ann Barton went to see Storm at Mother Blues, a fancy blues nightclub in Dallas. Freddie 'Pharoah' Walden on drums, Jimmie Vaughan on guitar, Lewis Cowdrey on harmonica, and Keith on bass. Me, Buck, Jackie and Lou Ann had a blues band in Ft. Worth around 1971 or '72.

Keith's dad's name was John Ferguson. His dad was a gentleman, very soft spoken and kind. When I met him, he was retired and working part time at a record store in Houston. He would sometimes walk over to Rockin' Robin to talk to me on his lunch hour. He was always concerned about Keith's health and drug use. We were all concerned about his drug use. Keith's mom and dad were beautiful people. John was a classical pianist. I'm sure some of this musical talent rubbed off on Keith.

I moved to Houston from Ft. Worth in 1980. It was sometime after that that I met John Ferguson for the first time. Margret lived in Austin at that time, and I never saw the two of them together. I don't know if they were separated or divorced. Keith lived next door to his mom's house as long as I knew him. Cool house. A friend of mine, a writer for *Guitar Player* magazine, lived upstairs for about a year. His name is Dan Forte; he is also known as Teisco Del Rey.

Keith had deep Mexican roots -- music, fashion, food and culture. He spoke fluent Spanish. I never saw John Ferguson's record collection. Keith had a nice collection of old blues and Mexican music. He gave me an album of Mexican music and I still have it.

I worked on several of his basses. He had me sol-

Freddie: "Photo of my band in 1967. I'm on the far right of the photo. The bass was mine and I gave it to Ray in the photo. He didn't have a bass. I bought it from a pawn shop for $65 in 1966. I was 19 years old when this photo was taken."

Courtesy of Freddie Cisneros

Keith and his dad, John Ferguson.

Courtesy of Daniel Schaefer

der the volume and tone controls so they would be all the way on at all times. On one of his basses we bypassed the tone control and went straight to the output jack from the volume pot. He had fun with his vintage basses. He would put stickers, decals and reflector tape on them. It drove the guitar collectors crazy. They couldn't imagine someone doing that to a vintage instrument. Keith had many basses. His favorites were the Tele-style basses, and his favorite pickup was always the Seymour Duncan Tele Bass replacement. He mentioned this to me several times. I remember Keith's blue flower bass; he only had it for a short time.

The bass amp I remember Keith using most was a Fender Bassman head covered in faux red snakeskin. He used this in the '70s. I worked at Rockin' Robin from about '83 to '91. Someone off the street sold us an old P bass. My good friend Phil Florian, who also worked at the shop, saw an article about Keith's bass in a magazine and the serial number matched the description. We called Keith.
Phil, by the way is another great bass player. He played with Freddie King, Lightnin' Hopkins and Jimmy Reed.

The Thunderbirds often played Rockerfellers, an old bank building converted to a nightclub in the Houston Heights, an old neighborhood. After the show, Keith spent the night at our house down the street. My wife had prepared a spare bedroom for him, complete with a chocolate mint on his pillow. The next morning we said our good-byes, and when Mary Jane went to clean up Keith's room, there was a big chocolate smear on the pillow case. I sure miss that guy.

Freddie: "That show was 1978. The other band on the poster is me in the big picture and left to right are Craig Semicheck, Cadillac Johnson and Steve Springer. Keith has his eyes closed for the photo. He would do this on purpose to piss off photographers."

Courtesy of Freddie Cisneros

Keith Ferguson(ex-Trick) now of Tail Gators with Lit' Jr. of the local band Sheet Rockers and Keith's '52 Fender bass which was stolen 5 years ago. He was re-united with the missing bass by Rockin' Robin who will hurry it on to Keith.

Freddie and Keith with Keith's '52 Fender Precision that was stolen around the early '80s and then found at Rockin' Robins.

Courtesy of Freddie Cisneros

"He had fun with his vintage basses. He would put stickers, decals and reflector tape on them. It drove the guitar collectors crazy. They couldn't imagine someone doing that to a vintage instrument."

-- Freddie Cisneros

Taken at Rockin' Robin Music Shop in Houston, a rare picture of both basses Keith had owned. Keith is holding #0171, already refinished; Freddie Cisneros in the middle; Carlos Barbosa is holding #0172.

Courtesy of Freddie Cisneros

Perfect choice of notes

Cadillac Johnson

Interview by Detlef Schmidt, October 2012

(Rewritten and edited by Cadillac, March 2014)

Cadillac Johnson was the bass player for ZZ Top prior to Dusty Hill joining the band. He played with Freddie Cisneros (Little Jr. One Hand) in their band The Blasting Caps at the Bluebird in Ft. Worth. He returned to Houston to join Uncle John Turner and Alan Haynes in the original Step Children. Cadillac is now in full-time ministry and has a gospel/blues group, The Revelators, and lives in Ft. Worth.

Cadillac Johnson.

Courtesy of Steve Wheeler

Keith and I first met in Houston back in the early '70s about the time he was playing with Rocky Hill and prior to my moving to Ft. Worth. Our real friendship developed later while he was playing in the Thunderbirds and I was playing with Freddie (Cisneros) in the Blasting Caps. I had known Lou Ann from our days together in her first band in Ft. Worth, Rockola.

I had grown up in Houston and had been friends with Billy Gibbons since his early days in The Coachmen and then The Moving Sidewalks. The original ZZ Top included Dan Mitchell from the Moving Sidewalks and Lanier Greig on Hammond B-3. They later added Billy Ethridge on bass when Frank Beard replaced Dan Mitchell on drums. When Ethridge left, Gibbons called me to join him and Frank Beard on an interim basis until Dusty could fulfill obligations in the Dallas area. That was about six or seven months.

You've asked me if I'm aware of Billy looking elsewhere for bass players or if he ever contacted Keith about playing for him. I have no firsthand knowledge of that happening. I think that due to the extended time that Dusty and Frank had playing together with his brother Rocky Hill in The American Blues, there was great appeal in the unity and tightness of Frank and Dusty together. From where I was sitting, it was always going to be Frank and Dusty.

In those early ZZ days, Bill Ham, their manager, was still negotiating with London Records for them to get a record deal. The early 45s were released on the Scat label. We were doing local and regional openers for people like Fats Domino, Grand Funk Railroad, Chuck Berry and Bo Diddley. Bill Ham was hard at work plotting the now famous course that ZZ would follow. I remember him coming into rehearsal one day telling us that ZZ Top would open for the Rolling Stones in the not too distant future. Sure 'nuff, he was right.

There was a little black juke joint called Irene's down in one of the Wards of Houston, and Gibbons used to like to slip in there and blow harp. It had to be underneath Bill Ham's radar since there was an unofficial "no sittin' in" policy in place. Keith and I went there a couple of times. It was during this time Keith was doing some work with Rocky Hill, and they were regulars at Irene's. Keith especially liked Houston's own Joey Long's style of guitar playing. There was a lot of great music coming out of our hometown of Houston. There were lots of musical influences for us all to draw from.

I don't know much about Keith's days in California, although he did mention the Black Kangaroo project as a failure. I always found it amusing that Keith was so nonplus in his stories of playing with the cats that he did at Antone's over the years. Certain things were just business as usual for Keith.

Keith did enjoy some of the Lightnin' Hopkins stories. He had also played with him on occasion. Keith liked the story about Lightnin's drummer, Spider Kilpartick, who was with Lightnin' when I played with him. Spider used to tell people that his favorite things in the world were hamhocks, womens and strikin' red. Keith loved that story.

As a bass player, I guess the most that Keith imparted to me regarding playing was his technique of varied attack, positioning and phrasing. Just subtle nuances that I've kept to this day. Keith's influence on blues bass players is monumental!

Keith always played things in his own unconventional yet innovative style. Being left-handed certainly accounted for part of that, but not all of it. His positioning and ability to stretch made for a beautifully captivating study of technique and application. An excellent example is his work on "C-Boy Blues". His choice of notes is just perfect. It's just Keith.

While Freddie Cisneros and I had the band Little Junior One Hand and The Blasting Caps, we had a memorable night at After Hours, a now defunct blues club in Austin. We did a Battle of the Bands, with T-Birds vs. Blasting Caps. Long story short, we somehow won the contest that night, after which Freddie, Keith and I retired to Keith's house. Freddie recalls us finding some tamales frozen solid in Keith's freezer. Keith's oven didn't work so we were forced to thaw them out and heat 'em up with a Bic lighter! Those were fun days for us all!

Keith and I also shared a friend in Ft. Worth, Ruth Little. Ruth had grown up with Mike Buck and Freddie Cisneros and worked at the Hop. Ruth dealt in some of the finest hard-to-find vintage fashion wear for men and women. Ruth was a contributor to much of Keith's clothing in the early days. She came up with some great stuff for us!

I was at Keith's house for a visit once and Kim (Wilson) showed up to pick up Keith for a European tour, which I think had slipped Keith's mind. He packed an extra pair of his baggy pants, his passport and an extra shirt into his bass case, and turned to me in his typical dry wit and said, "I guess I'd better go do this".

I went back to Houston and was working with Freddie Cisneros and Jimmy Don Smith in The Cold Cuts. We did many an opener for the T-Birds in those days, and it was during that time Keith's dad showed up at several of Keith's gigs. From what I saw, Keith loved his dad, and I know his father was genuinely proud of Keith.

Who could ever forget those little rigs Keith played on in the early days. I say little because by today's standards they were. Keith was always about tone first and then volume. We watched him go from the Fender Showman amps to Bassmans and then to the little Peavey TNTs and combos for a while.

With Fergie, he'd sound the same on just about any amp. His tone came from his hands and from deep within his creative spirit via a plethora of diverse influences, which he had cultivated and formulated into his own provocative style. There have been some great live recording to surface lately from his T-Bird days, wherein you can really hear the emotion and intensity Keith delivered.

I know he was proud of his work with Don Leady in The Tail Gators. Those records still hold up today! There will only be one Fergie. Often imitated, yet never duplicated.

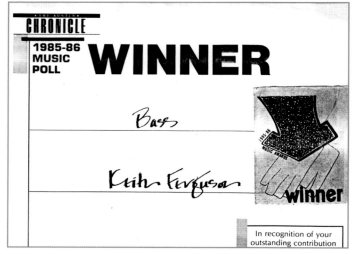

Keith won the *Austin Chronicle* Music Poll for Bass, 1985-86.

Courtesy of Keith Ferguson Collection

Early Antone's and Los Lobos

Carlos Barbosa
Interview by Detlef Schmidt, October 2011

Carlos Barbosa, a good friend of Keith since the early '70s, followed Keith's life for more than two decades and could tell lots of colorful stories. Keith told him how to play bass, and he still has one of Keith's old basses.

Otis Lewis and Keith with Jimmy Reed and Eddie Taylor at the old Antone's on Sixth Street
Courtesy of Billy Cross

Clifford (Antone) had a store and import clothing store. His family was Lebanese. He was that rich kid that lived on the lakeshore. I met him and his sisters when he was like in the fourth grade. We often went over there and played. His mother would make a something to eat. Clifford then had the food store, and they would jam back there -- Jimmie, Bill Campbell and Denny and Keith, too. This was early '70s. My family started to come to Austin about '68 or '69. Clifford was going, "We got to get a club." It was all about the blues; white boys wanted to do the blues. Coming from Port Arthur, we would hear some serious R&B while growing up. My cousin Bobby Ramirez was a drummer, and he played with The Boogie Kings. I started going across the river to Louisiana when I was about 12 years old and listened to his band.

Back in those days, Sixth Street was nothing but conjunto. And Keith knew all those guys. The only white thing was the color of his skin; he was Mexican to the bone. He spoke good Spanish -- pachuco, which is slang. The guy who told him how to play bass was a Mexican guy; I don't remember his name.

Bill Campbell told Clifford, "We have a building." It was a furniture store. We went there -- I believe it was Bill Campbell, Clifford, Keith and I think it was Jimmie. It was just a big, open, old building. And it was big. And the whole front was all glass, so you could see right into it. And the price was right, so he got it for peanuts. Then we went to work. Put in a dance floor. We built the bandstand; you had steps on either side. Right in the back, it went upstairs. That's where the office and the dressing room was. The bar was opposite to the stage; it made an L to the door.

It was all Port Arthur people, the girls that worked there. And Clifford said, "We got to have a band. We got to have an opening band." I don't remember if it was Keith or Bill Campbell who made the suggestion to bring up a band from down there, and it was Clifton Chenier, zydeco and Cajun.

As kids, we used to go and see Clifton Chenier for 50 cents. Those were the segregation days; the only black people was the band on the stage. Clifton would play from 4 to 8 non-stop. And it shut down at eight o'clock because everybody was a refinery worker, and they got to get home and get a good sleep because Monday they had to go to work.

I first met Keith through Billy Cross about 1974 or

The Fabulous Thunderbirds with Otis Lewis on drums and Angela Strehli at the old Antone's on Sixth Street.
Courtesy of Becky Stapleton Crissman

Keith wearing his Afghan coat.
Courtesy of Becky Stapleton Crissman

1975. They already knew each other. The first time I saw him, I will never forget this. He was always dressing very flamboyant. Billy, too. They would always do something with their hair. He had on that Afghan coat with all that sheep fur, and he's coming down the street.

The first night of the club opening, nobody was prepared for what was going on. They ran out of ice. "Who the hell is playing next week?" They don't even have a band for next week. We could go there early; they didn't open until 9 p.m. They still had conjunto clubs down there on Sixth Street. Keith would go there before the show. And he knew all those Mexican players. I am talking broad daylight, one or two o'clock in the afternoon.

And all the blues guys that played there requested Keith to play with them. Those guys, they loved us. We took care of them. At that time, the guys didn't do one-night shows -- they stayed there for a whole week and played every night. Antone's was open seven nights a week, 9 p.m. to 2 a.m.

Another part of my job at Antone's was to pick up players from the airport, making sure that they got

Carlos Barbosa and his 1952 Fender Precision bass. Carlos points to the identation Keith made playing the bass left handed.

to the club on time. Big Walter was one of them. John Lee Hooker, I picked him up, too.

There was a saloon called the Long Branch; it opened up at 7 a.m. I was down there with Campbell, Eddie Taylor, Hubert Sumlin and Big Walter. We were there at about eight o'clock, drinking long necks. They were telling stories. Hubert and I became friends. Hubert told the story about how he got connected to the Wolf. The deal was that his father, who was the sharecropper, owed money to the Wolf, a gambling debt. And for a payment, he gave him Hubert to work his fields. And Hubert was very young; he was about 11 or 12. Hubert said that in the evenings, when the work was done, Wolf was rehearsing in the barn. He was just fascinated by the sound of the guitar. So when they were done, he would go over there, pick up the guitar and play. The Wolf, the big man -- the guitar looked like a ukulele in his hands. The Wolf

was booked for Antone's, but he died before he could make the gig.

Melanie Guernsey, this girl is the original poster-maker for Antone's. Danny Garrett made the best posters for Antone's. At that time, all the different clubs, the Soap Creek and so on, had artists who made the posters. Melanie Guernsey made the original posters and they were signed M G.

The curtains of Antone's came out of the Ritz theater. Clifford Antone did a wonderful thing in supporting all the old blues greats -- Muddy Waters, Jimmy Reed, all these great blues guys. And they all loved to play in the club.

I lived about three blocks from Keith with my cousin Irene, who was dear friend with Lou Ann. It was my birthday, 1981 or '82, and Keith came over for the

Keith in front of his house, late 1970s to early 1980s.
Courtesy of Margaret Ferguson

I have seen Keith break a string, I guess it was a D string, and he changed it on stage, never missing a lick. When he gave me bass lessons, he was standing in front of me so that the necks were pointing in the same direction. And he was pointing with his fingers on my fretboard and giving me directions. When he would take an instrument and flip it because it was a right-handed instrument, that would always turn me up.

We spent a lot of time hanging around. Keith would just love nothing more than hanging on the front porch. And grandmother Effie, she cooked every day. She walked across the yard, sometimes in her bare feet, bringing the plates. I usually got half of it. Margaret didn't live there yet.

When he invited me first to the new house, I had to ask for the address. And he said "Second Street; you will know the house." And he was so right -- a tourquise house. If that porch could talk. We had some great times down there, drinking beer, see who could burp the loudest, spinning wax and listening to music. Keith would sing in Spanish.

One night, Keith was coming back from the gig in Waco, and he called me up to meet him at the house. We were going to see a conjunto band at the east side. I drove over there and had some beer and was waiting on the porch. The next thing I know was that two or three cop cars stopping in front of the house. Margaret saw somebody sitting on the porch and had called the police. I didn't know Margaret then. She had just moved in. They had the spotlight on me and then I saw Margaret and said, "Margaret, it's me -- Carlos."

Keith could play guitar, too, and he could play the bajo sexto. There was nothing more wonderful than being on the porch and drinking beer. He'd be spinning wax, it would mostly be conjunto or Cajun, and he had just all the information that you would want to know about the records. You never knew who would show up. Him and Johnny Winter were good buddies. Johnny was from Beaumont.

Keith was a very generous person. I have so many things that he has given me over the years. Other than his grandmother Effie, the main thing he loved was being home, waiting for the mailman and who else showed up. And it was always real fascinating cause you never knew. I never went over there without bringing cigarettes and beer. Keith was like a

birthday party. He said, "I have a few offers to sell this, but I don't really want to sell it. But I would sell it to you, if you like to buy it. I'll take $1,000 for it." And I said, "OK." And he said, "But I don't want the money. When I ask you for $100, give me a $100." At that same night, he gave me an Ampeg B18 fliptop as a gift. Later, it got stolen.

He had three or four basses at that time. One of his favorites was a big, old Kay hollowbody with F-holes and everything. An ugly thing -- turquoise or green color. He swapped in and out basses like you change shoes.

Keith's orange bass, orange like a pumpkin. He didn't like it because it was so heavy. The reason that Keith had it for that time was because he played for a Halloween gig.

I remember when I asked Keith to teach me bass, he said, "Give me $20 and I'll show you everything I know." I gave him $20 and he went, "If you use this finger of your right hand, use this finger of your left. And if you use this finger of your left hand, you will use this finger of your right."

lizard; he loved the heat. He never had air-conditioning.

Newman Jones was a guitar-maker. He lived here in Austin. He was very popular amongst the country and western scene. He made the acoustics. We were sitting on the porch, I was on the swing, the phone rings. Keith sticks his head out of the door and goes, "Carlos, you want to meet Keith Richards?" He said, "Keith Richards is at Newman's. He is picking up a guitar Newman made for him. He has asked us to come over." I said, "Yeah, cool, let's go over." Then we go over there, pick up some beer. That was before the Thunderbirds opened up for The Rolling Stones in Dallas and Houston. I don't know how they knew each other. Keith knew a lot of people. Jimi Hendrix gave him a scarf. He was in the band in the Bay area with Lewis Cowdrey and Angela Strehli. The girlfriend that Keith was going out with at that time, her friend was dating Jimi Hendrix. So they got to see each other and Hendrix gave him that scarf.

I remember the first time Stevie came to town. He used to sleep on the pool table. Stevie used to call Keith "Fado", like father figure to him. When Stevie died, Keith called me that very night. He said, "Man, we lost another one. Stevie is dead." It was just hard to believe. Me, Keith and Larry Davis, who wrote "Texas Flood", and John McVee rode to the funeral in Dallas. Larry and Keith knew each other. Stevie Wonder was there and Bonnie Raitt.

When Santana invited the T-Birds for the *Havanna Moon* recording, he had Keith stay at his house where his studio was -- not the band, just Keith. I have seen photographs of the studio. Carlos had set up his rack next to Keith. So before the session started, Santana's rack had flowers and candles on it. The next photograph was the after-session photo. Santana's rack looked the same. Keith's was just trash city -- the bass was on the floor, ashtrays and cans of beer.

All his dear friends in Houston were Mexicans. When the T- Birds played Rockefellers, a club in Houston, they always played two nights. Keith did always go with me; he never rode with the band. On Sunday mornings, we would go to his friend Freddy Cisneros of Little Junior and The Sheet Rockers. They lived out in the Heights; very beautiful. Mary Jane, Freddie's wife, had a garden. It was always great

"Second Street, you will know the house."

Courtesy of Liz Herny

fun. You never know who would show up at the gigs. When Johnny Winter would come, Keith would have me sit with him, get him drinks, have conversation.

Billy Gibbons had a place at Greens Point, East Houston, a hotel. We would go out there to party. Keith knew Lightnin' Hopkins. Keith and Billy Gibbons were good friends. To my knowledge, Billy Gibbons called Keith when he was trying form a trio, ZZ Top. He wanted him to come play. Keith was not interested and gave him Dusty's number. The rest is history. Billy Gibbons had a band in Houston, The Moving Sidewalks. They played in a club called The Cellar. We used to see ZZ Top at the Townhouse in Groves, Texas for 75 cents, before they were popular. They were knocking it down.

Every now and then he would call me to go to Houston to see his dad. Not many people knew his father. His dad had an unreal music collection. His music room was huge. He had shelving from floor to ceiling on at least two walls with albums and reel-to-reels and tape decks. And it was always classical music playing. We never visited long. And I don't really know how their relationship was, but he would go and see his dad from time to time. There were times when we would go there from Austin to Houston, and he would be in there for five minutes and then we would go back. On the other times, we would stay visiting for a little while.

Joey Long, who was a friend of Keith, played at a club -- it was Houston's hothouse for daytime romance. It was me, Keith, Denny Freeman and some guy from a record label. I forgot his name. Joey did a weekly gig there, from Monday to Friday, from 11 in the morning till three o'clock in the afternoon. So we drove down there. We came to the club at about 12 o'clock, and you would lose all concept of day or night. No windows and packed. We went and sat over in the corner, and Joey was playing a song. Right in the middle of the song, he said, "Excuse me, ladies and gentlemen, we are going to be back in a minute." Then he got off stage and walked right over to our table.

Carlos Santana jamming with the Thunderbirds.

Courtesy of Becky Stapleton Crissman

Keith hated to be touring; he wanted to be home. I have postcards that he sent me, mostly from Europe. He would make cutouts and put them on the postcards. Keith gave me a pair of Stacy Adams shoes. He said: "Don't worry, I didn't wear them." He was a dresser, very flamboyant. He always stood out, he always did something different.

When Pinky (Preston Hubbard) came to town, Keith would call me and introduced me to him. "This is the new bass player of the Thunderbirds." Keith and Preston Hubbard were friends. Keith was not jealous or anything. He just said, "Good luck."

Keith enjoyed The Tail Gators. He didn't have to mess around with all the bullshit. They were a pretty good band. A lot of times after that gigs, he would go to the eastside and sit in with Mexican bands -- Ruben Ramos from The Revolution, a dear friend. Keith always would say that Ruben's brother Pia was the best bass player he ever knew. With Keith, we would always go to Mexican restaurants on the eastside, Joe's. It's still there.

The first time the band Los Lobos came to Austin in 1980 or 1981, they'd been playing for a reunion festival at the campus. I was watching the whole show. That night, I brought them home to my house and made them something to eat. Keith was out of town, they were playing somewhere else. Me and Los Lobos have been friends since that day on. Whenever they played in town, they would come to Keith's house. Cesar and David Hidalgo would play Mexican ballads and corridos on their bajo sextos. We would be there until the sun gets up, run out of beer. But Keith would have that connection with Big Al from a liquor store, so we could get what we wanted.

We went to see John Hammond Jr. one time. And as soon as he would finish his gig, he would come to our table and say hi to Keith.

I was at the house when Billy Gibbons came and brought the two red guitars for The Tail Gators. Billy drove up and then he presented them. They had a little alligator under the finish. Keith didn't like the bass and later sold it. We were on our way to a conjunto concert, and Keith told Billy that we were in a hurry. Later on, I asked Keith why he didn't ask Billy to come to the concert. Billy liked conjunto music, too. And Keith said, "Well, I forgot." He was just a man of very few words.

Joey Long

Described by *Guitar Player* magazine as "one of America's great unknown guitarists", Joseph Longoria was born in the small town of Zwolle, Louisiana, on Dec. 17, 1932, into a poor family of sharecroppers. His first musical influence was a black blues guitar player named Charlie Wiser. In the early 1950s, he teamed up with Sonny Fisher; together they formed one of the earliest rockabilly groups, appearing on the *Louisiana Hayride* radio show and recording for Starday Records. In the mid-'50s, Long moved to Houston, Texas, and teamed up with legendary Cajun and country musician Link Davis, recording with him off and on from 1958 until 1970.

Reluctant to travel and promote himself outside of his home state, Joey Long mostly made a living playing Houston-area clubs such as the Cedar Lounge and doing session work, most notably for producer Huey P. Meaux. Long even took over lead guitar duties from legendary bluesman T-Bone Walker on sessions produced by Meaux. Along the way, Long released several singles of his own under the pseudonyms Tee Bee Fisher, Curley Long, Wee Willie Smith, and Him (the excellent blues guitar instrumental "4 A.M." backed with "It's A Man Down There"). Besides two LPs for Meaux's Crazy Cajun label, Long also released the LP *Stoned Age Man* on Scepter Records in 1970 under the name Joseph.

Despite keeping a low profile, Johnny Winter and Billy Gibbons have cited Long as a major player and influence; Winter has called him the "godfather" of the white blues guitar players in Texas. Joey Long did make it to Europe once for the Blues Estafette festival in Utrecht, Holland, in 1992. After suffering a stroke in the 1980s, he battled various health issues, but refused to curtail his musical activities, and he died in March 1995 from a heart attack.

Klaus Kilian (sources: Texas State Historical Association website; Blues & Rhythm *magazine no. 99, May 1995)*

Above: Keith in The Tail Gators.
Courtesy of Gregory G. Carlson

Right: Cesar from Los Lobos with Keith.
Courtesy of Daniel Schaefer

Below: Keith on a Tail Gators gig playing the red bass (note the alligator inlay) Billy Gibbons had given to him.
Courtesy of Margaret Ferguson

Postcards from touring

In days prior to emails and facebook, letters and postcards were the way to stay in contact. Keith was very good in staying in contact with his friends and some of them kept the postcards until today as a memory. So I am able to show them here, thanks to Becky Stapleton Crissman and Frank Sarro and Jillian Bailey.

Postcards To Becky Crissman

April 28, 1978
I hope you liked Jerry as he is a nice fellow for someone in this business. I haven't been to Houston because I stopped working for Rocky (added by the author: meaning Rocky Hill) and also we're leaving on another of our trips north.

May 6, 1978
Hello – I am here in New Hampshire. So far we have been to Pennsylvania, Mess., and here and tomorrow is Rhode Island. I'm anxious to get back to my house and where people don't have accents.

Nov. 8, 1978
Lou Ann and I have a little house at 3402 S. 2nd Austin, which my mother owns, so I guess that means its mine.

Sept. 29, 1979
It's hard to write anything about this "tour" without complaining – the only good thing I can think of is that it's almost over. I am tired and it gets more and more difficult to stay "top of the hall". I labour under the assumption that it'll be better next time and it's better than welding out in Arizona with my uncle.

Oct. 29, 1979
Hello from Mississippi.

Jan 30, 1980
So far all is good – Rockpile are super
people, too.
(I promise to get something for you from
Dave by the way)
Nick Lowe is a riot, too. Couldn't ask for
better people to tour with – real party
dogs.

May 19, 1980
Hello from Hamburg.
I am on our second annual T-Bird tour
of Europe and UK. It's much better this
time out, we're headlining so it's better
treatment all around. John Hammond
opened up for us last night and he is still
real good.

Aug. 18, 1980
We just played Chicago Fest and it went
quite well.

Oct. 15, 1980
Hello from L.A. So far our new record is
moving right along. The other night at
our gig in San Francisco, Carlos Santana
gave Jimmie a very old Fender Esquire
Guitar. That was nice.

Nov. 22, 1980
Right now we are in St. Louis, I think.
Then its Knoxville, Nashville.

Feb. 2, 1981
Last night Cheap Trick sat in with us. I
guess that means we've arrived.

1981
Tom Petty and his people are pretty
decent as are the crowds. Soon we are
going west which is fine for me.

March 22, 1993
Dear Becky, Happy birthday and may all
your dreams come true in 1993.

Postcards To Frank Sarro

Nov. 22, 1977
Playing with Muddy Waters was real
good, too.

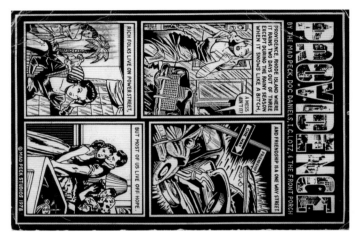

May 18, 1978
I really like Mobile – except that they treat us so well I can't remember anything after the second set. We're going to New Orleans tomorrow. Marshall Chapman sat in with us in Atlanta. I am having a good time, but I'll be glad to get home.

Aug. 19, 1978
The SF blues festival and tonight we're doing a radio broadcast. It's a lot better than going east for sure. None of my old friends recognize me – I love that.

May 1979
Next week we're going to Dallas to record. We got some sort of a deal with a West Coast label to make an LP. Lou Ann's group already made one.

Nov. 1979
Our current outing (with John Prine) is actually fun. Concerts are much easier than bars.

Nov. 13, 1979
Hello from Hollywood. Playing with John Prine has been a real piece of cake.

Jan. 29, 1980
We're being well received and Rockpile are nearly as sick as I am which helps. Soon it's to be Holland, Germany and Paris. What a drag.

Feb. 28, 1980
I am three night off in London. Last night I saw Joe Ely of Lubbock and the Clash. Lou Ann wants me to marry her when I get back. What have I done wrong?

May 9, 1980
Hello from London,
Much better over here this time. Money is still slow but they treating us better. Also we are playing clubs instead of colleges - and I hate colleges.

Sept 21, 1980
We are playing with Marshall Tucker for a week or so.

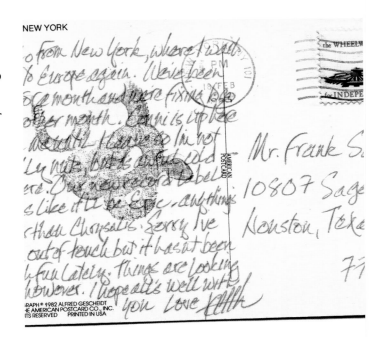

Oct. 15, 1980
Hello from L.A., we just got here from San Francisco, where Carlos Santana gave Jimmie Vaughan a great guitar at one of our gigs. He's a better guitarist than I thought, too. We should start recording tonight or tomorrow.

Postcard from Finland

It's colder than a whore's heart here. Everyone speaks rapid martian and drinks a lot. Everyone also loves us here. There are a loads of beautiful girls here but they all smell like goats.
We're playing with Link Wray in Amsterdam, it's a good thing I remember Rawhide. I should stop this shit and get a job.

March 1981
Hello from Seattle, I really like it here. So far the gigs have been very good even though I'm not used to my new amp yet. The reviews have been good, too. I haven't met Eric Clapton yet but he's bound to be luck out soon.

198?
Hello from Detroit and my little Eric Clapton tour.

April 7, 1982
Hello from Monterey, this little tour has been fun, I've tonight off even. Carlos Santana sat in with us again with the Roomful of Blues Horns. That was San Francisco. Anyway we're going home soon which is good as I am ready to kill to see Conni.

Feb. 18, 1983
Hello from New York, where I will go to Europe again. Conni (Hancock) is up here with me until I leave so I am not totally nuts, but it's awful cold up here. Our new record label looks like it'll be Epic, anything's better than Christalis.

June 21, 1988
We are playing in Big Austin Saturday 2 July in the Continental Club. I am happy with my old bass back.

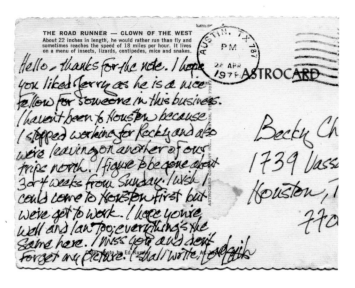

Postcards to Jillian Bailey

From New York 1983
I go now to play with Robert Gordon.

Postcard for Keith's 40th birthday.

Courtesy of Kathy Murray

Postcards from Keith.

Courtesy of Daniel Schaefer

199

Keith and the Lowriders

Written by Tito Aguirre

At one time, Keith was our El Presidente around 1980-1981. Now, this might bring up a wheelbarrow full of question marks to those who thought they knew him well. "Why, that's impossible," might proclaim a few masters of Keith trivia.

How could someone who didn't drive be the president of (during the late '70s), one of the largest car clubs in the Southwest of North America?

And how did Keith, with no car parked in his wooden, on-its-last-legs, back-of-the-driveway garage without doors even get close enough to share his Cheshire cat grin at those within the inner circle of thee los L.B.'s?

The second question is far less complicated to answer than the first. Even easier to answer is the one question yet asked: Who be Thee Los Leisure Bros. State of Mind con/safos?

The L.B.s were comprised of hot rodders from all parts of Austin and the surrounding area. Hot rodders of American brands of automobiles, already paid for and, although distinguished by brand loyalty, united in the natural, perhaps genetic, need to be faster with motor modifications and unique with paint combinations. In some areas on the east side of Austin, there were at least a few hot rod carruchas and trokas per block, many having passed from father to son or daughter, tio to nephew, sometimes just sold to the hombre next door.

And if one were to lift up the dusty tarp in the corner of any given end-of-the-driveway garage, one would more than likely find an old Harley, also customized. No, we weren't rich, just talented at taking the discarded, non-working two- and four-wheeled machinery and making them work ... again. Restoring them to showroom floor status -- sometimes, even better than before.

At first, the L.B.s were shared between just a few Vietnam vets, but membership very rapidly spread, eventually to the Califas coast. How the success? Easy. The L.B.'s were a state of mind -- an easy trip for a true hotrodder, no matter what other affiliation or other club one belonged to already. And our efforts were solely used in one direction: charity. All proceeds always went to groups like a summer camp for the poor, and/or to an organization which provided, free of charge, clothes and school supplies for the poorest of Austin.

The L.B.s were created by a group of men and their mujeres (Thee Ladies of Leisure) as a way to promote positive community vibes at a time when public perception was bad on the street for all customized vehicles.

Now, back to Keith. One sunny afternoon, the L.B.'s were sponsoring a hundreds of cars and Harleys parade around the capital of Austin, followed by a party at the now-gone Duke's Royal Coach Lounge, Third and Congress. The band scheduled to play for our gathering did a no-show.

So we arrived, chingos de Harleys, lowriders and hot rods, as did a band van, which was picking up its PA from the night before. The band, The Fabulous Thunderbirds, said, "Fuckit, we'll jam!", replugged their amps and rocked the block into the sunset that late afternoon, for free. And that's how everyone became friends, especially Jimmie Vaughan and Keith, the epitome of pachuco.

There is a huge, twisted storyline which involves many other incidents and stuff, but eventually, one early morning, me and Keith and someone else were cruising down South First Street in south Austin. We was bouldered. (There is stoned, but before that, a little stoned -- pebbled, then after stoned, really big stoned -- bouldered.)

Keith asked, "Can I drive your bomba?" My personal bomb ('51 Panhead in the garage), a '48 Chevy Fleetline, lowered, candy apple carmel white with gold glitter on the roof and fenders.

I said, "Sure," pulled over and we switched seats. The ride turned into a slalom between telephone poles, with Keith scoring 100. The passenger in the back woke up during the ride, proclaiming, "Allah chingada, you can't drive for chit!"

Somewhere between there and another time, a visitor asked Keith, "But, I thought you didn't drive?" He replied, "I don't."

In a later sharing of the telephone pole avoidance drive down South First, someone joked, "Ha, he can't drive for chit. He don't even have a driver's license. He should be our next president."

A vote was taken. And that is the how Keith Ferguson cs/f, became the non-driving president of a nationwide car club, Thee Los Leisure Bros. State of Mind con/safos.

El Tito Aguirre con/safos

Chapter 5

The Tail Gator Years

1985-1989

DON LEADY   GARY "MUD CAT" SMITH   KEITH FERGUSON

THE TAIL GATORS

Promo shot of The Tail Gators for Restless Records.

Courtesy of Don Leady

Chapter 5

The Tail Gator Years 1984-1989

The Tail Gators

Don Leady
Interview by Detlef Schmidt, October 2013

Don is the guitar player and mastermind of The Tail Gators. He also was a member of The LeRoi Brothers in the early 1980s, with whom Keith recorded their first album. Don was a member of *Big Guitars From Texas* and won a Grammy nomination for this album. Don currently lives in Austin and has a solo recording out, *Hillbilly Boogie Surfin' Blues*.

Don Leady on his Telecaster guitar.
Courtesy of Tracy Hart / The Heights Gallery

I first met Keith back in the late '70s in Dallas. Steve Doerr and I used to go over and see the Thunderbirds in Dallas because we were living in Fort Worth. That's why I know Ted Tucker, Wes Race, Jim Colegrove, Johnny Reno and Sumpter Bruton. We all used to hang out at the Bluebird, but the T-Birds played Dallas frequently at a club called Faces.

We knew Keith, like all the fans did. He was pretty cool with all his tattoos. We knew Christina Patoski, Johnny Reno's wife and sister of Joe Nick Patoski, the writer (author of "Stevie Ray Vaughan: Caught in the Crossfire"). So, when we moved down to Austin,

It all started in Austin, Texas, in 1985. Don Leady, a co-founding member of The LeRoi Brothers, decided to venture out on his own to pursue his own style -- a combination of original swamp pop and Louisiana-style rock 'n roll -- which later he would name "swamp rock". Gary 'Mud Cat' Smith joined him on drums after playing with then-14-year-old Charlie Sexton (The Eager Beaver Boys). Jack Moore, one of Don's old friends, volunteered to play bass temporarily to get the band started. Just two months later, Keith Ferguson walked into a club on Sixth Street in Austin where The Tail Gators were playing and said "Hey, I'll play with you guys." Right then and there, Don told him, "You're hired!" Keith had just left The Fabulous Thunderbirds and had always been one of Don's heroes from the '70s. The original Tail Gators trio was formed. The Tail Gators' debut album, *Swamp Rock*, was recorded a couple of months later.

The Tail Gators recorded several albums over the years in the styles of swamp rock to surf. One song, "Tailshaker", received a Grammy nomination for Best Rock Instrumental in the late '80s. (Just prior to that time, Don and Keith had been playing with another Austin band, Big Guitars From Texas, which also received a Grammy nomination.) Over the years, The Tail Gators constantly toured all over the world. After several years, Keith decided to quit touring and leave the band. J.J. Barrera then replaced Keith and has been the trio's bassist ever since.

Source: The Tail Gators Homepage[2]

Mudcat and Keith, playing the cowhide bass.
Courtesy of Tracy Hart, The Heights Gallery

Swamp Rock, the first album of The Tail Gators.
© Wrestler Records

we were living in Joe Nick's house for a while, about a month or so, right during the flood they had in Austin. We watched some cars floating down Shoal Creek from the car dealership next door. They were floating down the creek with their headlights on.

We kind of knew all of the T-Birds from Faces. Keith, surprisingly, was a really nice guy. You thought he was going to stab you with a knife or something. He was real nice, and we kind of became friends. Every time they came up to Dallas, we went to see them. Then I moved down to Austin in 1980 to start another band, but it wasn't The LeRoi Brothers. It was to start a band with Mike Buck and Keith Dunn, the harmonica player. So we started a band called The Headhunters with Mike Buck on drums and me and Steve on guitar and Alex Napier on bass, Keith Dunn on harp.

So we played a few gigs with that band, and then we started a new band with Lou Ann in the same configuration -- Lou Ann and The Fliptops -- that lasted a little while we played several gigs over a few months. Then we decided to start the LeRois with Buck in

there. On the first recording, "Moon Twist", we had Alex on bass. Then we were going as a trio with no bass. So when we recorded *Check This Action*, we got Keith to play bass on that one. This was the second recording of The LeRoi Brothers. We were touring as a trio, like super loud. Steve always tuned his guitar to D and was playing power chords. We were really loud. There is a funny story. It was up in Wichita and we were playing at a place called the Spot, and then got a noise complaint. The cops came in and looked around and said, "God damn, there's only three of 'em."

Two Tail Gators releases, *Mumbo Jumbo* (above) and *Tore Up* (below).   © *Wrestler Records*

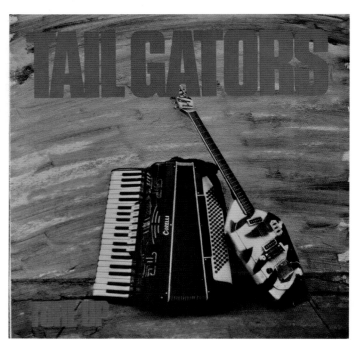
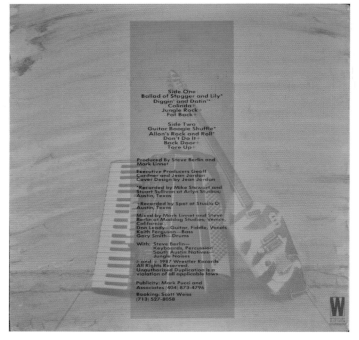

So Keith got on this recording, and this was our first playing with him. He didn't play gigs with the LeRois. Then, in about 1984, I quit The LeRoi Brothers to do my own thing. So I decided that I was going to start my own band and do the swamp rock type of stuff. I had a friend named Jack Moore, so when I started, I got him and Mud Cat. He was the first bass player for The Tail Gators. He only lasted about two months or so, maybe about 10 gigs, because he didn't really want to do the band thing. He only played because I asked him to play.

One time we were playing down at Sixth Street. Keith came walking in there and was hanging out there for a while. Then he walked up to me and said, "I am your new bass player." We said, "What?" And he said, "I just got out of the Thunderbirds and am looking for a gig." So I said, "Yeah, we would love to have you."

I talked to Jack and told him that we got Keith. He was good with that. Then we started playing gigs with Keith -- first locally, then we started minor touring the Midwest. With Keith, he didn't travel very well. So what we did in the beginning, when we went somewhere, we just flew. We just used whatever gear they had to offer. We were flying to a place, rent a car, do a little circuit around and go back. So Keith didn't have to kick his habits. Keith was mad at the Thunderbirds at that time. But he was kind of complicated

Don Leady singing and playing a Tele.
Courtesy of Tracy Hart / The Heights Gallery

The Tailgator bass and guitar, presented by Billy Gibbons, shown here on the album *OK, Let's Go!*
© Restless Records

when it came to travelling -- and those guys were travelling all the time. So he was mad when he got out, but I think he got over it.

Keith and I were asked to play on a four-guitar band called Big Guitars From Texas. Gary Rice, who used to manage The LeRoi Brothers, was involved in it so they picked me, Evan Johns, Frankie Camaro and Denny Freeman. So Keith got in on bass and Buck was on drums. By then, Keith was already playing in my band.

We got more radio airplay with that then with anything. We did some live things with that band because the record was so successful. I am not sure how we got it. Somebody heard it and liked it. We all went to the Grammys; I don't remember Keith going there. We were in Hollywood for the presentation. It was pretty exciting. The funny thing was, we had got nominated. We had the final cut where we had to be in the audience. Stevie Ray Vaughan also was there. So we had big hitters there except the Big Guitars From Texas. Jeff Beck ended up in winning the

Grammy. The cool thing was that Bruce (Sheehan), who had the record label Jungle Records, put the record out; he went out there with us. We had this rental car, and Bruce was driving, and he could not find a parking spot. I guess if we would have known we were going to miss the announcement, we would have jumped out. We were all in the car driving around. So we got in there and they had already announced who won. So we got in there, found out that we didn't win. We were not that disappointed. They had an open bar. So we just all got blasted. All of us were drunk, except Angela Strehli, who was with us in the car. Finally, Bruce let Angela drive. We used to say that we owe our lives to Angela.

The Tail Gators album _Hide Your Eyes._

Keith playing the cowhide bass.

Courtesy of Tracy Hart / The Heights Gallery

We had some gigs after that Grammy nomination, some video deals. We did Dixie's Bar & Bus Stop (YouTube video), the Continental Club. We never made any money from the record, which isn't unusual, but we got some songwriter royalties.

The same guy that did the painting on my sparkle Telecaster guitar made the guitars that Billy Gibbons presented to us. And he actually made the guitars for Billy Gibbons. John Bolin, Bolin Guitars, is his name. He is still up in Idaho. These guitars ended up at Keith's house. Keith said, "Come on over here, I have got a guitar for you." So I went over there and he said,

"Billy Gibbons gave us these guitars. Check them out. Wow, these are red." We never did use them a lot live. I still have mine, but I think I took the pickups out of it. I believe Rick Gonzales ended up having Keith's sparkle bass. I don't remember how he got it, but he ended up getting it. It might have been in a pawn shop. Keith told him, "Go there and get it." So he went up there and got it. It has an alligator inlay on the front of it. Billy thought we would look cool with the two sparkling guitars. Billy had said that we were his favorite American band, so we wrote this in our press kit. That helped us a little bit.

The Miller Beer cooperation was an idea of the guy that was our manager at that time. So he thought we should get with Miller and get our free beer and posters. They gave us guitars, too. They gave me a guitar and Keith a bass that had "Miller" on them. Both of us sold them, I think. They were gone like in a week after we got them. I guess we both pawned them. They were good, but they were like the new kind of guitars. They were not blues guitars. Mine was shaped real funny, like a Miller sign. We didn't like them, mostly because they said "Miller" on them.

208

Keith playing the cowhide bass through a the Fender Showman, the classic Keith setup.

Courtesy of Tracy Hart / The Heights Gallery

We didn't drink much of the Miller, but we gave it away to everybody. Backstage, every gig we had two cases of beer. Keith did drink the Miller.

People from all over were trying to duplicate his bass rig, but it is not in the rig. He had it in his fingers. He had the sound in his fingers. He got his sound on any rig he ever played. It didn't take much -- he just turned it all the way on bass and turned it up. That was it; the rest was his fingers.

Some rigs sounded like they were going to blow -- the Fender rig especially did. Keith's bass playing kind of defies description. He had more than one thing going on at the same time. What comes out is a little bit different to what goes in. Sometime I don't think his amp could take all of what he was playing.

I think it had to do with his finger technique on his left hand. A lot of times he would hit a lot of notes, but most of the times it didn't come out of the amp. Maybe it was because of his tone setting. It came out as a roar instead of picked notes. If he had treble on his bass, these picked noted would have come out more than they did. With The Tail Gators, we didn't

do hardly any overdubbing on the recording, just a little bit.

We did a lot of Norway and Sweden. I don't know if we ever went to Finland with Keith; we might have went to Finland with Keith one time. We ordered a pizza one time and we got a reindeer pizza. It was reindeer, horsemeat and tunafish. We thought it was good until we found out what it was.

We never played England. We did play Belgium, Holland, Germany. I don't think we ever went to Spain with Keith. I used to take my neck off the guitar when we were on the road, flying in a plane. I think Keith did, too. They used to have this overhead compartment, where you couldn't fit guitars in. So we'd take the neck off, leave the strings on and just kind of folded the guitar to fit it in. When it didn't intonate the right way, you pop it on the one side, then on the other side. OK.

I wrote a song that is on one of our Tail Gator albums, "Hallelujah, I'm Coming Home". That is a song about Keith because he would get so happy coming home. He used to say that he was dreaming all the

Rock 'N' Roll Till The Cows Come Home

© Wrestler Records

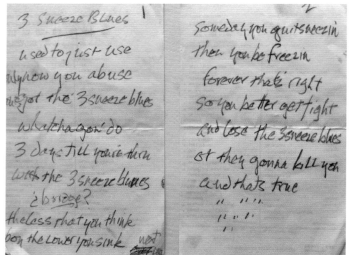

A blues song Keith and Don composed together.

Courtesy of Don Leady

of the car when he took his shoes off. So some friend of his had told him to take a brown paper bag, soak it in vinegar, then wrap his feet in that. And then he put his shoes on with the feet wrapped in vinegar. So he got in the van one time, and everybody was going, "What is that smell? It's terrible." And then Keith goes, "You must be talking about this." Then he showed me his feet all wrapped in a paper bag. I said that it was worse than it was before, because he had his feet right under the heater. And he asked me if he should take off his shoes. I said, "No." I think Keith did drive one time when we were really tired. He said, "If you need me to drive, I will do."

Keith didn't talk much about his California days. I didn't meet his dad. The only thing that Keith told me about his dad was that he wasn't around. At the end, I guess he didn't see him very much.

Keith used to say something when a guitar player played too much: "Hid a lick." And he was going, "Hidalickhidalickhidalick."

He had a Telecaster bass with the blue pickguard. I may have made it or gave the material to Keith, but I don't remember. I don't think he used the bass in The Tail Gators. He did use the cowhide bass or the red Fender Precision bass. He had this National bass one time, and I had this Airline guitar that looked just like it.

Keith just got tired of touring, so he got out of the band. He just wanted to stay at his house. Every time we did go on the road, he said, "I have to go home. My grandmother wants me." Effie died after he got out of The Tail Gators. I think that this grand-

way back to seeing his grandmother. Keith did some co-writing with me. "Mumbo Jumbo" was a song of The Tail Gators he wrote with me.

Basile Kolliopolos was a real nice guy. He and his brother came from Oklahoma. They used to open up for us a lot of times when we played in this club in Oklahoma City, VZD's. He recently passed away. We hung out with them and knew them all pretty well. Their name was Fortune Tellers. We used to have fun in Oklahoma City, for sure. I think Wes Race came up there a few times.

Keith was famous for feet that would knock you out

Keith playing the cowhide bass.

Courtesy of Don Leady

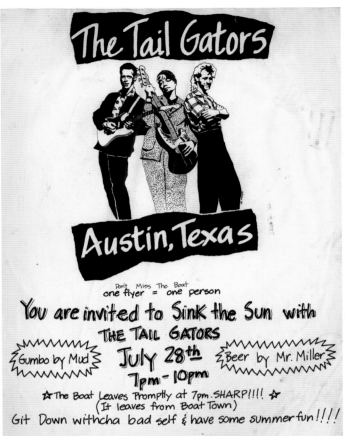

Tail Gators gig poster.

Courtesy of Keith Ferguson Collction

mother thing was a codename for something else. When we were out on the tours, he was good for some days, but then it got hard. He had his connections, but not everywhere.

Mud Cat is somewhere down in Arizona. I think he got tired of doing gigs on the road, too. I kind of lost contact to him for years. We played around 100 gigs a year together since 1984. I guess he left the band around 1992. Now I am just doing different types of gigs mostly local whatever comes along. I released an instrumental CD a year ago called *Hillbilly Boogie Surfin' Blues*. I plan on doing some touring with that band and also a new band playing obscure rock 'n roll and rockabilly called The Under Yonder Boys. Mike Buck is playing drums in this newest bit of craziness.

I'd like to say that Keith was a great artist in every way and could do amazing pencil drawings. I can't find any at the moment, but someday I hope they turn up. Knowing Keith and playing music with him was some of the best times in my life.

Miller Brewery advertisement.

Courtesy of Keith Ferguson Collection

211

Miller beer print advertisements.

Courtesy of Keith Ferguson Collection

English advertisement for the first Tail Gators album (note the mention of Keith).

Outtakes from a studio photo session.

Courtesy of Keith Ferguson Collcetion

KEITH FERGUSON   DON LEADY   GARY SMITH

the **TAIL GATORS**

WRESTLER RECORDS   BOOKING: ELECTRIC ARTISTS (409) 298-2891

Promotional and live photos.

Courtesy of Don Leady

214

Top: Keith, the cowhide bass and a Peavey amp and (above) The Tail Gators in a Low Price Motel.
Courtesy of Don Leady

Left: Keith and his red Fender Precision bass.
Courtesy of Tracy Hart / The Heights Gallery

Shots of Keith on stage (left column) and offstage (right column).

Courtesy of Don Leady

Recording The Tail Gators

Mike Stewart
Interviewed by Detlef Schmidt, 2011

Mike Stewart was the sound engineer for The Tail Gators recordings *Mumbo Jumbo* and *OK, Let's Go*. He is a bass player and watched Keith closely during the recording sessions. He currently lives in Amsterdam, Netherlands.

Don Leady is and was the main cat in The Tail Gators. He is a guitar wizard and, like his sound, rough and ugly. I had seen Don play several times and really liked his approach to guitar. Soon after I moved to Austin, Don asked me to record them. He wanted to do a recording very quickly, for budget reasons and to keep their live energy that they were so famous for. This band played a lot in the U.S. and Europe -- probably close to 200 shows a year.

The bass player was Keith Ferguson, who was one of the coolest cats in Austin. He had played for the T-Birds for years. Gary Smith was the drummer and he was very, very good at this rocking, Cajun style of music.

We did the *Mumbo Jumbo* record in four days at Arlyn Studio in Austin for Wrestler Records, and Dusty Wakeman remixed it at Mad Dog in L.A. Dusty is a really cool guy who has produced, engineered and played bass on some very great recordings (Lucinda Williams, Dwight Yoakam and Jim Lauderdale).

On The Tail Gators sessions, Keith used any Fender amp he could find, usually older and always tube, not necessarily in good condition. His most basic rig was a '70s Fender Bassman head and a 1-15 cab with stock Jensen speakers. Since his rig was often unavailable, perhaps in the pawn shop, he was borrowing anything he could scrabble up, really!

On the recordings I did with Keith, we usually used a DI (direct input), probably a simple Countryman, into various available tube preamps. And I think both records were made into a '70s API console, so it could have gone first into the API preamps, which

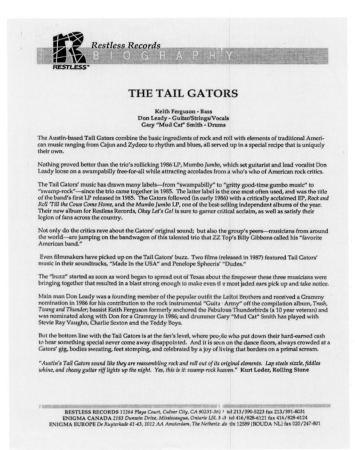

A press kit for The Tail Gators.

are very good for bass. I almost always used Pultec EQs and Tube Tech compressors in those days, but the API EQs and comps were often a choice, too. Hard to say what exactly was used.

One of the nights, he broke a bass string. He also, at the time he broke the string, had somehow wrapped himself up in his headphone cable and bass cable, which freaked him out immediately. Trying to get untangled, he got even more tangled up in the cables and in the frenzied moment, kind of tossed his bass down and dragged the cables off himself, then left the studio as quickly as he could.

We did not see him for two days, when he came back with an old replacement string. This was before cell phones and we just did not hear from him. Don and Mud Cat and I finished a couple of tracks without him, vocal and guitar overdubs, mostly.

Keith was a special and unusual bass player. Young

217

bass players today are mostly trying to be way too technically good. If new and young bass players could understand what it was that Keith had and try to play with the feel of it, rather than with an impressive, notey style, bands would be better.

I mostly saw him with old '60s Telecaster basses, with maple necks, small headstocks. But I did see this Harmony one day, too.

The second recording two years later was called *OK, Let's Go!*, and we recorded and mixed this in seven days, also at Arlyn. We did this recording for Restless Records, which is how I met Ron Goudie when he was doing A&R for them. Ron is a producer and now lives in Amsterdam, too. Small world.

He (Keith) liked the strings on his bass when they were at least two years old and searched hard around town with other bass players to find a used string of the same gauge and type to replace the broken one. I am a bass player and learned a lot from watching Keith and listening to him play. I have tried to use old strings ever since then and usually hate the sound of new strings.

Keith was one of the best bass players ever to get the groove going and roll his sound in and around under the rest of the band. Sometimes hard to distinguish his notes, but always undeniably on the groove, driving the band along, walking his bass from section to section and never fighting with the drum groove.

These recordings were the first where Don Leady experimented with playing instruments other than his Telecaster, playing fiddle and lap steel guitar.

Don has kept the Tail Gators on the road for all these years.

Letter from Daryl Hall:

I was introduced to Keith by my drummer, Sam Alford, in 1989 and knew him until 1995 when I left Austin. I came into his living room once and Sam said, "Here's someone who likes your bass playing, Keith!" I told him that when I heard "Rock And Roll Till The Cows Come Home", I said to myself, there's a bass player who's got his shit together! He laughed and said he couldn't even remember what he played on that!

Don Leady on a Telecaster.
Courtesy of Gregory G. Carlson

Tail Gators with Evan Jones and the H-Bombs.
Courtesy of Don Leady

Bajo Sextos

JJ Barrera
Interviewed by Detlef Schmidt, October 2011

I first met Keith when he played with The Fabulous Thunderbirds. In April 1986, I met him with The Tail Gators at John F. Kennedy Airport in New York City and was reacquainted. That's when I played with a group called The Commandos. We were leaving the States to go tour in Finland to promote our new CD. After our arrival in Helsinki, we heard about the world's worst nuclear power plant explosion of Chernobyl, Russia. People joked about us back home as "the band that glows together". At that time we weren't able to eat any vegetables because of the radiation fear. What's funny is that before the leaders of The Commandos decided to make the trip to Finland, they were afraid to travel there for fear of the terrorists from Libya! Some years later, when I returned to Scandinavia with Don Leady and The Tail Gators, we wouldn't be able to eat the reindeer meat because of the same radiation from the Chernobyl disaster.

Anyway, back in Austin ... Keith and I came together through conjunto music and our mutual love of the bajo sexto (12-string, acoustic bass guitar) instrument that is used to accompany the button accordion. We would talk about regional Tejano conjunto music and norteño music from Mexico touching about the many recording artists in those genres throughout the years from the '30s to the '80s. We talked about the instruments used in this music and its evolution from acoustic to being amplified and anything else that had to do with the music. Turned out later ... we each had bajo sextos being made by Guadalupe 'Lupe' Reyes from Gregory, Texas. After some time, Keith called me up and said, "He has them ready and wants us to meet him in San Antonio. Let's go!" I picked Keith up at his house and off we went. We met Lupe at the Allen & Allen lumber yard, where he used to get his choice wood to make his instruments. I can tell you Keith and I were happy as can be to get our new bajos. You can see this in the photo where Keith had us pose in front of the lumberyard fence with a large sign in the background that says HICKS! Ha! Keith humor! When Keith wasn't touring or playing with a band in Austin, he

The Tail Gators

REPRESENTATION:
ELECTRIC ARTISTS
214/748-3825

The (new) Tail Gators: Don Leady, Mud Cat Smith and JJ Barrera.

liked to go see what conjunto or norteño group he could, whether it be the annual Tejano Conjunto Festival in San Antonio, and/or the Johnny Degollado's Cinco de Mayo Austin Tejano Conjunto Festival. Tejano conjunto and norteño music have their roots from when German, Polish and Czech immigrants in the 1800s brought their music via the accordion to the Americas. There is the story of Narciso Martinez (considered by many as the "father of Texas-Mexican conjunto music") who had a friend of his visit the German dances in Texas. And he would memorize the music he heard and return to Narciso where he would whistle the tunes so Narciso could replicate them on his accordion.

Keith told me that he once invited Los Alegres de Terán, a norteño group popular for their corridos (which are songs sung about true life events), to his house after their gig. At his house, Keith pulled out their first recorded 33 LP, and they were astonished. "Ha, hijo, you have got that album?!! We don't even have it ourselves anymore." You know, his dad had that music store and this is how he had these albums. Eugenio Abrego and Tomás Ortiz asked Keith ... "Can we buy this album from you," and Keith turned to them and said, "No, but I'd like you to autograph it for me." Keith humor.

I can tell you, the first rock 'n roll garage band in Laredo, Texas, with my brother Georges Barrera, Joe Ruiz, and Lauro 'Sonny' Guerra in the late '60s,

Keith and JJ Barrera in San Antonio to pick up their custom made bajo sextos. In the middle is the now deceased Guadalupe 'Lupe' R. Reyes, luthier of stringed instruments in Gregory, Texas.

Courtesy of JJ Barrera

was named The Dismal Swamp. As we went through personnel changes, and I switched from playing guitar to bass. Our guitar player, named Dan David, had always spoken to me about his musician cousins and uncle living in Houston and about Keith Ferguson, who was their friend who hung around with them who learned to play bass guitar from Armando Compean. His dad was an important orchestra musician and as his son grew up ... he ended up in L.A. as a studio musician and was recording for many well known stars. Anyway, back in Laredo, when we began toying with the idea of renaming our band, Dan David suggested the name "Keith." So we switched the name.

I love Keith's style of playing bass and I try to emulate some of it, especially with The Tail Gators. I would study his work. Of course, nobody can play exactly like somebody else, but I allow inspiration to guide me. Like Keith, I was self taught; everything he did was by ear. Also, he had listened to that music as a kid. And it helped that he grew up with the Compean musical family kids in his barrio (neighborhood), which helps to explain his 'pachuco' wit, charm and swagger. And he could curse as well as any Chicano.

So he had all that in his background, plus the blues, the conjunto/norteño music. His dad had all that music in his store, so he had a rich background of

listening to all this important stuff. So that's why he is special. And his personality was tops. He had friends in every corner of the globe that he traveled or lived in.

Yes, I used to own the cowhide bass before Keith. I bought it for $75 in Laredo, Texas, from a friend of mine named David Curiel who had converted his mom's living room into a music store. David Curiel was also a songwriter and composer of songs. When I moved to Austin in the early '70s, the first person that saw this '65/'66 Fender Precision was Don Bennett, Marsha Ball's bass player. I picked him up when he was hitchhiking near the center of Austin. In conversation, he mentioned he also was a bass player and had also recently moved to Austin for the music. He wanted to see the bass I had on my backseat. So, I pulled over and took it out of its original leather case. To this day, whenever I see Don Bennett, he always remembers me because of that bass!

Upon hard times, I put this bass on consignment at Ray's Heart of Texas Music. And a couple of days later, Billy Gibbons heard about it, bought it and gave it to Keith. Someone had stolen Keith's older Precision bass, which showed up years later at Rockin' Robin music store in Houston. When I next saw the bass I used to own, Keith had converted it for playing left-handed and he put the cowhide pickguard on it.

Showing the tattoos

Wes Race
Interviewed by Scott Ferris, October 2012

I first met Keith when he started touring with Don Leady and The Tail Gators when they came through Wichita. Basically, after the gigs, me being a third-shifter, Don put two and two together and let me keep Keith company. So we'd just go back to the hotel after the gigs. We'd be up until 5 or 6 in the morning. I worked third shift, so I couldn't sleep anyway. It was kind of cool, watch the TV with Keith. He loved movies and came out with pretty cool remarks about them.

I loved posters and Keith did, too. I ended up with old Robert Ely and Sue Foley posters. He rescued me one time at Don Leady's wedding. I drove down from Fort Worth and I got a little drunk and loaded during the wedding, and I showed up at Antone's where Keith was playing. So he told me, "Why don't you come over to my house."

He really liked that Joe Hill Lewis. He collected switchblades. I guess he got them earlier on when he was living in Houston. Every time he came to the Kansas/Wichita area, we would hang out. I could show him all the good Mexican restaurants.

Wes: "The pictures were taken out at the Coyote during a double bill of The Tail Gators and Doyle Bramhall. It was Keith's birthday and somebody had brought him a birthday T-shirt. We showed our tattoos."

Courtesy of Dave Ranney

Chapter 6

Late Austin Years

1990-1997

The always-stylin' Keith Ferguson.

Courtesy of Mike Steele

Chapter 6

Late Austin Years 1990-1997

The Excellos

David Watson
Interviewed by Detlef Schmit, 2011

Drummer of The Excellos and former member of Anson Funderburgh and The Rockets, another famous Texas blues band.

David Watson and Keith in The Excellos.
Courtesy of David Watson

Promotion photo of The Excellos.
Courtesy of David Watson

I met Keith through my uncle, Doyle Bramhall, in the early '70s. Keith was a genius in music but never reached his full potential. I went with Keith to where he was from in San Antonio, Texas, and met some of his family and went to a Mexican restaurant owned by relatives. Keith was influenced heavily by Mexican music and could play Mexican music on a nylon-string. large guitar upside down, tuned right-handed. Doyle, Keith and Stevie Ray Vaughan played together, and each one of them had a huge personality. But if you tried to do an interview with Keith, you would get nothing from him. He was shy until you friended him, then he would be the center of attention. He was smart, funny, witty.

In 1980, when I was playing in Anson and The Rockets, the Thunderbirds were recording *What's The Word* album at Sumet Burnet studio in Dallas. They rented my drum set for some of those recordings. Keith and Kim Wilson came to our gig that night at Poor David's Pub.

I first met Anson Funderburgh when my uncle, Doyle Bramhall, was backing up Lightin' Hopkins at The Granada Theater in Dallas when I was 18 years old. Hopkins was playing a country set and Doyle was playing drums like he was backing Bobby Bland. Lightin' stopped the band and kept giving Doyle hell about his playing. I was in the second row and could see he just wanted a click track. Lightin' stopped the band and asked for another drummer. Doyle pointed at me and I very nervously got up there and played a click track where you lay the stick on the snare and tap to the beat. I started when he started and stopped when he stopped. Lightin' was a storyteller and stopped to tell stories often. Then he stopped and looked at me and I thought I did something wrong. My heart was in my throat. Lightin' said, "Now that's a drummer." Anson called me later, and I played in a band he put together called Delta Road in 1973 that led to Anson and The Rockets.

Mr. Conrad was not his real name. He used Conrad from a 1970's detective TV show with William Conrad named *Cannon*. His first name was Theodore with a Greek last name. His father was Greek and Conrad talked like the Sopranos. Mr. Conrad is from

The Excellos on the Blues Cruise in Corpus Christi, Texas, May 1992: Mr. Conrad, guitar; Freddie Walden, drums; and Keith Ferguson, bass
Courtesy of Dutch and Eunice Koontz

The Excellos: Mr. Conrad, David Watson and Keith.
Courtesy of Dutch and Eunice Koontz

Mr. Conrad, David Watson and Keith in The Excellos.

Courtesy of David Watson

Keith posing on a surfboard.
Courtesy of Dutch and Eunice Koontz

Buffalo, New York. Conrad's dream was to move to Austin and play with Keith and Freddie Walden. I met Conrad on Sixth Street during a jam.

We talked and I told him I knew Keith and where he lived. We went to see him that week. Keith was playing local gigs only with several bands. Kathy Murray and The Killowatts. I knew Bobby Arnold from Fireside Recording Studio, so The Excellos did a budget recording. With that cassette tape and Keith's name, I booked an every-Monday-night gig at Babe's Burgers Club in Austin, then Maple Leaf in New Orleans, a Dallas gig, a few San Antonio gigs. The van I bought broke down near Houston. I walked to a phone and called someone to pick up Keith and Mr. C. I had a friend tow me back to Austin and that's where it sat. I did this all at my expense. I had enough and left the band.

Conrad lived in Austin about six months. The band played four months with me and a handful of gigs with Freddie. In this time, we recorded a tape at Pedernales Studio (Willie Nelson's studio) in 1992, and a live recording at KUT radio in Austin.

I feel like I've just started the story. To describe Keith's bass playing is impossible. Watching him, his

Mr. Conrad, Keith and Freddie Walden.
Courtesy of Daniel Schaefer

fingers look sloppy, flailing all over the bass, but the sound made you move and groove. It made my playing much better. Most creative bass lines ever played. I loved him but was uncomfortable and in fear at the same time.

Keith was a target of police in Austin. Cops would hang out around the corner of his house, watching the traffic that went in and out of there. Hanging out on Keith's front porch was a show in itself. The music poured out of there. Many stories told. The house he lived in was a scene out of a '40s movie. Old, wooden floor, rugs, pictures on the wall … was all like an old Billie Holiday movie. He played blues and Mexican records from an old turntable. Upstairs was more modern -- carpeted floors, cabinets sinks and kitchen was modern. Keith kept a switchblade or a long case knife for his own protection. When he took one out of his pocket to clean it, a chill would come over you because you didn't know if he had intent to use it. Then he would slice and apple and eat it. Keith was taken in after a gig we did on Sixth Street when we were loading equipment out. He was bailed out soon, and I never heard anything about it.

I moved to Eureka Springs, Arkansas, about 12 years ago. Jimmy Thackery moved there just after, and I did a gig with him. He had a bass player named Larry Boehmer, who was the Zoo Bar owner in Lincoln, Nebraska. Larry moved there after retiring. We started a band called The Tablerockers. We used various guitar players until we found Jason Davis. Larry knew club owners in the Midwest area and booked us regularly. We also backed up James Harman, Charlie Musselwhite, R.J. Mischo, Magic Slim from Chicago, and others.

David Watson and Keith in The Excellos.
Courtesy of David Watson

Mr. Conrad and Keith on the Blues Cruise.
Courtesy of Dutch and Eunice Koontz

227

Ted Lambros (aka Mr. Conrad)
Interviewed by Detlef Schmidt, March 2012

Guitarist and singer of The Excellos.

I met Keith over the phone, through my old bass player, Joe Skinner, who'd met Keith when the T-Birds played at The Belle Star, a club in Colden, New York, in the '70s. Joe reconnected with Keith over info on a stolen bass he thought may have been Keith's and also told him about me. Joe called Keith and introduced me and we spoke a few times on the phone after that. I told Keith I may visit Austin and said to come by.

So, in the summer of 1990 I went to Austin to visit my friend Phillip 'Modboy' Plyler from L.A. who'd moved back to Austin. I mentioned I'd spoke with Keith and, as it turned out, he knew him from when he lived there in the '70s. We called to see if we could come by the house, Keith said yes, so we went over. This was the first time meeting Keith in person.

We hung out all day and Keith told stories, played some cool records for us, showed us his bass and old photo albums. He seemed very happy to have us come by and want to hang with him. I also played him a live tape of my band (with Joe) in Buffalo. He asked if that was me singing and playing guitar. I said yes, and he said if I ever wanted to come down and play with him, let him know. Great, I thought!

I also met a girl named Linda Gracey, and she took me around and showed me the clubs and introduced me to other players. One night we ended up at The Black Cat, and I got to sit in with Alan Haynes and Tommy Shannon! Wow, I was really starting to dig Austin!

Toward the end of my visit, I ran into James Hinkle, who was playing with Marcia Ball and who I met at a Marcia show in Buffalo the year before. He invited me to come up to Ft. Worth to a show and then hang with him a while. So I rode up with the band in the van, saw the show, got to sit in and stayed with Jimmy a few days, then took the train back home. I had a ball and thought, maybe one day, to move there. I really dug Austin!

So, it came to pass that I was finally divorced and needing a complete change of scene. I called Keith and asked him if he still wanted to do gigs. He said he would. I said I'd be there Wednesday. He said, "I'll be home, bring beer." On Jan. 29, 1992, I stood on his front porch with a 12-pack of Busch beer, back in Austin ready to play.

I'd also contacted Linda Gracey and she introduced me to another guitar player, Keith Bradley, who let me me stay for a time at his apartment just down the road from Keith's house. I also stayed at Ferguson's house for a short while before I moved up to North Austin.

We played what I call the I-35 circuit -- Dallas, San Antonio, Corpus Cristi, Freeport, Galveston, even New Orleans once. We had a regular Monday night at Babe's on Sixth Street, too. I, needless to say, had a ball.

I also felt like I got better as a player just from working with Keith. He never said much in the way of advice or do this or that. But I got the one and only compliment when he turned to me one day at a show and said in that Bogart kind of voice, "Hey, yer gettin' better," as he walked off lighting a Kool. Well, that was all I needed to hear. That made it all worthwhile to me.

I was just some kid from Buffalo with a guitar who could carry a tune, but he accepted me, seemed to like my original songs and choices, and, in his quiet way, encouraged me to be better. It was the best musical year I ever had.

I went home to see my family for Christmas, December '93. When I got there, I found my mom had sold the house (where I had all my stuff, record collection, etc.) and we had to be out in seven days. So, I had to sell everything I owned because I couldn't move it. And at that time, my health started to fail me and I had to go into treatments. So I got stuck back in Buffalo. I called Keith to tell him about this situation and that I couldn't make it back to Austin. I know he was disappointed (as was I) but it couldn't be helped.

I lost track of Keith during this period and, unfortunately, we never reconnected. When I moved to L.A. in '98, I got a call from Ronnie James to tell me of Keith's passing. I was very saddened and wish we could have reconnected before this but life gets in the way, I guess. I'll always be grateful to have played with and encouraged by El Mero Guero -- the one and only Keith Ferguson.

Keith with Liz Henry's Squier Precision bass (note the cowhide under the pickguard).
Courtesy of Liz Henry

Mr. Conrad and Liz Henry and The Excellos (note Liz playing her black '53 Fender Precision bass.
Courtesy of Dutch and Eunice Koontz

Freddie Walden on drums.
Courtesy of Dutch and Eunice Koontz

Freddie and Keith in The Excellos.
Courtesy of Durch and Eunice Koontz

"I also felt like I got better as a player just from working with Keith."
-- Mr. Conrad

Conjunto Music

Daniel Schaefer
Interviewed by Detlef Schmidt, October 2012

Daniel was a professional photographer and good friend of Keith and took some of the classic pictures of Keith of incredible quality. As a close friend, he could get great private photos.

I met Keith when they were recording *Butt Rockin'*. I had my photo studio in the same building. I used to go in the darkroom and print and listen to Mexican radio.

All of a sudden I hear this knocking on the door, and the guy is talking to me in Spanish. I walked out the door of my darkroom and said, "What can I do for you?" He looked at me kind of strange and asked if there is a Mexican guy in there. And I said, "No, I am listening to that."

And so we started talking and he said, "You need to come over to my house." And Keith gave me my education in conjunto music and nortenjo music. I could translate stuff; I was useful to him. I had been living in a commune in Mexico with a bunch of Mexican hippies. We did a lot of things together. We went to clubs that people weren't interested in going to, except me and Keith.

One day, Keith knew that I had some money in my pockets. He told me to get in my car and drive over to South Austin Music. We went in and he grabbed that bajo sexto, gave it to me and said, "Buy this." So I bought the bajo sexto, and then we drove over to Benny Romero's house. He owned a bunch of conjunto bars down at Sixth Street. He owned the Plaza and the Green Spot, just before Sixth Street was Sixth Street. There were only blacks and Mexicans. He told Benny, "Show him the three chords." That's how I got started. I have had two or three bands, and I've made four CDs on my own, and Liz and I played together. Keith just knew what to do with everybody. Playing the bajo sexto is just the joy of my life.

Keith affected everybody's lives in a very dramatic way. He seemed to have a way of doing the right

Above: Keith teaching Daniel how to shine shoes.
Courtesy of Tino Mauricio
Next page: Keith's 40th birthday.
Courtesy of Daniel Schaefer

thing with people -- if you were OK. I used to have a beer in the fridge for Sunday morning, because Keith needed a beer on Sunday morning.

As a kid, he used to go down to New Braunfels in the summers, where his grandmother Effie lived. Effie was great. She took care of Keith. She was kind of a buffer between Keith and Margaret. Margaret was the one that bought all that corner lot in 3402 South Second. First Effie moved there, then Margaret had a house moved over there and took care of Effie.

Keith told me the reason why Clifford Antone and him had fallen out. One day Clifford showed up at

Bajo sexto collection.

Courtesy of Daniel Schaefer

A bajo sexto birthday cake for Keith's 40th.

Courtesy of Daniel Schaefer

Daniel Schaefer and Liz Henry.

Courtesy of Daniel Schaefer

Keith's house with a girl. He was trying to impress this girl, which was really stupid to bring her over to Keith's house. She fell immediately in love with Keith. I don't know what it was, but Keith did something that really pissed Clifford off. Keith told me that this was what really turned Clifford against him.

Bradley Williams and Keith were very good friends. Bradley is an accordion player. He's one of the few white boys who can do it right. I took Bradley over to Keith's house. One of the things that Keith really hated was when the musicians came over to his porch, took their instruments out and played. That would drive him right up the wall. So when I showed up with an accordion player, especially a white boy, Keith was ready to kill me.

Darrell Burnett was another good friend of Keith. He worked for record company. He knew more about blues than almost anybody. He and Keith could discuss stuff that nobody else could, in terms of blues. Los Alegres De Teran was Keith's favorite conjunto band. Tomas Ortiz, bajo sexto and Eugenio Abrego, accordian. We went to see them a couple times. On the photo you can see Keith just fumbling over his heroes at that point.

Here is what Jimmy said at the Memorial: "He taught us how to tuck in our shirts. He taught us how to tie our shoes." You got to have your shoelaces like the Kansas City or Chicago musicians. If you had a pair of Stacy Adams shoes and the laces were criss cross like on tennis shoes, you have to take your shoes off and he would make them right, because those things were important.

If you do look at Stevie's (Ray Vaughan) wardrobe, there is a lot of reminiscence of Keith. Mike Steele and Stevie were real tight. Matter of fact, Stevie lived a while at Mike's house.

> **Keith affected everybody's lives in a very dramatic way. He seemed to have a way of doing the right thing with people -- if you were OK.**
>
> -- Daniel Schaefer

Keith playing a bajo sexto.

Courtesy of Daniel Schaeffer

The cover shot of the *Chronicle* article, after Keith's death, I did the photo on that. Billy Gibbons gave him the guitars. Keith was not impressed by stardom. He was not starstruck.

There were actually two memorials. That was a big memorial with 100 or 200 people. And when we buried Keith's ashes, there were about 20 people there. His ashes were buried in a box that was made by Albert Macias. Bradley was the person who asked Albert to make the box. The Macias family makes the Stadivarius of bajo sextos. Albert's dad, Martin, started the business and Albert's son, George, continues. George has a son whose name I don't know, but it is my understanding that he is also making bajos. So you have four generations of guitar-makers.

Daniel: "It's a guitaron with the Spanish accent on the 'o'. Phonetically -- 'gee (hard 'g' like in 'good') tar own' -- gee-tar-own. Mariachis use it. It's a bass that can be carried around."

Courtesy of Daniel Schaefer

Keith and his heros: Los Alegres De Teran were Keith's favorite conjunto band. Tomas Ortiz, bajo sexto, and Eugenio Abrego, accordion.

Courtesy of Daniel Schaefer

A portrait of Keith.

Courtesy of Daniel Schaefer

Keith in front of his house.

Courtesy of Daniel Schaefer

Keith and an Airline guitar in the backyard of his house.

Holding court at the porch

Gerard Daily
Interviewed by Scott Ferris, 2012

Gerard Daily is a Texas pianist, a good friend of Keith since the Thunderbirds times, and a regular visitor to Keith's house in the '90s.

I first met Keith June 4, 1976. Otis Lewis was playing drums with the Thunderbirds. I played a gig with Freddie Cisneros, Mike Buck and Ray Campi at the Luckenbach World Fair, and then they took my down to Sixth Street and said, "You need to hear these guys."

Apparently, they had known Mike or Freddie from earlier. They played the first set and then came over to the table and hung out. They introduced me and that was when I first met them. They opened for Larry Davis that night, that "Texas Flood" guy. He was incredible that night and there were only six or seven people in the audience. When I first saw Keith, he had that long hair and a bandana around the head. Then I moved to Austin the summer of '77, and a couple of weeks after I moved, I got a call from Mike Buck. He said, "I am playing with the T-Birds now." He had moved down to play with them full time. He would take me by their houses and I looked it up in my diary. I went to Keith's house. I didn't know his last name. Kim was staying with him at that time. We walked in and thought it must be the life of leisure, because it was afternoon and they were just getting up.

They were playing at the Rome Inn on the Blue Mondays to a half-filled place, and then over the next few years it started to get really packed. I remember going to see one of the Fourth of July shows and Billy Gibbons had rented a bus to come up from Houston. And that lady, Ivy, was there because she had been friends with Billy Gibbons and Gretchen Barber, and all of these people from Houston came up. Just like the lyrics to that song "Lowdown In The Streets" -- that was all those people.

Then I had a pair of high-waisted pants made at Ace Custom Tailors downtown Austin. The guy said, "I

Luckenbach World Fair: Mike Buck, drums; Ray Campi, bass/vocals; and Freddie Cisneros, guitar.
Courtesy of Gerard Daily

haven't made one of them." That was a long time ago, pre the swing craze. Mike said, "Keith really dug your pants. He'd like to talk to you some more." So he came up at the end of the show. Keith was always the mysterious one. He would never talk to anybody unless he really liked you. He said, "I really like your pants. Where did you get them?" And we first really got into talk.

We were from San Antonio and Keith had some great stories. His grandmother had worked for a wealthy family there, and he told me that he had seen The Rolling Stones play their second show in the United States. It was at a Teen Fair in Texas in '64 in June and he told me stories. "Oh, I went to see that gig." George Jones was opening for the Stones.

Then the T-Birds were doing tours and Mike Buck left the band, and I saw him less and less. Then I moved up to Fort Worth to play with Johnny Reno. We played at a party -- James Brown was playing there and the Thunderbirds. Doyle Bramhall was playing with us, and Keith and Jimmie stood and watched us. It was the weekend that Mike Buck was going to get married and Keith said, "Do you want to ride down in the bus with us and go to the wedding." But I had to do something else.

I remember when we played in Houston with Reno, Billy Gibbons would come backstage because he knew Doyle. He couldn't sit in because of that con-

Margaret Ferguson and grandmother Effie.
Courtesy of Daniel Schaefer

Keith and his friend Rollo Banks in Rollo's car.
Courtesy of Daniel Schaefer

tract thing with Bill Ham, but he would always come. You can tell he and Keith were all long-time buddies. I remember that Keith used to tell me that he did some gigs with Rocky Hill early on.

When I moved back to Austin in 1990, I started going over to his house. That's where we really started hanging out. He had quit the T-Birds, and I think he was already out of The Tail Gators by then, too. When he needed a ride or beer, I would go over and take him around.

I played a gig or two with him. There was an Italian restaurant that needed a house band, somewhere in South Austin, and I played piano with them.

I got to meet all the people that were over at his house. I got to meet Hector (Watt), and Mike Steele was always there, and there were people from Houston that would often show up. Carlos was there when he could make it and Daniel Schaeffer. There was one guy that was an old club owner of The South Door.

He was an 18-wheel truck driver and he would show up and park his wheels up there. You would never know who would show up.

People who were touring through, that's where they would go before the gig or after the gig. Or they were just visiting. I remember seeing James Harman there a couple of times. Everybody came to Keith; he never went to you. You either had to show up at his house or you went somewhere and you had to take him. He always bought Busch, some low-dollar beer. And you had to bring some beer over. If you want to come visit, you had to bring presents.

Tony Dukes is the guy who hunted up vintage guitars for people and who used to go hunting with Ted Nugent. Tony also came by.

Keith was pals with Gary Scanlan, one of the early partners of the Vulcan Gas Company. They would always come over and talk about that stuff. I don't know if they knew Keith from Houston from the early days. So there were always people dropping by. Keith rented out his upstairs. There was a couple people living there. Dan Forte, Hook Herrera, Corey Keller. He was a big gecko guy. He loved to see shows on reptiles. He would always call people up and go, "Hey, listen what is on *National Geographic* channel."

Keith did have a film that someone took of him and Johnny Winter, back in 1968 or 1969. It was pretty weird. It was Keith, Johnny and some topless hippie chick. I don't remember if everyone was nude or just the hippie chick. I remember he found the footage one day under his bed. It had been taken with some kind of movie camera that used a speed that wasn't in use anymore. People had to look all over, and the only movie projector we could find using that speed was the old ones school districts used to use to show film strips and educational films with, like "Don't Drink and Drive" or "How to Recognize Venereal Diseases". They tried to get the film transferred to video, and I saw about 10 minutes of it. It was really bizarre, and Keith just couldn't stop laughing. There was Johnny Winter combing his hair and scratching himself and this chick was lying across their legs. I have no idea who filmed it or why or where the video ended up after Keith died.

I asked Keith about Johnny Winter, and he said, "We were the only guys we knew that were into lowdown blues. He told me stories that when Johnny Winter had moved to New York, Keith would go up and visit

The backyard of Keith's house and the steps to the little roof apartment that he used to rent to friends.

A recent shot of Liz Henry sitting on the porch, showing how it currently looks.

him and hang out at The Scene, that club up there. He would hang with the band because he knew them all real well. And, of course, they would hang out at the club because that belonged to their manager.

One of the bands that Keith met at The Scene club was Lothar and The Hand People. They were one of the first bands to use theremins and early electronic instruments. I had their two albums on Capitol Records. Keith thought that was very funny because not too many blues fans also had albums by Lothar and The Hand People. When he found out I had them, he then started telling me stories about seeing them live in New York.

Somewhere in an interview with Johnny Winter, Johnny mentioned that Keith and he were married at the same time in the '60s. I asked Keith, "Who were you married to?" And he claimed he couldn't remember her name.

The three houses on the corner that Keith's mom bought were for Keith, Margaret and Effie, Keith's grandmother. He always got along great with the grandmother. The grandma lived on the corner and the mom in that other building. They had a great relationship. She loved Keith for what he was, no matter what he was. Margaret would always come up with ways to stop him being a junkie, but it was never effective. I used to take Keith to see the grandmother when she was moved into the care facility. I used to work nights at the Municipal Court in Austin and I would go over to see Keith in the morning sometimes. He would often sit out on the front porch and feel horrible, going through heroin withdrawal. Then the door would open at Keith grandmother's house and she would come walking across the lawn

in a robe and slippers, old and half-blind, and come up and give Keith a $20 bill and talk to him a little bit. And then Keith would wait until she was back in her house and then go call his connection. Sometimes I would have to drive him, or sometimes the connection would come over, but in a little bit Keith would be feeling much better. He loved his grandmother a lot, just because she was so nonjudgmental and loving.

We opened up a show for The Tail Gators in Dallas. They played really loud. They never stayed overnight. They always drove home right after the gig. When Keith did have to stay somewhere overnight, he was not a happy camper -- and you didn't want to be around him when he was not a happy camper. I remember Keith did a lot of pickup gigs on Sixth Street. I saw him play with Kathy Murray for a while. I always helped to get his equipment out because I had a station wagon, and I'd come back at the end of the night to pick them up.

Keith had told me that he had met Mike Ledbetter, the English blues writer, at the record store in Houston. Keith told me some stories about meeting Chris Strachwitz; it was like '60 or '61. I had gone to California in the mid '70s and had gone to Downhome Music, which Chris Strachwitz ran, and he talked to me about who I knew in Austin. Then we talked about Keith the whole time. Keith also listened to that conjunto music, and he and Chris were buying that stuff. Keith would hook him up with the record company owners. He had a fabulous collection of Mexican music.

The dad worked at a record store named Daily's. He was like the salesman there. But there also was a big

Keith displaying a birthday cake.

Courtesy of Liz Henry

distributorship, and his dad had to listen to all kinds of music. I had met his dad for a couple of times, and I had always heard stories that Keith and his dad never got along, but that was as far as from the truth as it could be. I remember coming over there one day and asking, "Who is this old guy talking to Keith?" They were all laughing me up. "It's my dad."

When his dad died a few years later, he left him his stereo and his record collection. His dad had some fabulous classical records and stuff. I remember taking them with Keith around to Antone's and some other places to sell the records, and they were worth some money. Keith's dad might have stayed a couple of days in Keith's house in the front room. If they didn't like each other, they surely hit it well.

His grandmother had lived in San Antonio, and Keith had spent the summer down there. Conjunto music is on the radio down there all the time, so maybe this was how he got into it. He had known a couple of guys down there; one was a guy from a radio station, a deejay. I was over at his house and the guys would show up. They were conjunto musicians and said, "We're playing a show with Flaco Jimenez tonight." So they knew him from somewhere. He definitely was one of the few white guys who was listening to that stuff. He had a huge collection, under the bed and all over. It was tons of records. He had a left-handed bajo sexto made for him. He was going to make a company in Mexico to make bajo sextos and import them, but that never happened.

A couple of times, the guys from Los Lobos came to his place. The songs that won them the Grammys were the songs he told them to learn and to play. It was either the first EP or *How Will The Wolf Survive?*, and Keith was the one who told them to play the songs. There was a guy called Mouse, who was the

road guy from East L.A., and he would always hang around Keith when they were in town.

When Keith died, and they had that benefit at Antone's. There were a couple of big Hispanic bandleaders who played gigs there.

When Bradley J. Williams showed up, Keith took him around and told them, "Hey, this guy is cool." Keith told him, "When you going to play this stuff? You don't need to be in San Fransisco, you need to be in Austin. Here, you can play gigs with conjunto bands and Cajun bands."

I remember going to some conjunto gigs with Keith and Daniel. These were Sunday afternoon gigs, and we were definitely the only white boys there. They were always glad to see him there. Daniel has been in there forever and knew all the guys personally from taking their pictures. Keith was always playing the bajo sextos around the house. You don't see many white guys with a bajo sexto playing around.

I was not there when those guitars from Billy Gibbons arrived, just a couple of days later. Keith would rather play his old Fender bass. It was two of them, I think, a six-string guitar and a bass. And they went to the pawn shop within a week or so.

I remember taking him down to the pawn shops. He always used to go to Doc Holliday down on Lamar. He knew the guy there because they were both musicians. Sometime when I was down there, they said, "Hey, have Keith call me because I have something for him." Then Keith would say, "Take me over there." Then they would talk about old guitars and he would ask Keith what he would think of this bass or whatever. There were a couple of pawn shops. They all knew him and sometimes they would call and say, "We got something in."

I was over there when he bought that Harmony bass. He really was excited over this one. I heard the story that he was going to sell it and Sean Ono, the son of John Lennon, bought it.

I remember when he got the cowhide, it really stank. He told me that when it got really hot, it would really stink. So you can imagine the cowhide bass in his gig bag along with his socks. It's like all that other stuff -- as soon as he did it, people saw it and started to do it themselves. Like the see-through shirts and the bandana.

I am a keyboard player, not a bass player. I was doing some home recording and needed a bass. The opportunity to buy it (the cowhide bass) from Mark Hickman came up and I had some extra cash at the time. I figured it was better to keep it in the family of Texas musicians, so to speak, rather than let some lawyer or Japanese businessman buy it and have it wander off, never to be seen again. I think Keith used it on some recordings or maybe a gig or two. At one point, the pickup was starting to fail so he took it to some repairman in Austin who put in a different pickup. I think he just did that as a favor to Keith because I didn't pay for it. I don't know who Keith was playing with back then; I don't think it was anyone full time. He only wanted to play around town or in Texas then. He didn't want to do any trips overnight.

I was once over at Keith's and I brought the movie *Jimi Plays Berkeley*, and you can see Keith in the audience. Keith would go, "That's me, right there." He always got a chuckle out of it when I would bring it over to watch. He had great stories of dodging the riot police and the tear gas to get to the hall. Keith is seen for only one or two seconds, so here are some guidelines on how to find him. He is seen in the song "Voodoo Child". (Get out your stopwatch.) Jimi says, "Thank you and goodnight", and immediately starts playing. About 4:28 from that point, there is a shot of some people sitting on the stage, including a girl with a shaved head. At around 4:49, Jimi starts singing again. (Get ready.) Around 5:17 or so, there is a crowd shot. A black girl with sunglasses and short hair is in front of Keith. She moves her head out of the way and there is Keith in profile. The camera does a close-up on Keith for a second.

I saw that letter that Stevie (Ray Vaughan) wrote him from the rehab. It was on Keith's refrigerator in a little plastic display thing with a magnet to hold it. Last time I saw Tommy Shannon, he was over at Keith's house. He had brought over a couple of basses for Keith to borrow, and they actually kept in touch. Keith told me when Stevie came home and found his wife gone and his furniture gone, he called Keith

Keith with an Airline guitar on the porch of his house.

Courtesy of Daniel Schaefer

and Keith told him to come over to calm down. Keith said, "I had to calm that boy down." Keith went up to Stevie's funeral. I think he went up with Larry Davis and somebody else. I don't know who drove them.

Keith had a massive record collection, and he was always pullin' out some stuff that you had never heard or you would think it was ridiculous. "Listen to this, this is great." He was like a deejay and he had bizarre records, like a midget bass player in a Mexican band. When CDs were coming out, he would really go for them, because of all the alternate versions you could get on them.

"Everybody came to Keith; he never went to you. You either had to show up at his house or you went somewhere and you had to take him."
-- Gerard Daily

From fans to friends

Eunice Koontz
Interviewed by Detlef Schmidt, 2011

Being 82 years old when I interviewed her, Eunice is still a huge blues fan. She and her husband, Dutch, went out to concerts three or four nights weekly in Austin. Both were friends to Keith, and she had some great stories to tell.

When we were first married in 1950, we listened to the radio about four o'clock in the morning because we had to get up early. The only station that was on was a black station, and they played the blues and we just loved it.

We went out to a lot of live music, and one of our favourite bands at that time was The Little French Band with D'Jarma Garnier and Daniel Santo, and Ponty and Keith. Keith was a very interesting person. I saw that he was unique. We wanted to get to know him, but it was very hard. We tried to get him to come to our house to dinner, but he couldn't do it. We had to go to a kind of intuition where he could find out that he could trust us. He trusted us then and we became good friends.

One time Keith got in trouble with the IRS, the income tax, and they were checking out the form he filed. He was scared to death. An authority figure was on his trail, so he called my husband. So we made some phone calls to see how he should proceed, because he didn't know. So my husband went with him to the federal courthouse and settled things. Things went very well. After that, we met some friends of Keith and they said to my husband, "Oh, you were the one that took him to court."

My husband and I went to a mall that had a young artist who did T-shirts and we wanted to have him make a T-shirt for Keith. So to make it, we had to give him a book that was pretty valuable. We got the book back and we got the T-shirt. It's very realistic (image of a lizard on the right shoulder).

First time we went to the Conjunto Fest in San Antonio with Keith, he introduced me to Chris Strachwitz. At that time I didn't know who he was; I

Eunice: "Liz and Keith and my husband and I on our front porch. He dressed very well, very unusual, clean, neat."

Courtesy of Dutch and Eunice Koontz

An old shot from Keith's California days that he used as an autograph photo.

Courtesy of Dutch and Eunice Koontz

Chris Strachwitz, owner of Arhoolie Records:

Keith, he was a very sweet and nice guy who was a fellow fan of Mexican border music and helped me become aware of and find some very important records, like "Rinches de Texas" on ORO Records -- and some on Del Valle. He was a good friend for being interested in Mexican music. He had a number of items he told me about which were especially important. He also told me about the stash of 78s in the basement of a store in San Antonio, in Rangel's basement -- which, unfortunately, I never got to until after the man's death and when the records were literally dumped in the back of his house. And Salome Gutierrez of DLB Records rescued the records and did bring in quite a few into his shop -- including Decca 7000s -- Peetie Wheatstraw and such!I got a lot of blues records on Decca, and Blue Bird, I think. Those were the days when 78s were still floating around, also 45s but I neglected them since they were still in use and not so cheap! I think his father had been a salesman for records and that is how Keith had found out about the stash in Rangel's basement.

Arhoolie Records Story by Chris Strachwitz

On November 3, 1960, the first Arhoolie LP arrived from the pressing plant: 250 copies of Mance Lipscomb's *Texas Sharecropper and Songster*. I had recorded Mance Lipscomb, the remarkable songster and guitarist from Navasota, Texas, during my first extensive trip to Texas, Mississippi and Louisiana in the summer of 1960. Mack McCormick, who had introduced me to my idol, Lightnin' Hopkins, in Houston the previous summer, was a very informed and generous host and also came up with the name Arhoolie for my new record label. I decided to start a record company, primarily to capture Lightnin' Hopkins at his inventive best: live, at the beer joints where I heard him the previous summer.

In the summer of 1960, I met up with British blues aficionado, author and vernacular architecture scholar Paul Oliver and his wife, Valerie, at the legendary Peabody Hotel in Memphis, Tennessee. Paul was making this trip, his first to the USA, to produce a series of radio programs to be broadcast by the BBC, and interviewing historic blues musicians at the source was a major goal of his trip. Paul had sent me in advance a list of names of blues singers who had recorded in Dallas and Fort Worth in the 1920s and '30s, hoping I would perhaps do a little research on my way to Texas from the West Coast. Driving with Bob Pinson (now of the Country Music Foundation Library) into Texas, we both made many inquiries which led to meeting Lil' Son Jackson and Black Ace, a singer who accompanied himself on a National steel guitar. With Mack McCormick, I was fortunate to meet and record the remarkable Mance Lipscomb and later on the return trip to the West Coast with Paul. We also met Alex Moore in Dallas, an extraordinary character and pianist from the early era in blues history, as well as many other artists in Texas, Louisiana and Mississippi.

By the late 1960s, The Rolling Stones helped to boost the interest in blues all over the world, and sales for real blues records have continued to climb ever since. Fred McDowell was a remarkable blues singer and slide guitarist from Como, Mississippi, who had been introduced to the world by Alan Lomax via several incredible cuts on an Atlantic LP. After several LPs of Fred's music on Arhoolie, The Rolling Stones put his version of "You Gotta Move" on their *Sticky Fingers* album.

In February of 1964, my idol, Lightnin' Hopkins, introduced me to one of his wife's cousins, Clifton Chenier, at a little beer joint in Houston, and I recorded our first session the very next day! Over the years, Clifton's amazing zydeco music proved to be a steady seller for Arhoolie. Another extraordinary accordion player, Flaco Jiménez from San Antonio, Texas, also became a good seller for Arhoolie and won us a Grammy with the album *Ay Te Dejo En San Antonio*.

Taken from http://www.arhoolie.com/. Used with permission of Chris Strachwitz.

since learned. He knew Keith very well.

Keith got some guitar from Mexico and he wanted us to come over and see it. The two of us came over and it was beautiful, inlaid wood, gorgeous. And I said, "This would look wonderful on a wall." Well, that was not the thing to say. "You should never hang a guitar on the wall, it should be played," Keith replied.

They played on a blues cruise out of Corpus Christi. They would go out on the ship when it was still light, and they would come back when it was dark.

David Watson, Eunice and Keith in San Antonio at the Conjunto Fest, May 1994.

Courtesy of Dutch and Eunice Koontz

Mike Steele: "Keith was in the band for a couple of years and it consisted of Stretch Williams on guitar, Keith on bass, and Gilbert Gonzales on drums. Stretch and Gilbert had day jobs so the band didn't play on a regular basis, just as their time and schedules permitted. They were a great trio and Stretch was a really good slide player, often using a beer bottle or whiskey bottle to play slide."

Courtesy of Mike Steele

The very realistic T-shirt with a hand-painted lizard (note Eunice's record collection of blues and jazz).

Courtesy of Dutch and Eunice Koontz

Pickup gigs for Keith in *The Austin Chronicle*:

- Aztec Pimps in Emo's (featuring Hunt Sales, Will Sexton and Keith Ferguson)
- At Joe's Generic Bar, Hook Herrera featuring guitarist Alan Haynes, bassist Keith Ferguson and drummer Tony Voleman.
- Keith Ferguson play at Joe's Generic Bar with the Roadaires.
- Stretch Williams and Keith Ferguson are at Babe's.

The San Antonio Conjunto Fest where Dutch and Eunice went together with Keith in 1992.

Courtesy of Dutch and Eunice Koontz

The Little French Band

Ponty Bone
Interviewed by Detlef Schmidt, 2011

Ponty Bone is an authentic Texas accordion king. For two decades, Bone has led his band, The Squeezetones, to popularity throughout the Southwest, the rest of America and across Europe. Over seven prior years with Joe Ely, he helped change the face of country music. He has shared the stage and studio with such varied musicians as punk rock stars The Clash, Tom Petty & The Heartbreakers, fellow Texas accordion king Flaco Jimenez, country-rock superstar Linda Ronstadt and English rock legend Ronnie Lane.

Painting of The Little French Band.
Courtesy of Keith Ferguson Collection

He (Keith) was a great character who liked me from the start and always admired my accordion playing. Once he came to Lubbock when I was still living there in the '70s. He wanted to be taken to a local Mexican record store, and I left him there while I attended to a couple of other things. When I came back, he was -- despite his attire at that time, which included very long hair, many tattoos, much cologne and just a bigger-than-life persona -- in a heated conversation with the owner, in Spanish, about all the different recording studios around Texas where all the latest albums had been cut.

The Little French Band at Griswald's Restaurant, 1996.

Courtesy of Dutch and Eunice Koontz

Another time, much later, I was playing in a band which included D'Jalma Garnier on fiddle, Dan Del Santo on guitar, me and Keith. There came a time when we scheduled a rehearsal at Dan's house to go over some different material. Neither Dan, nor Keith or I, wanted to learn yet another version of a song which we already knew, preferring "more" rather than "complete". D'Jalma took us to task, noting that our dragging our feet on this issue was like "urinating on his grandfather's (a creole fiddler) grave". Keith, Dan and I just rolled our eyes.

The memorial for Keith was huge -- lots of us meeting one another for the first time; lots of us already musical friends.

The Little French Band: D'Jalma Garnier, fiddle; Dan Del Santo, guitar; Ponty Bone, accordion; and Keith Ferguson, bass.

Courtesy of Dutch and Eunice Koontz

Get a monkey or move to Texas

Notes by Bradley Williams, 2014

I have lived in Austin, Texas since 1993. I am originally from Saginaw, Michigan. Over the last 30 years, I've moved around the United States, living in the San Francisco Bay Area for 12 years, Southeast Alaska, South Florida ... mostly working in the seafood business and on fishing boats. I didn't play the accordion until I was 25 years old. I played other instruments before that -- trumpet, mandolin and guitar. I also play bajo sexto, cuatro, Chemnitzer concertina and bass. I am currently active in making music with Conjunto Los Pinkys, Susan Torres y Conjunto Clemencia, The Fabulous Polkasonics (Polish-American) and The Gulf Coast Playboys (Cajun).

While living in Berkeley, I heard Cajun and Tex-Mex music and also met Flaco Jimenez and his conjunto. I was already playing bluegrass and old-timey music on the mandolin and singing. I had an affinity for dance music and loved accordion music. I purchased a button accordion in 1986, began to teach myself to play and soon found myself in a folk-rock band in San Francisco called The Movie Stars.

In 1992, I came to Austin for SXSW and was busking on the street where I met filmmaker Lee Daniel and Keith's friend, Daniel Schaefer. Daniel took me over to the front porch of Keith's house on South Second Street and introduced me to the man I only knew from the picture on the *Butt Rockin'* album cover. With an accordion strapped on and feeling a little nervous, I played some polkas for him and we immediately became friends.

After that trip to Austin, I was going back to California with thoughts of returning to Texas. I had some problems with booking my band members with the original Los Pinkys there, and I really liked Austin. I wanted to be around Tejano music, lots of available players and be able to learn more about the music. So, I remember when I called Keith and told him about my situation. I asked him if he wanted to "help me out" on bass when I came down to Texas again, and he said that he'll do it, or that he'll find someone

Bradley Williams.

Courtesy of Daniel Schaefer

else to do it. And that was how it started. He (and Daniel Schaefer) started spreading the word.

I never had problems in finding musicians from that day I moved to Austin. Over the phone, he gave me the encouragement to move here. Doug Sahm sings "If you wanna live in Texas, you gotta have a whole lotta soul." I took that line to heart. His advice to me and my accordion dreams: "Get yourself a monkey and a tin cup OR move to Texas." He always was a sweet person to me. He gave me career advice and shared his love for music, tips on how to dress, how much you should ask for a gig. He always told me that I was worth a lot more than I thought because of all the different things I could do as a musician. I hired him to play with Conjunto Los Pinkys one time. He played it all perfect. At the end of the show, we always played a 6/8 huapango. To the surprise of our drummer and the rest of the band, Keith nailed it! He was a great bass player -- and dancer, too.

I really think his contribution to the music scene was much bigger than just being a musician and beyond being a bass player in The Fabulous Thunderbirds. From his front porch, I think he helped people in their careers, helped make them look good, make them sound good, picked the songs and material for them. He knew how to make you a better person and most of all, he always remembered what you liked and knew what was perfect for you. Keith always energized me and made me feel special. Daniel Schaefer also was a great help in starting a career for me in Texas. Without Keith and Daniel, it never would have happened. Period.

After a few years playing in Austin, it seemed everyone in my circle played with Keith or knew Keith. Many of the musicians that later played with me in The Gulf Coast Playboys, even musicians from Port Arthur and Louisiana (Carlos Barbosa, Bruce Lamb and Grady Pinkerton, Jr.) knew him from the T-Birds days. The original bass player, Danny Turansky, was using Keith's cowhide Fender Precision bass when we started the band. It was a good luck charm!

I got to know his mother, Margaret, after he passed, I soon realized where Keith got a lot of his wit, intelligence, good manners and kindness. It was a pleasure to meet her and see how much influence she had on his upbringing. She made a museum, a room in Keith's house that had photos, objects and drawings he did as a child and a teenager. He was a very creative person and a good artist.

When I met Keith, he was post-Thunderbirds and playing with The Solid Senders on Sixth Street. We never talked about the Thunderbirds very much. I didn't know him as the Thunderbirds bass player. Lucky for me, he was a guy that lived in my South Austin neighborhood. I think pretty often of Keith. He was a big influence on me, and I feel fortunate to have known him and his friends.

Ralph Ritchie
Interviewed by Detlef Schmidt, August 29, 2011

Ralph was Keith's closest non-musician friend.

I am originally from Chicago. I lived in Keith's neighbourhood. A friend of mine took me over to Keith's porch to drink some beers. He always liked Busch beer. So we started to get to know each other. After I had some troubles with my girlfriend at that time, and my sister died, Keith was very nice to me and said, "I will stay your friend."

I remember coming over to Keith's and Johnny Winter sitting in the living room. Another time, Billy Gibbons signed a dollar note for me with a funny drawing. I also remember Los Lobos being on the front porch; there were some of Keith's female friends there. Los Lobos were treated like they would be at home. He really liked The Tail Gators. He said, "I envy bands when they only have to divide the money through three musicians."

After Keith's death, Margaret gave me some of Keith's ashes. I put it in an hourglass. When I did so, I discovered a little metal thing with a number on it. That's what they do put on people's toes to identify them. Later, after Margaret had recovered a little, I said to her, "You must have given me the feet." We both laughed. Keith would have liked that morbid humor.

Ralph Ritchie with the hourglass. *Courtesy of Daniel Schaefer*

Living with Keith

Keith playing Liz Henry's '53 Fender Precision.
Courtesy of Liz Henry

Keith and Liz Henry.
Courtesy of Liz Henry

Liz Henry
Interviewed by Detlef Schmidt, October 2011

Liz Henry lived in Keith's house from 1991-1996. She began to play bass and has a deep insight and knowledge of his basses and amps.

I moved back to Austin in 1989, and early in 1990, I ran into a friend of mine, Mike Farmer, from whom I used to rent a room when I was going to the University of Texas in the late '60s. Mike was the person who first handed me a bass. Not only had I never touched one before, I couldn't even spell bass -- and from the first thump, I was hooked. There was one string for each finger, and I just loved the sound. I had to have a bass immediately, so I went and rented a bass and an amp from Rock N Roll Rentals and never looked back. Shortly thereafter, my next door neighbor, Myrna, told me, "Now, if you're going to be a bass player, you need to go hear Keith Ferguson. He's as good as it gets." Right after that, this guy who was installing an A/C for Myrna -- he was also a bass player himself -- introduced me to Keith. Well, we hit it off from the very first.

Keith and I had a lot of really fundamental things in common: We were within five months of being the same age. Both of us were only children, which is a bigger deal than one might think. Like, Keith was the brother I would have always wanted to have. Both of us had been married and divorced. Neither one of us had any children, by choice. And so forth. Anyway, we spent the next six or eight months getting acquainted, primarily on the telephone. It used to be so cool. Keith would call me with some hysterically funny joke that Mike Steele had just told him, and we'd both just laugh and laugh and laugh. One of the things that I've always liked best about Mike Steele is that he really knows how to tell a joke right and he always knows the latest ones. So, when Mike would hear a new joke, he'd call and tell it to Keith who would then immediately call and tell it to me. Although Keith had a wonderful sense of humor, a very dry wit, and very funny, he couldn't tell a joke worth a damn. That's why he'd have to call me right away, before he'd had a chance to forget exactly how the joke was supposed to go, so he could still tell it so it would be funny.

Towards the end of 1990 or early 1991, they raised the rent on the apartment in which I was living and I had to move. Keith said if I needed somewhere to stay while l looked for somewhere else to live, I could come stay with him as he had an extra room that no one was living in. So, of course, I took him up on his offer. After a couple of months, Keith said, "You know, I really like having you here, so if you want to stay, that's cool," and I lived there for the better part of the next five years. When Keith told me this, I was sitting at the table in the kitchen and he was across the room, kind of bent over, with the door open and his head stuck in the refrigerator so he wouldn't have to look at me while he said it.

When I first moved in with Keith, he had cable for his TV and every Saturday night was *Headbangers Ball*. And we religiously watched *Headbangers Ball*. Once upon a time, right after the final days of the T-Birds, Keith developed a small bald spot on the top of his head. He attributed it to nerves and allowed as to how he heard that getting the bald spot tattooed would make the hair grow back. So, he had this nice, life-sized blue eye tattooed on the top of his head. And yes, the hair grew back.

Danny Turansky is a dear friend and a really good bass player. He sold me my '53 P bass. He sold Erin her bass, I believe, and he owns Keith's '56 P bass, tobacco sunburst with cowhide under the pickguard that Keith played mostly in The Tail Gators, I think. I've got at least one picture of him playing my '53. He'd use it one night then the next night I'd have a gig and have to restring it right-handed. Then he'd have a gig the night after that and I'd have to restring it left-handed. And then the night after that ... let me tell you, I got real good at restringing basses.

Keith almost never used anything but GHS Brite Flats, long scale. He had to have long scale so they'd be long enough when he'd flip the bass over and re-string it left-handed. He played flat wounds because he didn't like the way round wound strings sounded ("If you need more punch, just play closer to the bridge."), and because round wound strings were too hard on fingers and frets. They just didn't feel as good as flat wound strings. One of the multitude of perks of living at Keith's was never having to buy bass

Keith playing the customized left-handed Fender Precision.

Courtesy of Liz Henry

strings. Periodically, Tommy Shannon would stop by and present Keith with a fist full of sets of strings, and Keith would very kindly pass a set of strings on to me. Keith didn't believe in changing strings. He'd say, "When they break, change 'em." And as hard as he played, he'd break strings more often than most. Also, I don't think flat wound strings get as groaty as fast as round wound strings do.

Once upon a time, Keith acquired a left-handed Fender Precision, tobacco sunburst, about a '62, if memory serves. He got it about the same time that I got my Fender Squire and decided that we needed to "tart them up" -- decorate them so they'd be unique. Gino, I think it was his name, had given Keith this cowhide-like suitcase or satchel sort of thing, and I got my friend, Mike Farmer, to make us two clear pickguards. Then I cut out pieces of the cowhide so they'd fit under the pickguards, and presto, cool basses!

I think Keith got the left-handed bass from Perry Petroni from Pittsburgh or Philadelphia or some-

Keith playing a reissue Fender '51 Precision.
Courtesy of Liz Henry

where like that, I think. Well, Keith never really liked that bass. He said the left-handed bass "just didn't feel right." So, about that time, it dawned on me what a fabulous opportunity I had to find out what playing a right-handed bass flipped over felt like to Keith. He let me restring it right-handed, and it made all the difference in the world. It was just amazing. All of a sudden the bass was balanced the way a bass should be, like whatever angle you put the bass at, it stayed where you put it -- where one didn't have to like support the neck with your fretting hand to keep it from slipping down. I was totally blown away with this revelation, but I couldn't get anyone else excited about it. I liked the way it felt so much that I moved the strap nut from the top lobe on my bass to the bottom lobe, and I love it like that.

The only other thing I've done different on my bass was to restring it with real heavy gauge flat wound strings and then tune it down to B. It's just like a five-string except it only has four strings; it doesn't have a G string. The only time I miss it is if I'm trying to read music, and that doesn't happen very often.

I'd hear somebody playing bass and think to myself, "Wow, they sound like they're getting down as low as Keith used to," and then I'd realize they were playing a five-string. I thoroughly enjoy having my bass tuned that way -- on the occasions that it's the thing to do. It's so much fun to be able to just romp down on that low B. It's also handy like when I'm playing with Daniel Schaeffer as he does lots of stuff in F, and it's real handy where it comes on the fingerboard with that tuning.

Keith did an album with Basile Kaliopolus, *El Grecco*. It's one of my favorites, if a trifle strange. The only copy I have of it is a cassette, which doesn't do it justice. Mike Steele has a CD of it. Keith did also work with the D'Jalma Garnier French Band. They were wonderful. I have a copy of a radio show they did.

Eunice is another of the multitude of people I met through Keith who has become a dearly beloved friend. She and her husband, Dutch, who died a couple of years ago, were music fans of international renown. They'd been retired for ages and went out to hear music three or four nights a week. They met Keith and then I met them, and they became dear fans and dear friends. Anyway, if memory serves, they videotaped a bunch of Keith's gigs, with several different bands.

That bass Keith bought for Angela Strehli -- they were out in California that time, then Angela had this bass. Then there is a big blank in the time. Keith had a Harmony bass and it looked almost the same as this bass. He did some recording for Lewis with it. Then Lewis said, "I have something for you," and he had this bass. And he goes "here" and Keith recognized it immediately. I think Keith played it then on the Lewis Cowdrey album. It's a Bruno Conquerer bass, made in Japan. The only other Bruno I have ever seen is Don Leady has a Bruno guitar.

My '53 Fender Precision bass -- the neck is a '53 neck and it's got Seymour Duncan hot pickups, fat frets and once had a broken neck, which is now fixed again. The pots are not original, too. But I think I have the original ones somewhere under the bed in a suitcase. The pickguard is a later one. By closer inspection we found out that the body most likely is a '53 body that was contoured to have the body feeling from a '54 contoured bass, then painted black. The serial number is 1287.

Keith also got a '51 Fender reissue, and it looked

right and it played right. He really liked it, and sounded great playing it. The only problem with it was that the pickguard stank. It smelled like cat piss. When he opened the case, it knocked you out. This would have been about 1994. He goes, "Maybe that's why they call them Pee bass." He played it for a pretty good while. Then he got it customized with gold hologram paper, pickguard and the headstock. When he'd be playing, the light would hit that hologram stuff and it would just take him into another dimension.

His Harmony bass had white binding and it just drove him nuts, so I took black electrical tape down on both sides of the neck. And when he got ready to sell it, the buyer said, "It's a shame it doesn't have the white binding, and I said, "It does," and took off the tape.

This is the last amp Keith owned. He rented it from Rock N Roll Rentals, and then he went to pay his rent on it and they said we don't own it anymore -- the rent is already paid for. And Keith said, "OK." He liked it because it was compact, easy to tow around and pretty loud.

Keith didn't have the patience to teach, but he showed me how to use my bass as a weapon without getting it out of tune.

Keith was banned from Antone's, probably about the same time he got fired from the Thunderbirds. One of the theories of a reason is that Clifford came with a girlfriend to Keith's house; she saw Keith and didn't want anything from Clifford anymore. It went so far that when Clifford reissued the "Picture of the Blues" book about Antone's, that it didn't have Keith on the cover anymore. The original version had Keith on the cover.

It took years before Keith would set foot in Antone's, and finally The Paladins were coming to town -- and they just worshipped Keith -- and said, "We are going to Antone's tonight." Keith said, "I don't know this place." And then Dave Gonzales said, "Oh, fuck this shit," and "Come on." And Keith said, "Fine." And then we went to Antone's and had no problems and had a good time. I guess a couple of times Keith went to Antone's while I knew him.

His interaction with fans or people that came to show homage, he was at his best. He rewarded them so much for liking him. He was so gracious with them.

Keith playing an archtop guitar backstage.
Courtesy of Angela Strehli

Keith and his refinished '52 with the T-Birds.
Courtesy of Liz Henry

"Keith didn't believe in changing strings. He'd say, 'When they break, change 'em.'"
-- Liz Henry

Above left: The Bruno semi-accoustic bass that Keith gave as a present to Angela Strehli and later was given back to Keith by Lewis Cowdrey. Above right: Liz Henry's '53 Fender Precision.

Above left: Keith's last bass amp. Above right: Liz playing with The Solid Senders.

Courtesy of Liz Henry

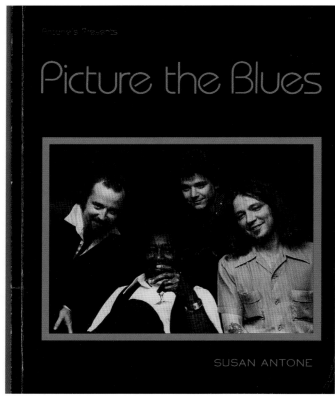

Above left: Liz holding her '53 Fender Precision. Above right: The version of the photo book by Susan Antone with Keith (and Kim, Jimmie and Muddy Waters).[13]

Keith playing in the Continental Club in Austin, 1991.

Courtesy of Eunice and Dutch Koontz

The Solid Senders

Spencer Thomas
Interviewed by Craig Higgins, 2008

Spencer Thomas was the lead singer for the Austin band The Solid Senders, and their last bass player was Keith Ferguson. Spencer currently lives in Kyle, Texas, where he and his wife own and operate a bakery and restaurant called the Texas Pie Company.

Solid Senders

Everything's gonna be allright

Album cover of The Solid Senders published by a Netherland label.
© Tramp Records; Courtesy of Tino Mauricio

I met Keith after all that stuff with the T-Birds happened. He was in The Tail Gators by the time I really got to see him at anything other than at a distance on a huge stage. It was like everybody divided up, either pro-Keith or anti- Keith, and it seemed like the Antone's school was anti-Keith. The Solid Senders never played an Antone's gig after Keith joined the band. I never really talked to Keith about what happened with the T-Birds, but he seemed bitter about things. He occasionally talked about places they'd play and people he knew. He used to talk about where he learned to play and stuff.

Keith knew everybody. And he had a funny way of sharing information -- sort of like commentary. For example, once going to a gig in the van, he says, "Check this out!" and he put in a tape of Earl Hooker. he says, "Earl Hooker's a kleptomaniac! You got to watch him if he comes to your house!" I don't think Earl Hooker's coming to my house, but it would not surprise me to see him at Keith's house! Once, as I was leaving Keith's place, I crossed paths with David Hidalgo from Los Lobos as he was coming to visit.

I grew up outside of San Antonio, Texas with a fascination for pop music in the '60s. Radio station KTSA played all the hits and I dreamed of being a singer, though I never had any musical training. By the time I moved to Austin in '80, I had learned to play a little guitar and I had a degree in English. I was born in '56, so I was 24 years old. I was writing songs and started doing open mics -- you know, just a naive kid thinking I could break into the music business. I knew about The Fabulous Thunderbirds, but I had no specific vision or musical direction ... yet.

Keith most likely playing a Fender bass copy.
Courtesy of Liz Henry

Having learned that my voice was my strong suit, I decided to find a band to sing with, and I answered a couple of classified ads in *The (Austin) Chronicle*. Hector Watt had placed an ad seeking a singer for his startup blues band. When we met, he played me records of Freddie King and Howlin' Wolf and Johnny 'Guitar' Watson and Guitar Jr., Ronnie Earl, all these guys I'd never heard. I just went, "Wow!" And the light switch came on and … that's what I wanted to do.

It was '86 when we got together. And we went to the Black Cat Lounge (venerable Austin music venue, mostly for rock and roots), and we did an audition there. The owner of the Black Cat said, "Well, you know, my neighbor right next door, Joe, is getting ready to open up his place." It was small. Joe Bates had a convenience store on Sixth Street. They sold beer, pens and paper and Rolaids and gum and stuff like that. But he had a little room in the back that he decided to put a bar in, and he got a beer license, and we played back there for a while. We were one of the first three or four bands that played at Joe's Generic Bar.

From our residency there we branched out to play all over town. When Hector started playing with Lou Ann Barton, who had seen us at Antone's, we took on a second guitar player who would fill in for Hector. His name was Johnny Katz. He's a guy that moved here from Toronto and went back after a while, but he was our second guitar player -- unless Hector had a gig with Lou Ann, and then Johnny was our first chair guitar.

Somewhere during this time, Hector had met Keith. I don't know where they met or how. I don't think it was through Lou Ann, because she was still in the Antone's crowd. But, maybe. The Solid Senders had a few break-ups and make-ups and personnel changes, and the next thing I knew, Keith was going to play with us. Actually, during one of those breakups, I had a band called The Spencer Thomas Band that was put together for me by a sax player. He arranged a few gigs with Keith on bass during that time.

We took him to a gig at an Alcoholics Anonymous party once. I think he was suspicious of an intervention. Now, when you did a gig with Keith, you were his ride, right? Even if it was in town. You'd go pick him up and get him there. So as we were approaching -- Michael Sweetman, the saxophone player, was driving and we're all in his van together -- and we're

Keith Ferguson - Bass

Insert of The Solid Senders CD showing Keith with his Harmony bass.

© Tramp Records; Courtesy of Tino Mauricio

Photo session shot that was used for the album cover.

Courtesy of Tino Mauricio

approaching the AA house when Keith goes, "What the fuck!? I don't know about this. What are y'all doing?" I said, "No, man, it's cool. It's a gig! It's a gig, you know. We've got your 12-pack here!"

Anyway, somewhere in there, The Solid Senders re-emerged, and Keith got involved in the band. We started learning a whole new set of songs and stuff. That was one of the things he really did for us, besides just giving us some credibility with his presence. He'd bring us mix tapes of songs he thought we should do, and songs from his vast collection he just

The Solid Senders playing a bar gig in Austin.
Courtesy of Paul Williams

Keith leaning against the wall, appearing to be sleeping.

Courtesy of Paul Williams

wanted to share with us for our edification.

It's that roots, regional roots music that Keith was into. If you went to his place, he'd most likely have on Amade Ardoin or Lydia Mendoza or somebody singing in Spanish and playing bajo sexto. And he just knew ALL that stuff. He was kind of teaching Hector some of that stuff too. He inspired all of us. I'm sure those roots traditions were what Keith and Don Leady shared in their band, The Tail Gators. Anyway, he made us tapes. Getting in the van and here he comes. "Oh, hey, I made you all a tape. Check this out." And it was just all this old Oakland and San Francisco proto-funk, this stuff that later came out on a Rhino collection of funk -- but stuff that was really obscure. He taught us who Dyke and the Blazers

were, and was always sharing information. He'd bring articles about weird stuff, or cartoons -- just strange things.

We had Keith in the band about '92 or '93, I guess. There was also a short time after The Tail Gators but before The Solid Senders when he was in a band called The Excellos which featured Canadian guitarist Mr. Conrad on guitar and Doyle Bramhall's nephew, David Watson, on drums. He also picked up gigs here and there. The blues scene was really hot during that time and there were gigs all over Texas.

I want to say 1994 we did that album, *Everything's Gonna Be Allright*. Eddie Stout got us a record deal with Tramp Records, from Holland. I don't even know if he heard a demo, but Eddie told the record guy, Paul Duvivier, that Keith Ferguson was in a new band, and Paul said he wanted to do a record. We did a real low-budget deal. I think the whole thing cost, I don't know, $4,500. We did it real quick and down and dirty. We travelled to Europe on the back of that one.

We went to Norway for about three weeks, and it was right in the middle of the World Cup competition, so it was as if we were playing against the Super Bowl every night. We heard ourselves on the radio in Norway and we had a few real good shows while touring the beautiful countryside.

In Holland, it was a weekend flash tour, basically. We arrived at the airport, got in the van, drove off and did a couple gigs, and came back to Amsterdam. The next morning we were in a plane on the way home. And that was our European experience with The Solid Senders.

We did about 22 tracks at that recording session, and we never finished most of them. Eddie Stout's production method is like this: The band plays a song; Eddie says, "That was great! Do another one!" Then, when the rough tracks were done, Hector spent most of rest of the time refinishing and fixing the guitar parts, and we never got to rework the vocals. We ran out of money and sent it over to Europe. Well, those 13 songs were put out on the first CD. The other 12, or whatever it was, were just left in the can and they were never finished at all.

After Keith died, the record company talked to Hector about the other tracks that we had done that we had never finished. Tramp released a second CD with

Keith on his last tour to the Netherlands. He borrowed his old Fender bass for this tour. The amplifier is most likely a Fender Bassman, 100 watts.

Courtesy of Paul Williams

the remaining tracks from that session plus one live track from Holland. I think the CD was called *Dig My Wheels*.

If you listen to that record, there's a song where -- this is kind of funny, really -- there's a song where I forgot the words, and so I just kind of hum through it, "da-da-da-da-da-da!" When you're recording the scratch vocals, you aren't really concerned about the sound because you know you're going to fix it. You

know you're going to do it again seriously. But we never fixed it! Tramp released it with the mistake. Well, now there's a young Dutch guitar player who has covered the song with his family band. His dad sings it phonetically correct, including the mistake I never got to fix. So he's going, "da-da-da-da-da-da!" at the end of one line. That's my contribution to scat singing.

Before one of those European trips, Keith's passport

Keith playing through an Orange amplifier supplied by the concert organizer.

Courtesy of Paul Williams

post office two days before Christmas, with people from every walk of life just winding around; the whole room's completely full. First we had to get in line at this little kiosk, to be directed to the appropriate line. We get in, go to the kiosk and I'm looking around and I'm going, "Oh, my God!" Every cashier, or whatever they are, has like 30 people in line. And Keith gets up there and everybody's kinda moving away from him and looking at him like, "Ohhh..." He'd always turn heads, airports and stuff, no matter where he goes. I liked to walk 15 feet behind him to watch the people stare at him. They were doing the same thing here, moving away. He gets up to the kiosk and he leans in and tells the man something. I was behind and didn't really hear what he's saying. But the guy in there looks over and he points to the one station with no line. There's a cashier station, unattended, and Keith is told to go there. Keith walks right up to it, and a guy comes from the back office, and in less than five minutes we were out of there with his new passport. And, I don't know. What the hell? I always felt they did that just to get him out of there.

He could always walk right through customs at the airport, too. He could just breeze right through. He always traveled light. He'd go to Europe with basically a paper bag for luggage -- that was all he'd carry, and his bass. And he would just walk through customs. Then Hector would come up behind him, and they'd stop him every time and search him. Something about Keith just became invisible ... he'd just slide right through.

Keith was a very sharing person. He was like a conduit for records, clothes, and articles of cool. Folks always gave him things, and he would wear 'em or keep 'em for a while, and then end up giving 'em to somebody else. It might be a lapel pin of a dragon or a tiger or a snake or whatever. And he'd wear it for a while on his scarf, and then he might give the scarf to somebody that thought it was cool and it would still have the pin on it.

Or somebody would come over to his house for the first time and be looking around in amazement at the museum of artifacts on the walls, and he'd say, "Oh, oh, I got something for you!" And he'd just give them some trinket, or magazine -- you never knew what he would come out with. So I'm sure there are people everywhere that can say, "Keith Ferguson gave me this!" And it could be anything. He just loved cool stuff, jewelry and clothes.

had expired, and he waited until the last minute and hadn't had it renewed. We had to go the Houston office to get it done in person. So I drove him down there -- like usual, if you wanted Keith to go someplace, you got to take him. So I picked him up at 7 in the morning, and he came out in slippers and camouflage shorts and just a dirty, grungy T-shirt with a big old picture of Jimi Hendrix on the front. It smelled like he'd had it on for about four or five days. We stopped and got a six-pack of Busch and headed to Houston.

We got there by maybe 9:30 or 10 in the morning, and by then he'd had a couple beers. He always drank the tall boy Busch. So we get to the passport office, and we walk in and it's just packed. It looks like a

He also loved to share cool information, not just music -- but books and recipes, whatever. You'd go over there and he'd say, "Hold on, you got to listen to this!" It doesn't matter what you went over for, he'd just go, "Here, check this out!" And it may be something he'd had for years. It's not like he was really out shopping and collecting all the time. It was more like, I think, someone might have brought him something. A lot of times it would be something he would dig out from under the bed -- something he was just into at the moment. He'd dig around and find something there and bring it out. It could be a Little Millette 45 from New Orleans, or a switchblade knife from L.A. You just never knew.

Keith was broke most of the time, and there are stories about him pawning his bass and maybe going back and getting it for a gig. Or maybe somebody else, one of his friends, would go get it so it wouldn't be lost forever, and things like that. He was not attached to things. He was generous and giving and always sharing. It wasn't just small stuff, either. Sometimes it would be a bass. He would give somebody a bass. Or somebody would give him a bass. And he might pass it on to someone else.

Keith's fashion style had changed when he played with The Solid Senders. He had mostly exchanged those kind of see-through, thin camisa shirts from the early T-Birds days, for a Band of Gypsies look. Maybe that look started during The Tail Gators. I'm not sure. Instead of the slicked-back pomade hairstyle, he let his hair grow out and really liked bandanas and scarves. He also liked draping elaborate prints.

He wore ponchos. He wore a poncho through the airport in London, catching a flight to Amsterdam or somewhere. This band from Peru came up to him and they were talking in Spanish, asking him where he was from. They were guessing, "You Guatemalan? Honduran? What are … who are you?" When he said, "No, I'm from Texas." they kind of looked incredulous and walked away.

He also had lost a lot of weight compared to the robust photos with The Fabulous Thunderbirds. The Solid Senders had a residence on Sixth Street at a small club called Headliner's East, where we played every weekend unless there was money to be made somewhere else. It was not uncommon for a music tourist on pilgrimage to Austin, who had followed the thunderous bass sound into the club expecting to

Keith playing in the Netherlands.

Courtesy of Paul Williams

The last album Keith played on, published after his death.

© *Tramp Records*

see Keith Ferguson, to be shocked to see he no longer looked like the guy on the T-Bird album covers that they expected.

But he would also nod out at the bass, and he would lean against the wall and be asleep -- but still be playing. Not just with us, but even before when he was with The Excellos, I think, a little bit of that. Sometimes we wondered if that was just his 'cool', you know? He would be like really slouched over and leaning and just really low-down, but he would be playing -- and playing well. Well, honestly we tell ourselves that, but his playing did suffer at times when his energy left him.

Keith was an animal lover, too. More than once he saved animals on the road and delivered them to safety.

Solid Senders concert poster.
Courtesy of Keith Ferguson Collection

Toward the end of The Solid Senders, we started booking all up and down these little restaurant/bars. in Houston. They all had decks with outdoor seating and live music. I guess people in Houston, after working all day in an office, wanted to get out and have a party on the patio. Anyway, we played at this place that had a crawfish boil on Friday evening or something. We had to pull our van up on the curb and hand all our equipment over the railing. So we pull the van up right next to the crawfish cooker. Somewhere along the line, Keith found an escaped crawfish that was crawling away. It was making its last ditch effort to stay alive. So he picked it up and kept it, kept it safe, until later. On the drive home to Austin, we pulled over somewhere around Columbus. There's a roadside park where we always stop for a break. There was a creek that ran through that, so Keith and Hector take the crawfish all the way down this muddy slope in the dark to get that crawfish down to the creek and they released him.

There was another time that we almost ran over a turtle in the highway. He made us stop, and he picked up this turtle and took it back to his neighbor, who

Promo shooting in front of Keith's house with his Harmony bass.

Courtesy of Daniel Schaefer

261

had kind of a pond in the yard. He said, "If you want to keep your turtle from running away when you leave, set it on the floor facing into the corner, and he'll be there when you come back because he thinks he's in a box." He had all kinds of helpful hints about stuff like that.

We got to know some of the people that he called his "family". I guess he hung out with these folks. There was a lady named Lucy, who was about his age. I guess they must've hung out a lot when they were young, and her children all just loved him. And Keith loved them all like a dad or a big brother or something. They were his chosen family. Whenever they would come to Austin he would include them. And they'd stay at his house, which was not so unusual since lots of people stayed at Keith's. But I could tell by the way that he reacted that this family was special to him. If we played in the Houston area. He'd go visit them, and the 'kids' would all come to the gig, and occasionally Lucy would come out, too.

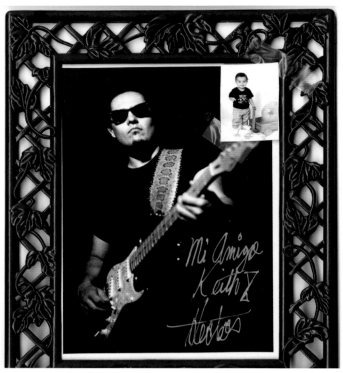

A framed picture of Hector Watt (also showing his little son) that was on a wall in Keith's house.
Courtesy of Keith Ferguson Collection

Hector Watt
Interviewed by Detlef Schmidt, 2012

I met him first on Sixth Street. I was playing there and he came and said he had a piece of plastic for my pickguard. He told me to come over to his house and we became friends.
He had cats; one was called Shithead. After a gig, he used to say "Let's get paid, I got cats to pet."

We were playing almost every night in Austin, Corpus Christi and Dallas. We toured Netherlands and Norway. I later played with Lou Ann Barton; I got them to hang out together. This was around '93-'94.

After The Solid Senders, I played with him on his last gig; this was in Houston with Paul Orta, Walter Hicks and Uncle John Turner.

A photo session shot for the first Solid Senders album with Keith and his Harmony bass.
Courtesy of Tino Mauricio

"He was not attached to things. He was generous and always sharing. It wasn't just small stuff, either. Sometimes it would be a bass."
-- Spencer Thomas

Tattoos

Daniel Schaefer was a close friend of Keith and therefore able to shoot some really special tattoo photos.

All photos courtesy of Daniel Schaefer

"Stevie Ray Vaughan: Caught In The Crossfire"[14]
Book by Joe Nick Patoski and Bill Crawford

Stevie wanted a tattoo. It couldn't be any tattoo, either. It had to be something unique that would stand out even around someone like Keith Ferguson, who was the closest thing to the Illustrated Man that Stevie knew.
After conferring with Keith, they paid a visit to one of Keith's acquaintances, Old Man Shaw, a tattoo artist in Corpus Christi. Shaw could give Stevie what he wanted, a phoenix-like bird that Keith described as a space eagle, inked across his sunken chest.

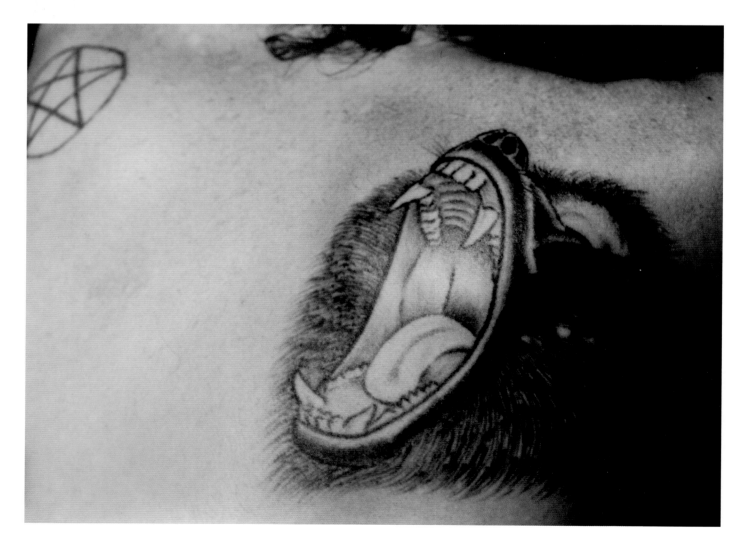

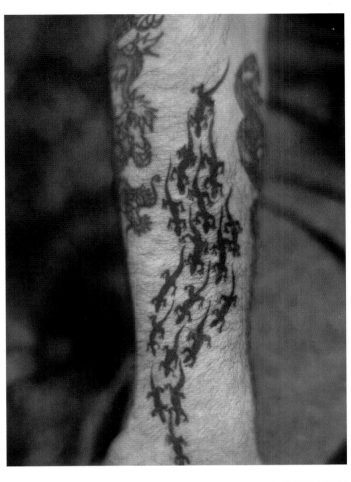

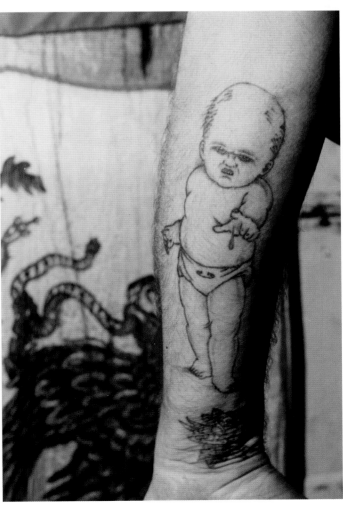

Memorial and Memories

The *Austin Chronical* issue after Keith died.
Courtesy of Daniel Schaefer

Keith Ferguson, celebrated bassist, dies at age 50

BYLINE: Michael Corcoran
DATE: May 1, 1997
PUBLICATION: *Austin American-Statesman* (TX)

"In recent years, Ferguson's health was a topic of worry for associates. According to longtime friend Ron Bates, Ferguson had been feeling especially poorly since bursting a blood vessel in his leg a month ago and finally was persuaded to go to Brackenridge on Sunday night.

Among those who kept a vigil at Ferguson's bedside on Tuesday night was guitarist Jimmie Vaughan, who had broken off contact with Ferguson after the T-Birds fired the bassist in 1984. The two reconciled after the death of brother Stevie Ray Vaughan, who played with Ferguson in the Nitecrawlers. Connie Vaughan, Doyle Bramhall, Doyle Bramhall Jr., Connie Hancock, Emma Little and Keith's mother, Margaret, also were at Ferguson's bedside."

Ralph Ritchie, Margaret Ferguson, Jimmie Vaughan and Mike Steele at the memorial.
Courtesy of Daniel Schaefer

Margaret Ferguson and Jimmie Vaughan at Keith's memorial.
Courtesy of Daniel Schaefer

Keith's inauguration in to the Austin Music Memorial: The plate (top); Conni Hancock and Margaret Ferguson (middle); and Margaret Ferguson (bottom).

Courtesy of Daniel Schaefer

KEITH FERGUSON
(1946-1997)

Keith was born in Houston, Texas on July 23, 1946. Keith became a legendary bass guitarist during his lifetime, playing gigs with several successful bands and performers in Texas and California, touring locally, nationally and in Europe. In 1985 he was named "Best Bass Guitar" in the Austin Music Awards. Keith did not receive formal musical training as a child, instead he began playing guitar with friends outside of school while he was still a teenager. He graduated from San Jacinto High School in 1964 picked up bass guitar when he was 20 years old, and flipped it over to play left handed. He soon discovered that he was naturally talented at being a bassist and taught himself to play the blues. Very soon after this he traveled and sometimes performed with different Texas music legends, such as Stevie Ray Vaughn, Johnny Winter and Junior Brown. He lived in California for awhile in the late 1960s playing with several bands such as Sunnyland Special, The Black Kangaroos, and he traveled with the Kracker Jacks. He moved back to Austin toward the end of 1970 and in 1975 he joined The Fabulous Thunderbirds with Kim Wilson, Mike Buck and guitarist Jimmy Vaughan. They started out as the house band at the original Antone's on 6th Street and quickly grew in popularity, bringing a re-vamped version of Chicago city blues back into style. Keith left the band in 1983 over disputes with the record label and played with the Tail Gators, a blues rock trio with Don Leady and Gary "Mud Cat" Smith, formed in 1984. They toured for five years together. Other bands he played in include: The Storm, Texas Sheiks, The French Band, Mystic Knights of the Sea, Excelos, and Stretch Williams. Keith had a love for the Mexican culture and its musical styles in Texas. Keith died April 29, 1997 and was inducted into the Austin Music Hall of Fame in 1997.

Los Lobos dedicated "Mas y Mas" to Keith Ferguson when they played the Super Bowl festivities in 2005[35]

Cultural blending has always been apparent in Tex-Mex music, for example. "The Germans brought the accordion, which is so huge in the legacy of Mexican music and Mexican-American music," he *(Louie Perez, of Los Lobos)* says. "Like norteño music. It wasn't till later on that we realized that the roots of it were in German polka, and there's no 'kinda' about it."

Perez adds that even today, Texans are more willing to embrace Spanish than Californians. One "Anglo Texican" the band counted as a friend was the tragic Sixth Ward-bred, Austin-based blues-bass boss Keith Ferguson. A former member of 1960s Mexican gangs in Houston, Ferguson parted ways with the Fabulous Thunderbirds just before they enjoyed their stay atop the mountaintop of the pop charts.

When Los Lobos played as part of the Super Bowl festivities here in 2005, they dedicated "Más y Más" to Ferguson. The Spanglish-language and careening, almost crazed, frontera rock of the song absolutely encapsulated Ferguson's full-tilt spirit.

And "Más y Más" also serves as a mighty roar in favor of cultural cross-pollination. Just as Mexico is the fusion of two cultures -- Spanish and native Mexican -- so Los Lobos are the fusion of Mexican and American.

"The way this band formed was the same way any other kids in America did it," Perez says. "We listened to rock radio and learned how to play instruments and we wanted to emulate our favorite musicians. And then we rediscovered the music that we had heard in the background all our lives. We picked up an acoustic guitar and tried to play a Mexican song and thought, 'Wow, we can't be so cavalier about this. This shit's kinda difficult.'"

http://www.houstonpress.com/2009-04-23/music/m-aacute-s-y-m-aacute-s/

Briscoe Center for America History, The University of Texas at Ausin[29]

The Keith Ferguson Collection consists of 307 LPs of Mexican and Tejano music of South Texas and Northern Mexico, collected by Ferguson over the years. Many of the LPs represent important early recordings by artists who became key figures in the conjunto and orquesta music of the region, and the fact that 35 of the records are autographed to Ferguson testifies to the musical bonds between Ferguson and these Latino artists.

http://www.lib.utexas.edu/taro/utcah/00681/cah-00681.html

Keith Ferguson in the Blues Hall of Fame.
Courtesy of Mary Lou Sullivan

***Bass Player* magazine, June 1998[30]**

Texas Blues: Keith Ferguson & Mike Buck

"The original Fabulous Thunderbirds rhythm section, the late Keith Ferguson and Mike Buck, played the T-Birds' tight arrangements with a loose feel. Keith laid down simple, greasy lines in an aggressive style that contrasted with Buck's more laid-back drumming. In turn the pair formed the perfect complement for guitarist Jimmy Vaughan and harp player Kim Wilson, laying down rhythm parts that were earthy but not sloopy. A lefty who played a right-handed Fender P-Bass upside-down, Ferguson put his own slant on traditional blues lines using alternate chord tones and substitutions, all delivered with a round but nasty tone. Both Ferguson and Buck had great ears and weren't afraid to use them."

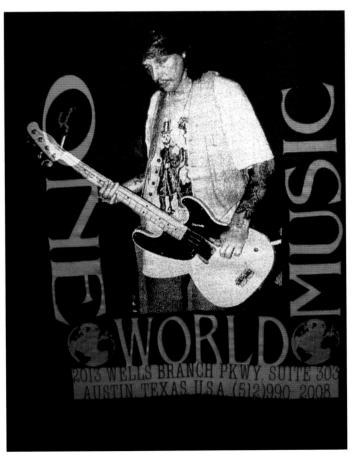

Memorial wall at the South Austin Popular Culture Center.

Courtesy of Mary Lou Sullivan

A T-shirt from One World Music on which they used Keith Ferguson's picture

Courtesy of Ted Tucker

After Keith's death, Margaret made the house in to a museum of sorts, showing it to visitors from all over the world. After she had to give up the house, all her collection was stored in Lubbock at the Texas Tech under the name "Keith Ferguson Collection".

All three photos courtesy of Ted Tucker

A letter from Chris Strachwitz to Margaret Ferguson explaining how important Keith was to the Mexican catalog of Arhoolie Records.

Courtesy of Keith Ferguson Collection

ARHOOLIE PRODUCTIONS, INC.
10341 San Pablo Avenue, El Cerrito, California 94530
Tel: (510) 525-7471 • FAX: (510) 525-1204 • e-mail: mail@arhoolie.com • Web Site: www.arhoolie.com

Austin Chronicle, May 23, 1999[31]

Antone's Keith Ferguson Blues & Pop Fiesta w/ Little Joe y La Familia, Ruben Ramos & Texas Revolution, Gulf Coast Playboys, Mistic Knights of the Sea, Texana Dames, LeRoi Bros., & many more

" ... Ferguson put his own slant on traditional blues lines using alternate chord tones and substitutions, all delivered with a round but nasty tone."
-- *Bass Player*

Austin American-Statesman Tuesday, May 6, 1997 E5 ENTERTAINMENT

Keith Ferguson: style and wi

Keith Ferguson, second from left, could be hilarious and cutting when talking about his former Fabulous Thunderbirds bandmates, from left, Jimmie Vaughan, Kim Wilson and Fran Christina. Ferguson died April 29.

■

Everybody seems to have a favorite **Keith Ferguson** story in the week after his sad passing April 29. Keith had a brilliant mind and when he'd go on a roll, especially with his ongoing tell-all monologue about his times in the Fabulous Thunderbirds, it would be the most hilarious and cutting thing you ever heard. Keith could be tears-in-your-eyes funny. Plus he had that element of danger that gives true comedy an edge. He was a true original and folks all over town, all over the country, are remembering him for his style and wit, and not so much for his addictions.

My favorite remembrance of Keith was the night of the 1986 T-Bird Riverfest. He had been kicked out of the T-Birds two years earlier, and he intensely hated his former bandmates. He didn't want any part of their yearly shindig on Town Lake, so it was surprising to see him backstage. But he had just come to remind Los Lobos about the party he was having at his house that night. While opening for a string of Los Lobos dates with the Tailgators, Ferguson had become fast friends with the fellow musicologists from East L.A. (even though he thought they blew it with their version of the sacred Tex-Mex standard "Ay Te Dejo en San Antonio").

He was in and out of the dressing room and then back home to get ready. A couple of Keith's old girlfriends had spent hours decorating the place and a few more were in the kitchen with him as he prepared a magnificent feast that would show those guys from East L.A. how we do Mexican in Austin. It was a great party that would get even better when Cesar and David and Louie showed up and started playing records with Keith.

But Los Lobos didn't show up. Their set was over at around 8 p.m., so even if you gave them a couple hours to unwind and shower, they should've been there by 10. When 11 p.m., midnight crawled on, you desperately wanted Los Lobos to show up because you could tell that Keith was disappointed, but it didn't look promising. Keith even went to bed at about 12:30. About half an hour later, however, Los Lobos finally did arrive, to the sight of six or seven people drinking Busch beer and reading the backs of old blues albums. When they found out that Keith had already turned in for the night, the guys in the band didn't leave. Instead, they picked up some of Keith's instruments — bajo sexto, maracas, guitarron — and surrounded his bed and started serenading him to life.

It's hard to feel sorry for Keith, even though some might say that he died 20 years ago but just found out. It was almost like he knew too much, and he spent the last twentysomething years trying to forget some of it. He had passion for what he loved, however, and I'm reminded of the time a friend and I wanted to start getting into conjunto music, so we asked Keith to recommend some albums. "Go down to Maldonado's," he said. "If you see an album with Mexican guys on the cover and one of them has an accordion, that's the good stuff."

There'll be no statue in the park for Keith Ferguson, but Austin was indelibly enriched by his mind and musicianship. ■

music

Keith Ferguson 1946-1997

In his house, wall-to-wall with posters, knicknacks, arcane musical instruments, photographs, postcards, and objets d'art, Keith Ferguson's precious collection of vinyl albums were divided into three sections: "Negro," "Mexican," and "Other." That, his friends will testify, was pure Ferguson, the white boy who was as black and brown as they come. Best known for his stint as the Fabulous Thunderbirds' original bassist, Ferguson died Tuesday, April 29 at 9:20pm in Brackenridge Hospital from complications arising from liver failure. He was 50.

It would be pointless to try and cram Ferguson's colorful and checkered career into a few words; suffice it to say that his bass lines thundered throughout the world. If their was a bottom-line reason Austin became known for its blues, Ferguson created it. Even the great Muddy Waters used to narrow his eyes and whistle in admiration at Ferguson's muscular soul. After departing the T-Birds in the mid-Eighties, he went on to play with the Tailgators and the Solid Senders. Ever led by the muse, he was surrounded by friends in his hospital room when he passed.

Keith Ferguson will be remembered by his friends on Saturday, May 10, at a service in his backyard at 3502 S. Second Street, where his ashes will be buried. However, with both Doyle Bramhall and Doyle Bramhall II playing Antone's this Saturday, May 3, I think I know where his heart and soul will be. *– Margaret Moser*

Bittersweet Grammy

AAS 6-12-97

"Anytime you win a Grammy, it's great," Vaughan said. "This one was a little bittersweet, though. It was nice to finally get to do the show and have it recognized for how great I thought it turned out. But, you know, you're doing it because Stevie's not here anymore."

While it didn't hit home as hard as the death of his brother, another of Jimmie's musical partners died recently: Keith Ferguson, longtime bass player of the T-Birds. Vaughan had ended relations with Ferguson when the T-Birds fired the bassist in 1984, but after Stevie's death, the two reconciled. The night Ferguson died, Vaughan was among those keeping a vigil at his bedside.

"What can a guy say?" Vaughan said. "He was my friend. I miss him. I think it sucks that he died. But he was a great guy. Everybody who knew him knew he was a great guy."

40 | THE AUSTIN CHRONICLE | APRIL 12, 2002

Keith Ferguson, celebrated bassist, dies at age 50

By MICHAEL CORCORAN
American-Statesman Music Writer

5-1-97

Notorious local music figure Keith Ferguson, whose bass playing with the Fabulous Thunderbirds helped lay the foundation for Austin's electric blues scene in the '70s and early '80s, died Tuesday night at Brackenridge Hospital from a combination of health problems including liver failure. The heavily tattooed southpaw, who dressed like the pachucos of his childhood in Houston, was 50.

Keith Ferguson: Helped lay the foundation for Austin's electric blues scene.

In recent years, Ferguson's health was a topic of worry for associates. According to longtime friend Ron Bates, Ferguson had been feeling especially poorly since bursting a blood vessel in his leg a month ago and finally was persuaded to go to Brackenridge on Sunday night.

Among those who kept a vigil at Ferguson's bedside on Tuesday night was guitarist Jimmie Vaughan, who had broken off contact with Ferguson after the T-Birds fired the bassist in 1984. The two reconciled after the death of brother Stevie Ray Vaughan, who played with Ferguson in the Nitecrawlers. Connie Vaughan, Doyle Bramhall, Doyle Bramhall Jr.,

Noted musician Keith Ferguson dies

Continued from B1

Connie Hancock, Emma Little and Keith's mother, Margaret, also were at Ferguson's bedside.

"In the last year or so Keith had taken a definite turn for the worse," Little said. "Last summer I took him to see Los Lobos, who are real good friends of his, and they didn't recognize him."

A two-decade addiction to heroin hindered Ferguson's touring activity and contributed to his firing by the T-Birds and his release from the Tailgators in 1990. In recent years he played mostly with pick-up bands or with the Solid Senders. His regard as one of Austin's most instinctive and original bassists never wavered among fellow musicians, however.

In a frank '96 article in the Dallas Observer titled "The Beautiful Loser," fellow blues musician Josh Alan Friedman wrote, "No bass player ever layered so much bottom" and compared Ferguson's style to "a swinging elephant trunk underneath the song."

No matter how much he abused his body, Austin's ultimate hipster never lost his rapier-sharp wit or his love for such regional music styles as conjunto and Cajun.

"He really was one of a kind," said former Storm singer Paul Ray, who dedicated his Tuesday night show on KUT to Ferguson. "His knowledge of music was tremendous. All those swamp rock influences in the T-Birds came right from Keith's record collection. He was also way into that border music years before anyone else" in the Austin music scene.

Keith Ferguson, right, was bassist for the Tailgators until he was released in 1990. Shown with him are Don Leady, left, and Gary 'Mud Cat' Smith.

Ferguson's dismissal from the T-Birds was a bitter one, as the snubbed bassist sued his former bandmates in '85, but lost in court. The firing of one of Austin's most beloved players split the local blues camps into pro-Keith and anti-Keith factions, with Antone's nightclub heavily in the latter group. Ferguson's anger with the T-Birds was especially enflamed when "Tuff Enuff," the band's first album with new bassist Preston Hubbard, sold more than a million copies.

A fruitful five-year run in the Tailgators, whose signature tune "Mumbo Jumbo" was co-written by Ferguson, helped him cope with his anger.

Ferguson was born in Houston on July 23, 1946, and grew up in "the Sexto," the mostly Hispanic Sixth Ward. Although Ferguson's estranged father John Williams Ferguson was a concert pianist with the Chicago Symphony, Keith didn't start playing music until he was almost 20. But he soon found himself playing bass for his record-collecting buddy Johnny Winter.

After moving to Austin in 1970, Ferguson quickly established himself as the premiere bassist on the local blues scene and he was often sought out by visiting musicians. One who approached him in the mid-'80s said he'd come all the way from Finland to learn the secret of Ferguson's style. He begged the master to teach him the essence and Ferguson agreed.

"You work your way all the way up the neck," Ferguson said, as the Finnish bassist leaned closer. "Then, when you get to the top, head back down." Such simplicity was the key to Ferguson's playing.

A memorial service will be in the back yard of Keith Ferguson's house in South Austin on May 10.

AC 5-2-97

music

Keith Ferguson 1946-1997

In his house, wall-to-wall with posters, knicknacks, arcane musical instruments, photographs, postcards, and objets d'art, Keith Ferguson's precious collection of vinyl albums were divided into three sections: "Negro," "Mexican," and "Other." That, his friends will testify, was pure Ferguson, the white boy who was as black and brown as they come. Best known for his stint as the Fabulous Thunderbirds' original bassist, Ferguson died Tuesday, April 29 at 9:20pm in Brackenridge Hospital from complications arising from liver failure. He was 50.

It would be pointless to try and cram Ferguson's colorful and checkered career into a few words; suffice it to say that his bass lines thundered throughout the world. If their was a bottom-line reason Austin became known for its blues, Ferguson created it. Even the great Muddy Waters used to narrow his eyes and whistle in admiration at Ferguson's muscular soul. After departing the T-Birds in the mid-Eighties, he went on to play with the Tailgators and the Solid Senders. Ever led by the muse, he was surrounded by friends in his hospital room when he passed.

Keith Ferguson will be remembered by his friends on Saturday, May 10, at a service in his backyard at 3502 S. Second Street, where his ashes will be buried. However, with both Doyle Bramhall and Doyle Bramhall II playing Antone's this Saturday, May 3, I think I know where his heart and soul will be. – Margaret Moser

Keith Rogers Ferguson

Keith, musician by heart and trade, died Tuesday, April 29, 1997. He was born July 23, 1946, and is survived by his mother Margaret.

He loved God's creatures and was gentle and kind. He loved the truth and was intelligent and elegant. He had a keen sense of humor and great integrity. He was an artist and loved beauty. He loved his friends and was loved by them. God rest his soul.

Memorial service will be in his backyard at 3402 South Second, Saturday evening, May 10, 1997, from 6:00 p.m. to 8:00 p.m., with eulogies by his friends and prayers by Rolland McLean, minister.

Austin-Peel and Son Funeral Home.

■ **Keith Ferguson dead at 50**

Keith Ferguson, a storied Texas blues bass player, died Tuesday night in Austin after a brief illness. Ferguson, 50, was a Houston native who moved to Austin just as the Capital City music scene began to boom.

Best known for a seven-year stint with the Fabulous Thunderbirds, a roots blues band he helped form in Austin in 1974, Ferguson played with a veritable "Who's Who" of blues and roots rockers.

With the Thunderbirds, Ferguson, a left-handed player whose motto was "Go halfway down the neck of the bass and then turn around and go back up," recorded albums such as "Fabulous Thunderbirds," "What's the Word," "Butt Rockin'" and "T Bird Rhythm." 5-1-97

San Antonio Express-News

That's A-Morte 10-31-97

Editor:

Blues fans in Italy were very disappointed at the patronistic coverage given in your newspaper on the death of bassist Keith Ferguson. A copy of your paper's feature was recently sent to us by request. We were surprised at the judgmental tone of the article, which unapologetically confused Keith's talent and musical legacy with his personal lifestyle. This was hardly the kind of treatment deserving of one of Texas' finest contributions to the blues, and a musical mentor to bassists worldwide. How one runs one's personal affairs is not a matter for the press' sermonizing. If America prides itself on defending individual liberties, and Texas in particular, makes such proud claims to independent thinking, the *Chronicle* might have limited its coverage to the simple respect that Keith or any other deceased person deserves. A heartless article, in keeping with the other death spectacle headlines Texas makes worldwide: prison executions.

G. Alessi and on behalf of Blues Musicians in the Emilia Romagna Region (Italy)

Some newspaper articles Margaret had kept from the time shortly after Keith's death.

Courtesy of Keith Ferguson Collection

Chapter 7

The Basses

Fender Precison Bass #0171 used by Keith on the first Thunderbirds albums

Chapter 7
The Basses

The Cowhide Bass

Danny Turansky
Interviewed by Detlef Schmidt, October 2012

Danny Turansky was an Austin bass player, a good friend of Keith Ferguson, and owned two of Keith's most famous basses. Danny had a lot of great stories to tell and was a great character. He sadly passed away in April 2013, shortly after this interview was taken in his living room. I had not typed the interview when the note that he passed away reached me. Looking at the five interview videotapes brought back good memories of an interesting afternoon in Kyle, Texas.

Carlos Barbosa took me over to Keith's house. That's where I first met him. From that day on, I would just go by and hang out with him. I became one of the porch monkeys. There was such a circus going on in those days. You never knew whom you were going to meet. This was about the late '70s, when the first Thunderbirds record came out.

1956 Fender Precision (aka the "cowhide" bass)

The tobacco sunburst cowhide showed up with an identical matching Stratocaster at Ray Henning's music store. Jimmie Vaughan went by the shop and discovered the bass. Jimmie immediately called Keith and said, "You got to come by and buy that bass."

Danny Turansky and the author with the 'cowhide' bass.

Keith didn't have any money at that time and couldn't do it. So Jimmie called Billy Gibbons and told him about it. Billy immediately sent a check to Ray Henning's for the bass and said it belongs to Keith now. Ray Henning called Keith up and said, "I've got your bass up here, you need to come and get it". Keith was like, "What bass?" Ray said, "This tobacco sunburst, the '56, come and pick it up."

So Billy Gibbons bought him the bass. I think this is all because Billy had wanted Keith as the bass player for ZZ Top before they got famous. Keith was in California and in love with Angela Strehli and didn't want to leave California, but he gave him contact to Dusty Hill who got the job then. Dusty later on sent Keith a postcard with a picture of him lying on a bed all covered up with money with some notes saying "Keith, thank you for the gig."

When the '56 was stolen, a friend of mine called me and she said, "I think I've got Keith's bass here." A mutual friend was a junkie and had stolen Keith's bass. He had it two blocks away and stashed in that little girl's closet. And she called me up and said "Hey, I just found something." Keith had panic. I

happened at Keith's house at that time and we drove right up there. And there it was, and then he got it back.

Collectors want everything original, and all that makes them more money. The basses that stay like that are the ones that sound like shit. There is one thing that I learned early on with solid body instruments. If you press them against your hips and you can feel the sound resonate, all that went through the neck and through the body, you got one that sounds good. You can always change your pickup, fix the bridge or do all the cosmetic stuff you want to do, but when you feel it resonating, you know it's a player.

We were sitting on the front porch and Carlos Santana was in town playing. It might have been with ZZ Top down at the Erwin Center. Santana pulls up in his limousine. He was sitting in the back and rolls his window down and asked Keith to come out and see him. And Keith just turned around and looked to the rest of us and said, "If you want to see me, you have to come up on to my porch." Carlos wouldn't get out of his car and Keith wouldn't bother go out and talk to him. Keith wasn't impressed by anybody.

Note the cigartte burn on the headstock, from a right-handed player. Pinetop Perkins' signature is on the backside.

Opposite page: Keith with his cowhide bass in front of his house.

Courtesy of Daniel Schaefer

Fender Precision Bass 0171

This bass now belongs to Erin Jaimes: "This is the bass that Keith Ferguson played on the first two T-Birds albums. The signatures are Pinetop Perkins, Wanda Jackson and Jimmie Vaughan. The indentation between the American flag and the pickup is from Keith's thumb. Keith refinished the bass because the wood was getting soft and smelly from being carried around in a gig bag with his dirty socks. He also changed the original black pickguard to the current tortoise-shell one."

Top right: Cigarette smoke darkened the lacquer on the unchanged headstock but the color under the decal remained lighter. Below: Signatures and decals adorn the front and back of the body.

Danny Turansky on Fender Precision Bass #0171:

The bass now belongs to Erin Jaimes in Austin, who still plays it in her band. That's the bass Keith learned on. The bass got painted because he put all his dirty socks and underwear in his bass case and the bass began to smell terribly. The wood was starting to get soft from the sweat, taking that hole out from his thumb. The hole was starting to get big, so when they refinished it, they didn't fill the hole. It might have been Marc Stevens who repainted it. He's a pretty famous luthier here in Austin. He had a vintage guitar shop back then, Stevens Guitars. It was unbelievable. When you walked in, it was nothing but all the old '50s and '60s basses lined up and guitars.

Keith put refection tape on it on the sides; changed the stickers from time to time. He played this bass until he got the '56 Fender Precision bass. The pickguard got broken and started to crack up, so he took it off and put a tortoise shell pickguard on. The tortoise pickguard that's now on Erin's bass is about the third one that was on. The first tortoise one got crystalized, breaking up and everything. He found some company in California that was making that material and had them make a new pickguard. That's the one that's on the bass right now.

The bass once got stolen when the Thunderbirds came back from Europe. It got stolen at the airport in Houston. It wound up actually at Rockin' Robin's (a guitar shop in Houston). There was an article in a magazine (Guitar Player, 1986) where the serial number was noted and that the bass belonged to Keith Ferguson. And when it showed up at Rockin' Robin's, they called him up immediately and said they had his bass there.

By then, he was so into playing the cowhide bass. When he got it back, he noticed that it wasn't so comfortable to play as the contoured body of the cowhide bass. So that was how I eventually wound up with it. He was pawning the bass and lost his hock. At the time we were going to the store, some other person was already taking it home. They refused to let Keith and I buy that bass from them. But Keith made a deal right there in the hock shop -- when the guy wanted to get rid of it, Keith would be the first person for him to call. A year or so later, the guy called Keith and told him that he wanted to sell the bass if Keith wanted it back. Keith immediately called me and gave me the guy's number.

So I called the guy, met him at a parking lot and bought it from him for $650. Actually, he wanted $600 for the bass, but he had a new Seymour Duncan pickup that he wanted 50 bucks for. I was not going to argue.

That was my main bass then. That was all I played until Keith went to the hollowbodies and decided that he was going to sell the cowhide bass. He hocked it and was about to lose it, so I went down and got the hock for him. Once Seymour Duncan came out with that single coil replica pickup, Keith started to use them. They sounded so much better than the original pickups.

Erin Jaimes playing Fender Precision Bass #0171 at Friends Bar on Sixth Street in Austin with Doug Day on drums. The bass was given to Erin by Danny Turansky, who received it from Keith after Danny and other members of Austin's blues family had rescued it from pawn shops multiple times. Erin: "The neck pocket is marked March 52 and serial number 0171 is on the bridge plate."

Courtesy of Scott Ferris

Erin Jaimes' 2007 release. Erin Jaimes came on to the Austin, Texas, blues scene in late 1994. To date, she has released two CDs, *You Had to Go* (2003) and *Soul Garden* (2007). Erin has toured regionally and internationally, plays regularly around Austin, and has been listed in The Austin Chronicle's music awards as one of the city's top bassists. She hosts the weekly Sunday Sixth Street Blues Jam at Friends Bar, a tradition that was started over 30 years ago by Walter Higgs & The Shufflepigs -- with Danny Turansky on bass.

Courtesy of Erin Jaimes

Fender Precision Bass 0172

This serial number immediately follows Keith's #0172 bass; what a coincidence. Keith used this bass in the early 1980s after his main bass was stolen. It can be seen in the Tracy Hart photos that are shown with the interview of Fran Christina. From the pictures, Keith used the bass until he was presented the "cowhide" bass by Billy Gibbons.

The bass is slightly oversprayed and has the reflector tape on the sides. One can see the identation from Keith's thumb. It has a Seymour Duncan hot pickup installed and a new pickguard. Also note the strap button on the backside, placed for Keith's left-handed playing.

Fender Precision Bass 0069

This bass once belonged to Mark Hickman of The Rockets. Then it was sold to Gerard Daily, who brought it to Keith and loaned it to him. Then the bass was sold to Scott Ferris, who still owns it. It's one of the best playing Fender basses I've had in my hands.

Fender Precison #0069 in Keith's bedroom (note the posters of B.B. King and Ruben Ramos on the walls).

Courtesy of Tino Mauricio

Gerard Daily: "The bed was a camping bed that folded up and supposedly belonged to a general in the Mexican army in the 1800s. I don't remember where Keith got the bed from."

Courtesy of Tino Mauricio

Mark Hickman and Keith in the 1980s. Mark was the bass player for The Rockets, another famous Texas blues band.

Courtesy of Mark Hickman

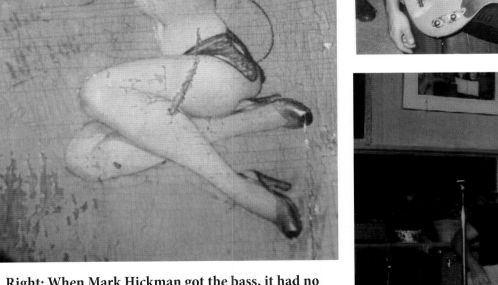

Right: When Mark Hickman got the bass, it had no pickguard and he put the retro one on it (note the pinup girl decal on the body).

Courtesy of Mark Hickman

Harmony H22-1

The semi-acoustic Harmony H22-1 bass is noted for its batwing pickguard and powerful pickup. This one belongs to Erkan Özdemir. He bought it from Keith around 1993 when he visited Austin. Erkan is the bass player for one of Germany's leading blues bands, Memo Gonzales and the Blues Casters. Memo Gonzales originally is from Dallas.

Keith's Harmony with the pickguad flipped.

Courtesy of Tino Maurcio

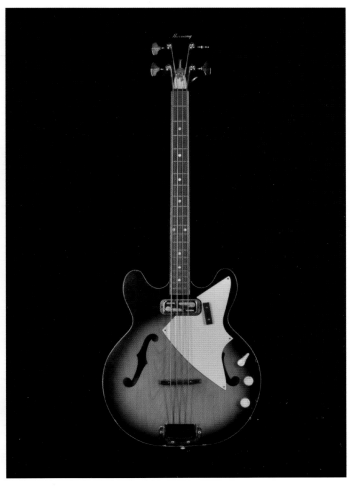

Other basses

Besides his main basses in the Thunderbirds -- #0172, #0172 and the cowhide bass -- Keith had a lot of basses throughout his career, especially in the late Austin days when he had a lot of basses for a short while. Most of them were pawned when he needed money; some were given as a gift to him and then pawned. Here is a few I discovered during research for this book.

Keith with one of his Harmony basses.

Courtesy of Daniel Schaefer

Keith with what looks like a newer Precision, noted by the very white dot markers.

Courtesy of Daniel Schaefer

Above: Keith and the red 1954-1956 Fender Precision. It's the same bass he used as a second on the Thunderbirds tour to Norway or Finland, and it can be seen in the Dave Gardner photos. Left: Keith playing a Gibson archtop guitar.

Courtesy of Angela Strehli

291

Mike Keller, current guitar player in The Fabulous Thunderbirds: "I think it's one of the last ones Keith owned. My brother bought it for him a few months before he died and Margret gave it back to him after he passed away. The bass is decorated with rhinestones and lizard earrings. It's also got a case that Keith drew a picture of a dragon on and put Virgin Mary/skull stickers on." This bass has two thumbrests installed.

Courtesy of Mike Keller

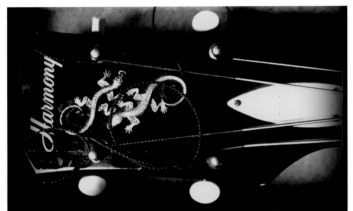

292

This bass is a 1968-1972 Fender Telecaster bass. Other than the pickguard, which is changed, somebody had installed some phenolic-type of saddles, maybe the same wooden ones Keith used to have on his cowhide bass. The finger indentations are from a right-handed person. Also there is muting foam underneath the strings.

Jeff Turmes, current bassist for Mavis Staples: "It had gold reflectorized tape around the body when I got it, but I took that off. At this time, Don Leady had a silver sparkle Telecaster with the same blue pickguard material."

Courtesy of Jeff Turmes

Robert de la Cruz on the National bass: "I never knew which bands he (Keith) used these instruments in. I last saw him at a pawn shop where he was asking for an extension for both the National bass and his Harmony bass. He really loved talking about the Harmony. I think it was his favorite at the time. This was proably less than a year before he passed away and he looked in very bad shape. The shop owner (who I knew) introduced me to him. He talked to me for a good 20 minutes and was so very nice. I wish I had bought the Harmony but settled on the National, which was a longscale bass and from 1968. It was unplayable above the 12th fret, but I guess Keith never went that far up! The Hondo bass (next page) has a broken truss rod so it is pretty much unplayable as well, but I love the look of the bass."

Courtesy Robert de la Cruz

Right: Keith playing a different National bass with only one pickup with Spencer Thomas and The Solid Senders at The Headliners East club.

Courtesy of Paul Williams

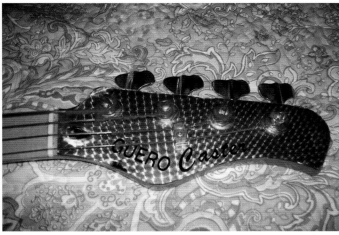

The Guero Caster, a Hondo bass heavily customised by Keith, how belongs to Robert de la Cruz.

Courtesy of Robert de la Cruz

Right: The original pawn shop ticket for the Hondo bass. (For some reason, Mike Buck had kept it. When he showed it to me, I told him that I knew the owner.)

Courtesy of Mike Buck

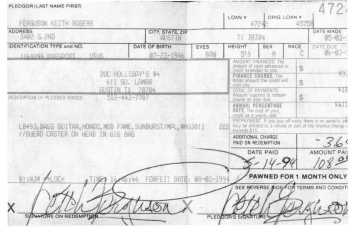

"He changed his basses like other people changed their shoes."
-- Carlos Barbosa

Personal story by Jon Penner

Jon Penner is a bass player who used to play with Junior Brown and still occasionally tours with him.

I moved to Austin, Texas, on July 4, America's birthday. That year, Willie (Nelson) had his annual picnic in town, in Zilker Park. My compadres and myself couldn't afford tickets, so we let the Colorado River bring the voices of the Highwaymen -- Kris Kristofferson, Johnny Cash, Waylon Jennings and Willie himself -- to us in the parking lot we were in on the north side of the river. My compadres and myself figured this was it. We'd come to the right place.

Later that night, I went to Joe's Generic Bar to see Keith Ferguson play bass. I can't remember who Keith was playing with, and Joe's isn't exactly glamorous, but I remember Keith distinctly. Eyes closed, back against the wall, in a sweet spot behind the beat but driving hard, with that unmistakable sound and his classic lines. Keith was mesmerizing. After the set, he stepped behind the bar (no dressing room), and threw up. From my vantage point, I couldn't tell if he'd thrown up on to the floor or into a garbage can, but he wiped his mouth with his hand as though nothing had happened, cracked open a fresh beer and joined the fans out front of the bar where he found a spot on the wall and resumed the same stance he'd had onstage.

I approached him at this point. "Hi, Keith, big fan, blah, blah, love your playing, blah, blah." He opens one eye and looks at me like I should be shot and says sarcastically, "It's not hard," and closes his eye again. That was so perfect and beautiful I had to laugh. He opened both his eyes and we had a brief and normal conversation. He was nice. Surprisingly sweet, considering how he looked. He looked at least 20 years older than he was but his eyes were soft and kind.

I'll never claim to have been a close friend of Keith's, so in a way I feel strange writing this, but over the next few years, I got to know him a little. In the last two years of his life, I lived just on the other side of South Congress, a short walk away from his house so

Junior Brown on guitar with Jon Penner on bass. Junior Brown: "Keith only played one gig with me, but it was fantastic. Keith was playing through a Fender Showman amp."

Courtesy of Jon Penner

I spent a little time hanging out on the front porch with Keith, Fred, Dave, Danny and Liz and others. At that time, Fred was living upstairs at Keith's on and off, and I was closer to Fred, having traveled with him a few years. Fred was a wonderful drummer and a wonderful man. Everyone loved him. Even northern women were charmed by him.

The scene on the porch was basically the same every day, but one particular event really stands out in my memory. Across from Keith's was an old house with an old woman in it. It was a big old lot, and from Keith's, it just looked like woods. There's a condominium there now.

One day, here comes a good-sized red snake from out of those woods. Keith spotted it first, and jumped up to get a closer look. Right at that same time, a truck comes downhill from the south, and runs over the snake, killing it, with the Tejano guy driving the truck laughing as he did it. Keith went berserk. It was the one and only time I saw Keith run, and he ran hard after that truck, picking up rocks and throwing them, and cursing that driver at the top of his lungs. The truck rounded the corner east towards Congress, and Keith came back in a state. He was livid. He was in tears. I had to leave. We all did. We could tell Keith wanted to be alone. Went back a couple of days later and the skin of that snake was nailed to the wall of the porch. Keith had given it a place of honor on his home, and he didn't say a damn thing about it.

Some time in those years, Danny sold me a bass he said had belonged to Keith. He had all of Keith's basses. He was keeping them safe. He said he'd asked Keith if it'd be OK if he sold it to me, and Keith had said yes, apparently. He gave me a good deal on it, $800, which even at that time was a low price for a '63 Precision. Of course, I still have the bass, along with a shirt Keith gave me once. I've sold basses in the past that I've regretted selling later. I won't make that mistake with this one. I don't know if it's a bass Keith ever played much, and I don't care. At least two times I can remember I went home drunk after gigs in Austin and left that bass unattended overnight in the open back of my girlfriend's truck -- and both times that bass was still there in the morning, roasting in the sun. I guess I'm stuck with it.

Before I ever moved to Austin I was, unbeknownst to me at the time, a part of a worldwide cult, dedicated to the love of the first Fabulous Thunderbirds album, *Girls Go Wild*. My Canadian buddies and me had no idea the cult even existed. We thought we were the only ones in the world who knew about this amazing blues album by a white band from Texas, really by far the best any of us had ever heard. These guys had IT. The thing. IT. We thought we were the only ones who

A '63 Fender Precision that once belonged to Keith.
Courtesy of Jon Penner

knew, and we wore the grooves off that record. Cult members around the world were doing the same.

I absolutely don't mean to take anything away from subsequent versions of The Fabulous Thunderbirds. They were all great bands. I saw the Preston/Frannie version of the T-Birds at the Town Pump in Vancouver, Canada, just before *Tuff Enuff* came out. It's the closest I've come to seeing The Beatles. They were incredibly powerful. Like they knew that they could have any girl in that room, and every guy and every girl in room knew it, too. They just stood there and played and had that much power, that much charisma. They floored the place. Billy Gibbons was there that night.

But for my personal taste, that first record, that first version of that band, had this bizarre, innocent magic. Jimmie, Kim, Keith and Mike Buck. I never knew Kim, but I got to know Mike through the record store mostly, and Jimmie just a wee bit in the years when I played with Junior Brown. Those three -- Jimmie, Keith and Mike -- the ones I knew just a little, always struck me as being very sweet, gentle guys, and that sweetness came across somehow on that first album, as nasty and raw as that album was. Again, kind of like The Beatles, or maybe more accurately, like Lazy Lester, who I got to know some and play with later.

This weird combination of power and vulnerability. Kind of feminine in a way, while still very masculine. Shy, but confident. Sweet, yet strong. Real strong. And besides what it did to girls, it really got to other musicians. They could have called it *Musicians Go Wild* because musicians were indeed going wild, too.

And that one album (in my opinion, and I'm sure many would agree with me) spawned that 20-year resurgence of the blues that happened in those years. It was because of that one record. All the white blues musicians who came after, and there were many very good ones, were trying to capture the magic that one record had. The only other albums that came close (again, in my opinion) were the Hollywood Fats albums, with another fantastic bass player, Larry Taylor. As good as Fats and those guys were, for my money, the T-Birds were much better. More brash, more balls, more original. More southwest Louisiana. More Texas.

I don't mean to glamorize Keith Ferguson's life. There is nothing glamorous about dying with a leg full of gangrene at 50. And I don't blame the T-Birds for parting ways with Keith, as much as I loved that version of that band. How can you go around the world with a guy like that? Keith was built for comfort, not for speed.

I didn't get to attend Keith's memorial, but somebody who was there told me that Jimmie spoke there and said that it was Keith that taught those guys how to dress and how to act, or something to that effect. I thought that was really cool of Jimmie. Like that snake Keith nailed to his porch, Jimmie gave Keith his due, in a public way. He honored him.

I miss those guys -- Keith Ferguson and Freddie 'Pharoah' Walden. They died close together.

Chapter 8

Keith's Bass Style

Keith's Bass Style

I succeeded in getting three great musicians to analyse Keith's bass style and to put down some notations and tabs.

Armando Compean is Keith's old friend and bass teacher from the 1960s.
Bird Stevens, a bass player from the Netherlands who plays in a Fabulous Thinderbirds cover band, Different Tacos, contributed some TABs.
Didi Beck is a German upright bassist and author of a rockabilly slapbass instruction book ("Rockabilly Slapbass - a slight introduction", published by Artist Ahead, ISBN 978-3-86642-004-5). He also published an instruction video and has played over 5,000 concerts with Boppin' B until now.[42] Being an old friend of mine since school days, he was also so friendly to overlook the notation and tabs.

Didi Beck.

Courtesy of Didi Beck

In The Style Of Keith Ferguson
Scratch my back

Armando Compean

In The Style Of Keith Ferguson
C-Boys Blues

Armando Compean

In The Style Of Keith Ferguson

The Tail Gators
Mumbo Jumbo

Didi Beck

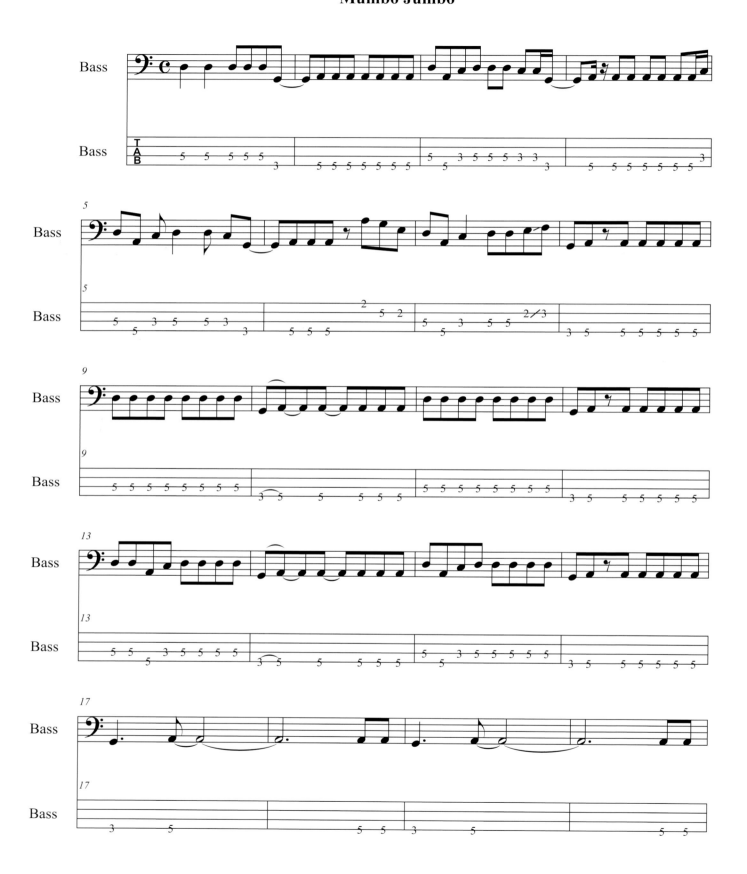

In The Style Of Keith Ferguson
The Fabulous Thunderbirds
The Crawl

Didi Beck

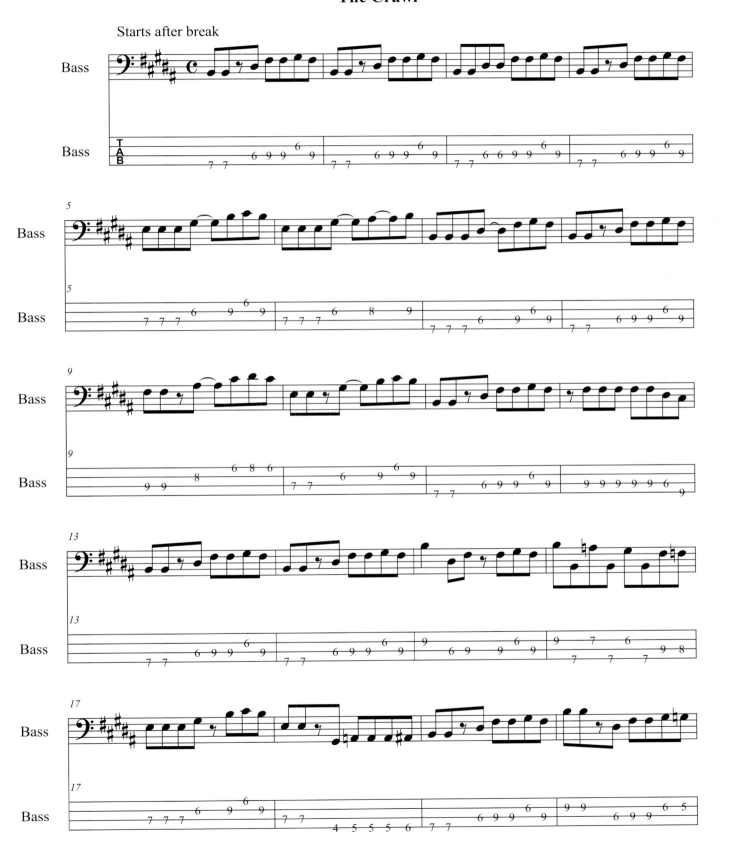

In The Style Of Keith Ferguson

Fabulous Thunderbirds
Extra Jimmies

Didi Beck

In The Style Of Keith Ferguson

Big Guitars From Texas
Boomerang

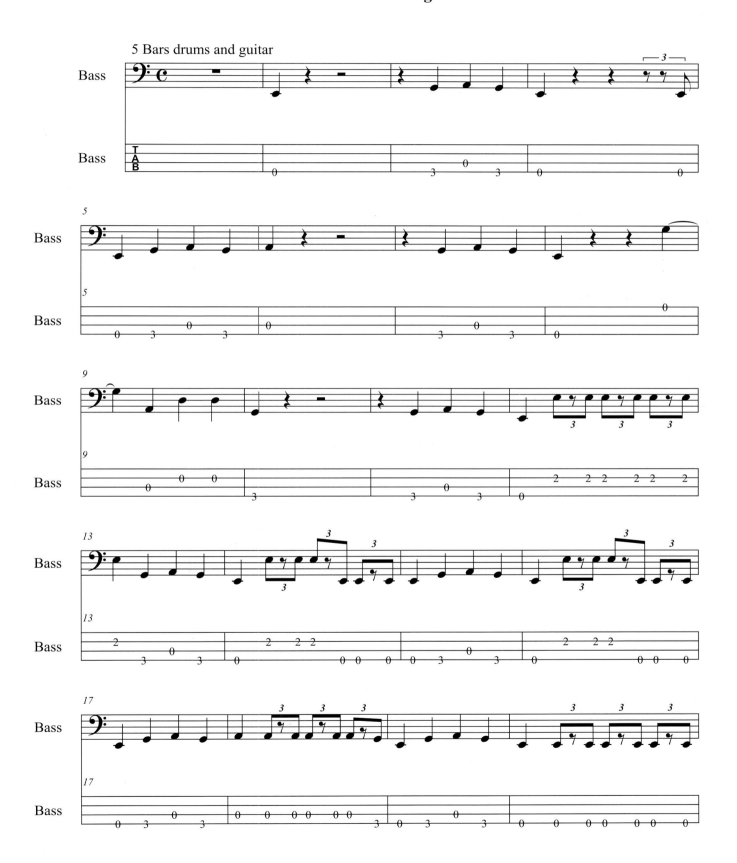

In The Style Of Keith Ferguson

The Fabulous Thunderbirds
Neighbour tend to your business

Didi Beck

In The Style Of Keith Ferguson
The Tailgators
Rock and Roll till the cows come home

Didi Beck

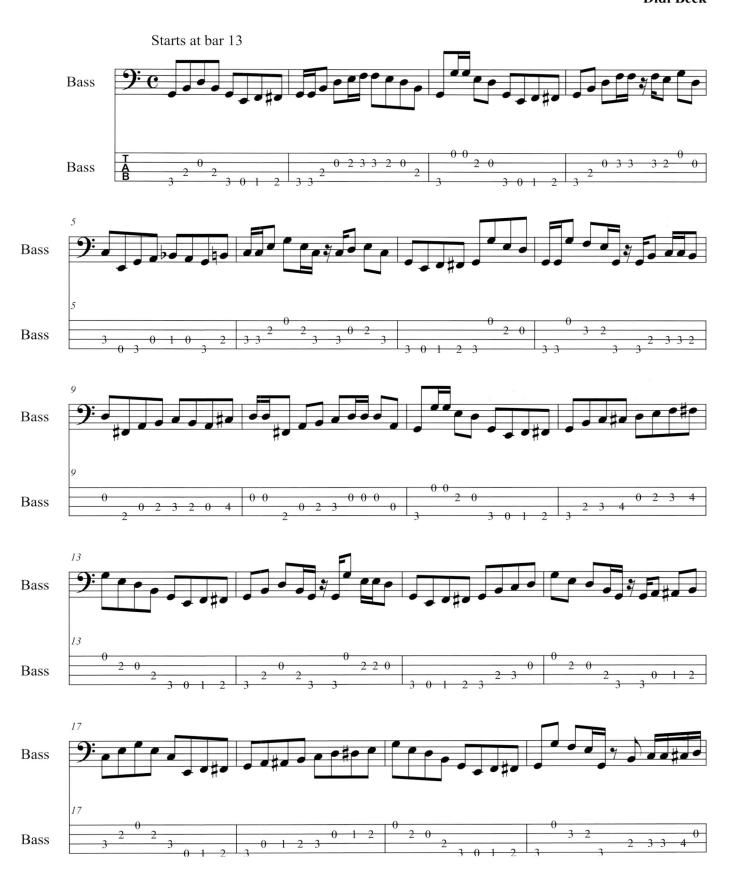

Keith Ferguson Discography

The Fabulous Thunderbirds:
- *Girls Go Wild*, Takoma, 1979
- *What's The Word*, Takoma/Chrysalis Records, 1980
- *Butt Rockin'*, Chrysalis Records, 1981
- *T-Bird Rhythm*, Chrysalis Records, 1982
- *Havana Moon*, Carlos Santana, 1983
- *VA: Austin Rhythm & Blues Christmas*, 1983
- *Different Tacos*, Benchmark Records, 1996, (and some samplers that were isssued over the years with old material)

LeRoi Brothers:
- *Check This Action*, Amazing Records, 1983

Big Guitars From Texas:
- *Big Guitars From Texas, Vol. I*, various Austin guitarists, Jungle Records, 1985

The Tail Gators:
- *Swamp Rock*, Wrestler Records, 1985
- *Rock N Roll Till The Cows Come Home*, Wrestler EP, 1985
- *Mumbo Jumbo*, Wrestler, 1986
- *Live at the Continental Club* (with various artists) 1986
- *Tore Up*, Wrestler, 1987
- *OK Let's Go!*, Restless, 1988
- *Hide Your Eyes*, Restless, 1990

The Solid Senders:
- *Everything's Gonna Be All Right*, Tramp Records, 1995
- *Did My Wheels,*, Tramp Records, 1997

Others:
- "My Back Scratcher" b/w "Do Something For Yourself", Sunnyland Special, Armadillo Records, 1969
- *Reunion of the Cosmic Brothers*, Freddie Fender & Doug Sahm, Crazy Cajun Records, 1974
- *May I Rock You*, Walter T. Higgs, 1989
- *VA: Austin Music Scene Vol. 2* (with Walter T. Higgs), 1990
- *Many Moods of Teisco del Rey*, Teisco Del Rey (Dan Forte), 1992
- *Lewis Cowdrey*, Lewis Cowdrey, 1992
- *It's Lewis*, Lewis Cowdrey, Antone's Records, 1994
- *Let The Dogs Run*, Mike Morgan & Jim Suhler, Black Top, 1994
- *Let That Right Hand Go...*, Joe Kubek, Bird Records 2012

The discography was made with the help of Paul Williams from the Netherlands.

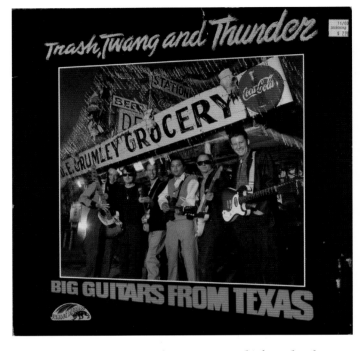

Above: Cover of *Trash, Twang and Thunder* from Big Guitars from Texas.

Below: Keith's profile on the back -- "Covered with mysterious tattoos and only speaking English when absolutely necessary, Ferguson is most dangerous in combination with Buck."

Only available on cassette, featuring the only bass solo Keith ever played. Just a great recording.

Courtesy of Mike Buck

Keith did the snake painting on Angela's album *Wang Dang Doodle*.

Basile Kolliopoulos

Basile sadly passed away in 2013 before he could contribute to this book.

In 1992, Basile recorded *El Greco*, which was actually a solo record. He went down to Austin and recorded it with Keith Ferguson and Mike Buck. At the time it was released only on cassette. This one features versions of Bo Diddley's "Willie and Lillie", Captian Beefheart's "Booglarise You Baby", and R.L. Burnside's "Goin' Down South". Also a couple of very strong Reverb Brothers standards from Basile, "Loaded" and "King of Beasts". An awesome instrumental, "Dark Notion", features Basile's guitar-god brother, Miho, on lead guitar. A couple of other songs and a lot of cool sounding experimental intros and segues.

Basile - vocals, 5-, 6- and 12-string guitars, exotic samples, little drums
Keith Ferguson - electric bass
Mike Buck- big drums
Miho Kolliopoulos - lead guitar on "Dark Notion"
Cover Design by Mr. Nodoe
Produced by Basile K and Doug Matthews

Carolos Santana's *Havana Moon* album, recorded with The Fabulous Thunderbirds.　　

There are some more recordings Keith is reported to have played on, but they were never published:
- Recordings with The Fabulous Thunderbirds prior to their first album
- Demos from The Excellos. I have heard them and they are great, too.
- Demos with Kathy and the Kilowatts; also great.

"She's Tuff" and "Scratch My Back" 45.
© Chrysalis Records
Courtesy of Keith Ferguson Collection

Cover of "Sugar Coated Love" 45.
© Chrysalis Records
Courtesy of Keith Ferguson Collection

"The Crawl" 45 rpm with Keith's tattoos colorized.
© Chrysalis Records;
Courtesy of Keith Ferguson Collection

A Christmas album that the T-Birds played a few songs on.

© Epic

YouTube is a great source for old videos. Here are my favorite videos where Keith can be seen:
- The Fabulous Thunderbirds at Rockpalast (entire show from 1980 that was broadcasted on German TV, where Keith uses his Fender Precision #0171)
- The Fabulous T-Birds Entire Show Baton Rouge (concert from the end of 1982; Keith plays the cowhide bass)
- The Fabulous Thunderbirds "How Do You Spell Love" (video for *MTV*; cowhide bass).
- The Fabulous Thunderbirds ACL 1984 (entire show for *Austin City Limits*; cowhide bass)
- "Boomerang" and "Do the Dootz", Big Guitars from Texas (cowhide bass)

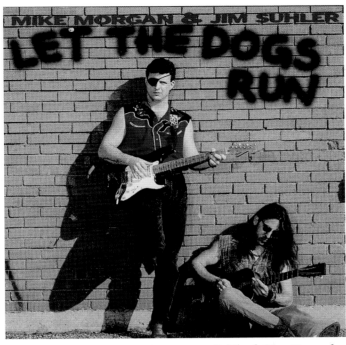

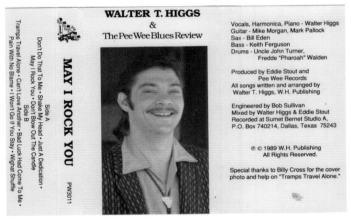

Walter T. Higgs cassette on Pee Wee Records with Keith Ferguson, Uncle John, Fredde Pharoah, Bill Eden, Mike Morgan and Mark Pallock, 1989; Bob Sullivan engineer.

Photo by Billy Cross; Cover courtesy Eddie Stout

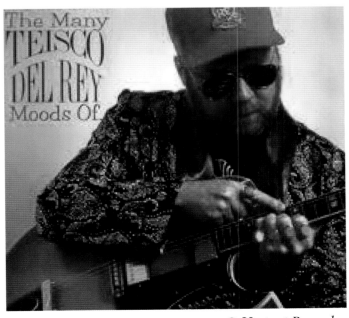

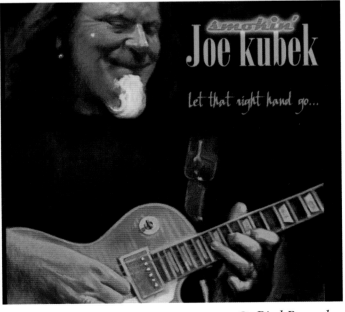

Sources

1) Keith Ferguson Collection, Southwest Collection/Special Collections Library, Crossroads Music Archive, Texas Tech University, Lubbock, Texas. In this book, the short form "Keith Ferguson Collection" is used.

"The Crossroads of Music Archive located in the Southwest Collection/Special Collections Library at Texas Tech University contains hundreds of collections from individuals and groups covering a wide array of musical genres. Focusing on the creative process, the Crossroads staff is actively collecting materials and oral histories from high profile entertainers, songwriters, and everyday musicians. The Crossroads archive is implementing online access to its collections. The archive helps educates the public about the collections through exhibitions and lectures.
www.crossroadsofmusic.ttu.edu"

2) Hopkins, Craig: "Stevie Ray Vaughan: Day By Day, Night After Night"
The book available online (www.stevieray.com) is the original, now collectible, limited edition signed by the author. The book was republished by Backbeat Books in two volumes: The first ("His Early Years, 1954-1982") was released in September 2010, and the second volume ("His Final Years, 1954-1982") was released in October 2011.

3) Hopkins, Craig Lee: "Stevie Ray Vaughan: Day By Day, Night After Night; His Early Years, 1954-1982"; Backbeat Books; 2010

4) Hopkins, Craig Lee: "Stevie Ray Vaughan: Day By Day, Night After Night; His Final Years, 1983-1990"; Backbeat Books; 2011

5) Friedman, Josh Alan: "Tell The Truth Until They Bleed; Coming Clean In The Dirty World Of Blues And Rock 'n' Roll"; Backbeat Books; 2008

6) Reid, Jan with Shawn Sahm: "Texas Tornado; The Times & Music Of Doug Sahm"; University of Texas Press; 2010

7) Gregory, Hugh: "Roadhouse Blues, Stevie Ray Vaughan And Texas R&B"; Backbeat Books; 2003

8) Tamarkin, Jeff: "Got A Revolution! The Turbulent Flight Of Jefferson Airplane"; Atria Books; 2005

9) Corcoran, Michael: "All Over The Map, True Heros Of Texas Music"; University of Texas Press; 2005

10) Govenar, Alan: "Meeting The Blues; The Rise Of The Texas Sound"; Da Capo Press; 1995

11) Koster, Rick: "Texas Music"; Martin's Press; 2000

12) Sullivan, Mary Lou: "Raisin' Cain, The Wild And Raucous Story Of Johnny Winter"; Backbeat Books; 2010

13) Antone, Susan: "Picture The Blues, Eleventh Anniversary"; Blues Press; 1986

14) Patoski, Joe Nick and Crawford, Bill: "Stevie Ray Vaughan: Caught In The Crossfire"; Back Bay Books; 1993

15) Leigh, Keri: "Stevie Ray, Soul To Soul"; Taylor Trade Publishing; 1993

16) Gibbons, Billy F.: "Rock + Roll Gearhead"; MBI Publishing Company; 2011

17) Govenar, Alan: "Texas Blues, The Rise Of A Contemporary Sound"; Texas A&M University Press College Station; 2008

18) Ludgate, Simon: *Record Mirror*, March 15, 1980

19) Forte, Dan: "The Tail Gators", *Guitar Player;* August 1986

20) *3rd Coast Music*, April 2002

21) Wheeler, Byron: "The Illustrated Keith Ferguson"; *Third Ear;* June 1983

22) Edwards, David; Callahan, Mike; and Eyries, Patrice: "The Starday Records Story"; www.bsnpubs.com/king/stardaystory.html

23) Monahan, Casey: "Somebody Loses, Somebody Wins"; *Austin American-Statesman;* November 4, 1989

24) Blackstock , Peter: "Suit Goes On"; *Austin American-Statesman*; January 31, 1991

25) The Tail Gators Homepage; www.thetailgators.com/

26) Claypool, Bob: "Keith Ferguson Is Still The One And Only"; *Houston Post*; October 23, 1986

27) Beuttler, Bill: "The Tail Gators"; *Down Beat*; December 1986

28) Reported Pick-Up-Gigs from Keith; *The Austin Chronicle*

29) The Keith Ferguson Collection; www.lib.utexas.edu/taro/utcah/00681/cah-00681.html

30) Rosier, Keith; *Bass Player*; June 1998

31) *Austin Chronicle*; May 23, 1999

32) Wilson, Burton: "The Austin Music Scene Through The Lense Of Burton Wilson"; Eakin Press

33) The Houston Press; http://blogs.houstonpress.com/hairballs/2009/01/sole_of_houston_airport_drive.php

34) The Houston Press; www.houstonpress.com/2001-05-03/music/treasure-hunter/

35) The Houston Press; www.houstonpress.com/2009-04-23/music/m-aacute-s-y-m-aacute-s/

36) Grigg, Andy: "Keith Ferguson, Real Blues"; June/July 1997

37) Birnbaum, Larry: "The Fabulous Thunderbirds"; *Down Beat*; Feb 1986

38) Jones, Allen: "Even Cowboys Got The Blues"; *Melody Maker*; March 5, 1983

39) Reynolds, Michael: "On Tour With America's Premier Bar Band"; *High Times*; October 1982

40) Pidgeon, John: "Fab Funbirds"; *Melody Maker*; March 15, 1980

41) Zaire, Tex: "Bus Rockin' With The Fabulous Thunderbirds"; *Austin Chronicle*; May 28, 1982

42) Beck, Didi: "Rockabilly Slapbass -- A Slight Introduction"; Artist Ahead

The author will be glad to answer questions, receive more stories, pictures, corrections, etc., and he can be reached by email at:
Bass52@gmx.de

Acknowledgements

There are a lot of people who helped on this book. I hope I don't forget to mention anybody, but surely will. I received hundreds of emails, collected some hundred "friends" on facebook for the research, skyped and wrote real letters (which I hadn't done for years). Of course, I want to thank everybody who was willing to be interviewed, shared memories of Keith, and contributed pictures, stories, records and posters. -- *Detlef Schmidt*

Europe

Susanne Kupka, the love of my life, for her support, understanding and time, for helping me with the typewriting and travelling and her general support of my life. **Erkan Özdemir**, the bass player for Memo Gonzales and the Bluescasters, for his friendship and the lending of Keith's Harmony bass that was standing in my house for over a year waiting to be photographed. **Georg Hoffmann**, from the concert agency Shooter Promotion, who helped me get in contact with Jimmie Vaughan. **Bernard Groll**, a German guitar player and collector, for his help on the Arlington Guitar show. **Nacho Banos**, the author of "The Blackguard Book", for his help in getting me in contact with Billy F. Gibbons. **Klaus Kilian**, the singer and harmonica player from Matchbox Blues Band, who shared his knowledge about records and early Thunderbirds concerts and wrote the article about Joey Long. **Claus Berninger**, the owner of the Colossaal club in Aschaffenburg, for his help with the Johnny Winter interview and generally for all concerts he brought to my hometown. **Paul Williams**, from the Netherlands, for sharing the pictures and memories of Keith's last tour and his help on the discography. **Neil Meldrum**, from Scotland, who contributed his huge collection of newspaper articles and who was an initial help for the start. **Bird Stevens**, bassist from the Netherlands, for his help on the tabs. **Paul Duvivie**, from the Netherlands and the record company that brought out Keith's albums with The Solid Senders. **Thomas Giegerich**, from Germany, for his help on layout questions. **Detlef Alder**, from Guitar Point, Maintal, Germany's biggest vintage guitar store. **Thomas Hesse** for some photos. **Steve Hooker**, from England, for help in getting information on the Thunderbird dates in England. Great to have played with you so many years.

U.S.A.

Paul Nelson, the manager and guitar player for Johnny Winter, who helped in getting in contact with Johnny. **Bart Wittrock**, from Rockin' Robin Guitars & Music shop in Houston, and his brother Tom for their support in getting some great pictures. **Eve Monsees**, from Antone's Records, for storing some of my personal stuff in her store. **Erin Jaimes** and her husband, Tom, for some great music, insight and a great afternoon in Tom's repair shop. **Mary Lou Sullivan**, who wrote the book about Johnny Winter, "Raisin' Cain", for her support with the quotes and the You Rock coffee mug. **John Lomax III**, for getting me in contact with Rocky Hill's wife and Bill Ham, the former manager of The Nightcrawlers and ZZ Top. **The Floyd Moore estate** for their help. **Gretchen Barber** for getting me the final contact to Billy Gibbons and lots of really supporting emails. **Craig Hopkins**, who wrote a book about Stevie Ray Vaughan and let me use the quotes. **Glenn Arnaud**, from Port Arthur, for the hosting and the ride in the Hummer. **Dicki de Luxe** for some Houston inside stories. **Angela Strehli** for adding some photos and a little story. **Terry Slade,** a friend of Basile Kolliopoulos, and **Heather Kolliopoulos**, the wife of Basile, both for helping me in the research. **Andrew Dansby**, from *The Houston Chronicle,* for his help with research. **John Nova Lomax**, from *The Houston Press,* for his research help. **Margaret Moser**, from *The Austin Chronicle.* **Joe Nick Patoski**, who also wrote a book about Stevie Ray Vaughan and gave some good advice. **Hook Herrera** for some funny stories. It was great meating you in Austin. **Carmen Ford** for the California Years. **Ted Tucker** and his wife for sending photos of posters and records. **Casey Monahan** for his support. **Eddie Stout** for some insights on the Lewis Cowdrey album. Hard to find out on which songs Keith actually played bass on this album. **William Michael Smith**, from *The Houston Press,* for his help with some of the quotes. **Tino Mauricio** for the photos and the mysterious lost interview. **John Conquest**, from *3rd Coast Music,* magazine for his help. **Minor Wilson** for helping in getting great photos from his father to the book. **Amanda Taylor** for getting Kim Wilson in the book.

My last special thanks goes to **Daniel Schaefer** and **Jeff Meverden** who were my biggest support in the last hours of compiling this book.

315

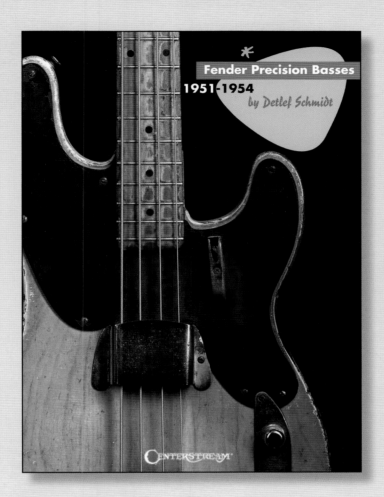

More Great Bass Books from Centerstream...

5-STRING BASS METHOD
by Brian Emmel
Besides discussing how to adapt to the differences in the 5-string versus 4-, this book explores the various ways of using the 5-string, practice tips, different techniques, and practical applications for various genres demonstrated through songs on the 37-minute accompanying CD.
00000134 Book/CD Pack...$17.95

ART OF THE SLAP
by Brian Emmel
This slap bass method book, designed for advanced beginning to intermediate bassists, is based on the understanding and application of modes. The focus is on the concept of groove sculpting from modes, and not on actual right- and left-hand techniques. The CD features recordings of all the examples, plus a split-channel option to let you practice your playing. Includes 13 songs.
00000229 Book/CD Pack...$16.95

BASS GUITAR CHORDS
by Ron Middlebrook
84 of the most popular chords for bass guitar. Covers: finger placement, note construction, chromatic charts, and the most commonly used bass scales. Also has a helpful explanation of the common 2-5-1 progression, and the chords in all keys.
00000073..$2.95

BEGINNING TO ADVANCED 4-STRING BASS
by Brian Emmel
This instructional video by noted instructor/author Brian Emmel leaves no stone unturned in explaining all there is to know about 4-string bass basics! Designed for the beginning to advanced player, Brian's step-by-step demonstrations form the foundation for understanding music theory and building bass technique. Topics covered range from common musical terminology, to playing in a garage band, to laying down tracks in a recording studio. 60 minutes.
00000374 DVD $19.95

BLUES GROOVES
Traditional Concepts for Playing 4 & 5 String Blues Bass
by Brian Emmel
This book/CD pack has been designed to educate bass enthusiasts about the development of different styles and traditions throughout the history of the blues, from the 1920s to the early 1970s. Players will learn blues scales, rhythm variations, turnarounds, endings and grooves, and styles such as Chicago blues, jazz, Texas blues, rockabilly, R&B and more. The CD includes 36 helpful example tracks.
00000269 Book/CD Pack $17.95

PURRFECT 4-STRING BASS METHOD
by Brian Emmel
This book will teach students how to sight read and to acquire a musical vocabulary. Includes progressive exercises on rhythm notation, 1st to 4th string studies, enharmonic studies, chords and arpeggios, blues progressions, and chord charts.
00000201..$9.95

ULTIMATE BASS EXERCISES
by Max Palermo
Bassist and educator Max Palermo takes you through more than 700 easy, step-by-step exercises for finger building, based on the 24 possible fingering combinations. 158 pages.
00000476...$19.95

HIP-HOP GROOVES FOR BASS
by Max Palermo
From the irresistible party jams of South Bronx to the urban sounds of today, hip-hop has maintained close links with its roots. Many of its characteristic sounds and beats come from funk, soul, and R&B origins. The electric bass plays a key role in creating the groovin' that gives hip-hop a unique, attractive feel. This book/CD set contains 90 authentic hip-hop licks that will lead you to the vibrant world of hip-hop style. All the bass lines are demonstrated on the CD's full-performance tracks and transcribed in standard notation and tablature. Jamming along with these patterns, you will improve your technique while you learn how to lay down the right groove. Just listen to the tracks and concentrate on playing with a good-time feel. Enjoy!
00001174...$14.95

P.O. Box 17878 - Anaheim Hills, CA 92817
(714) 779-9390   www.centerstream-usa.com

More Great Guitar Books from Centerstream...

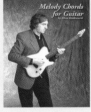

Those using
Centerstream
Books & DVDs

The Competition